REVOLUTIONARY
THEATRE

In the period following the Bolshevik Revolution a group of directors, playwrights, actors and organisers collected around the charismatic Vsevolod Meyerhold and attempted to achieve in the theatre what Lenin and his comrades had achieved in politics: the complete overthrow of the status quo and the installation of a new, utterly different regime.

It was in the practical experiments of the revolutionary theatre that Meyerhold, Eisenstein, Foregger, the 'Factory of the Eccentric Actor' and others produced their most telling work. They created a fusion of popular forms and intellectual preoccupations which owed as much to the circus, *commedia dell'arte* and the theatres of the fairgrounds as to the avante-garde experiments of the Futurists and Constructivists.

The rise of Stalin in the late 1920s and the accompanying imposition of state terror on all manifestations of non-conformity silenced this 'golden age' of modern Russian–Soviet theatre. As a consequence little has been remembered of the efforts of this idealistic and radical group or their influence on today's alternative theatre. In *Revolutionary Theatre* Robert Leach reveals in fascinating detail their roots, their achievements and their legacy.

Robert Leach is Senior Lecturer in Drama and Theatre Arts at the University of Birmingham, and a freelance theatre director. In 1990 he directed the Russian premiere of Sergei Trekyakov's *I Want a Baby* in Moscow, and in 1994 was artistic director for the Lichfield Mysteries. He is the author of a major study of Vsevolod Meyerhold and is editing a forthcoming history of Russian theatre.

REVOLUTIONARY THEATRE

Robert Leach

London and New York

First published 1994
by Routledge
11 New Fetter Lane, London EC4P 4EE

Simultaneously published in the USA and Canada
by Routledge
29 West 35th Street, New York, NY 10001

© 1994 Robert Leach

Typeset in Baskerville by
Ponting–Green Publishing Services, Chesham, Bucks
Printed in Great Britain by
Biddles Ltd, Guildford

British Library Cataloguing in Publication Data
A catalogue record for this book is available from
the British Library

Library of Congress Cataloging in Publication Data
Leach Robert,
Revolutionary Theatre / Robert Leach.
p.   cm.
Includes bibliographical references and index.
1. Experimental theater–Russia (Federation)–History
2. Theater–Russia–History–19th century.
3. Theater–Political aspects–Russia (Federation)
4. Meĭerkhol'd, V. É. (Vsevolod Émil'evich),
1874–1940–Influence.   I. Title.
PN2724.L4   1994
792'.0947–dc20   93–35722
ISBN 0–415–03223–7

To
Tatyana Sergeevna Gomolitskaya-Tretyakova
child to one Sergei Mikhailovich
'Baby' to the other

CONTENTS

CONTENTS

ILLUSTRATIONS

FIGURES

ABBREVIATIONS
AND TERMS

'Academic' theatres Theatres in receipt of direct government subsidy from 1918. Most of the former imperial theatres, plus the Moscow Art Theatre, the State Children's Theatre and others.

Agit-prop Agitational propaganda.

Biomechanics Meyerhold's system of physicalised acting.

FEKS Factory of the Eccentric Actor.

GEKTEMAS State Experimental Theatre Workshop, directed by Meyerhold.

GITIS State Institute of Theatrical Art.

Glavpolitprosvet Department of Political Education of Soviet Government.

Glavrepertkom Government Department for overseeing the theatrical repertoire; in effect, the censorship mechanism.

GosTeKomDram State Theatre of Communist Drama.

GosTIM State Theatre of Meyerhold in Moscow, 1925–1937.

GVYRM State Higher Director's Workshop.

GVYTM State Higher Theatre Workshop, successor to GVYRM.

LEF Left Front of Art, a group of radical writers and artists. Also the journal they published.

MastFor Workshop of Nikolai Foregger.

MastKomDram Workshop of Communist Drama.

MONO Cultural Department of Moscow City Council.

Narkompros People's Commissariat (i.e. Ministry) of Enlightenment, overseeing all educational and cultural policy. Commissar 1917–1929: Anatoly Lunacharsky.

NEP New Economic Policy, introduced by Lenin in March 1921, which restored a limited level of capitalism.

OBMOKhU Society of Young Artists.

Peretru Proletkult's itinerant agit-prop theatre troupe.

Proletkult Proletarian Cultural and Educational Organisation. Before the Bolshevik revolution, an organisation where working-class people could learn artistic methods and practices. Briefly enormously popular after the revolution, but from 1920 controlled and reduced by the Communist Party.

PTO Petrograd Theatre Department.

PUR Red Army political-educational department.

Rezhmas Proletkult's Director's Workshop.

ROSTA Soviet telegraph agency.

RSFSR Russian Soviet Federal Socialist Republic.

Skomorokhi Itinerant popular entertainers, pre-1648.

Taylorism System of economic and efficient movement, named after Frederick W. Taylor.

TEO Theatre Department of Narkompros, overseeing all theatrical activity apart from that of the academic theatres.

Te-Phys-Cult System of theatrical physical culture.

TePhyTrenage System of theatrical physical training.

TEREVSAT Theatre of Revolutionary Satire.

TIM Theatre of Meyerhold in Moscow, 1923–1925.

Ton-Plas Tonal-Plastic. A system of synthesising movement and word in performance.

TRAM Theatre of Young Workers.

Tsentroteatr Narkompros's umbrella organisation to oversee both academic theatres and TEO, 1919–1920.

Vpered 'Forward'. Group of Marxists, including Bogdanov, Lunacharsky, Lebedev-Polyansky, Gorky and others, who opposed Lenin before 1917 and emphasised the importance of culture and the arts in socialist society.

PREFACE AND ACKNOWLEDGEMENTS

This book tells the story of a group of absurdly idealistic theatre practitioners who believed that the Bolshevik revolution in Russia really might herald a new dawn of liberty, justice and commonwealth. They wanted to use theatre to find a model of social progress and integration which would be *of use* to the revolution, so they joined a struggle which they saw to be both political and artistic. The book is therefore not about the *avant-garde* as such, but more about that part of the *avant-garde* which was essentially politically motivated.

Their unquestioned leader was Vsevolod Meyerhold, and indeed many of them called themselves Meyerholdites. But this book pays less attention than it might to him, partly because much has been written about him in the last thirty years since his 'rediscovery' – I myself have contributed to the growing number of works which have sought to learn from him – but also partly because it is sometimes important to see such a colossus in context. To fully appreciate Shakespeare, we also have to find out about and savour Marlowe, Ben Jonson, Webster and others; to fully comprehend Mount Everest, we need to examine the Himalaya mountains. So some of Meyerhold's most brilliant 'revolutionary theatre', such as the productions of *D.E.*, *The Government Inspector* and *The Bathhouse*, is bypassed in favour of other revolutionary theatre work, which is less well-known but not insignificant.

The story of revolutionary theatre begins as an almost wholly political struggle in Petrograd in 1917, when it was believed that a state takeover would purge the theatre of all reactionary elements. When the Meyerholdites failed to take control of the organisation and management of all the theatres – partly because Meyerhold himself was taken ill and had to leave the north for health reasons – they tried to establish a series of theatres which they hoped would overrun the state organisation from below, as it were. These were the RSFSR Theatres which they numbered 1, 2, 3, 4 and so on. And when this device was blocked, a number of exemplary theatres pursued the goal of making such a startlingly 'new' theatre that audiences themselves would become dissatisfied with the fare provided at more traditional theatres. It is more apparent now than it was then that such an enterprise was inevitably doomed under an endlessly bureaucratic and domineering regime; the fact that the whole enterprise collapsed, with plays being banned, theatre workers silenced and some of the greatest artists among them, including Meyerhold himself, being arrested, tortured and put to death, still has the power to horrify.

Much of this work disappeared into an intellectual 'black hole' for decades, but with the current growing interest in 'physical' and 'visual' theatre and other comparable forms, it is now receiving increasing attention. This is surely a welcome development, but it carries with it the danger that these techniques will be used merely on a director's whim, or will become this month's fashionable 'experiment' to bring a dusty classic to 'life'. Revolutionary theatre grew out of a specific concrete political struggle, in which its founders were exhaustingly engaged, a struggle which involved the fusing of popular and *avant-garde* forms for a particular purpose beyond simply 'effective theatre'. The fact that revolutionary theatre is, in the abstract, 'effective theatre', is both its strength and its weakness, but I hope this book is able to demonstrate that this theatrical style can only be true to itself when it is yoked to a purpose beyond itself. Eisenstein had no interest in bringing *Enough Stupidity for Every Wise Man* to 'life', he desired to 'mould the audience' in a particular direction. To use such startling techniques for any lesser purpose is a kind of betrayal.

My own experience of work on *I Want a Baby* by Sergei Tretyakov confirms this for me. I first directed this play in England in 1989. The production was seen by Mark Rozovsky, director of Moscow's Teatr u Nikitskikh Vorot, who invited me to stage it with his company. This was the first production of the play in what was then the Soviet Union, and the penultimate dress rehearsal was watched by the theatre's Artistic Soviet, the body Stalin had imposed on every theatre in his struggle with the 'Left Opposition' in 1927. The Artistic Soviet of the Nikitskikh Vorot were shocked and outraged by the play, and almost to a man wanted to ban the production. The only person who defended it, interestingly enough, was one of the two women on the Soviet. The arguments eddied around almost exactly as they had in 1927: the Soviet public were not ready for such a play; the content was offensive; the style was primitive. Before the matter was resolved, the meeting adjourned, for it was 2 February 1990, the fiftieth anniversary of Meyerhold's execution.

At the vigil outside his flat, where hundreds of us held candles in the freezing winds and poetry was recited in his honour, it was impossible to stifle the feelings of amazement at such double standards. I am convinced that the members of the Nikitskikh Vorot Soviet were sincere in their desire to celebrate the Master; they were simply unaware that their kind of craven cowardice was precisely the reason he had been done to death five decades ago. Eventually the production was allowed to proceed, though it was to be reviewed again after three performances. By then, of course, it was clear that the 'Soviet public' was not only very ready for this play, but was enjoying it hugely. As I write these words, more than three years later, the production is still in the repertoire and doing good business. But Mark Rozovsky informed me that in the summer of 1991, a month and a half before the abortive Communist *coup* against Mikhail Gorbachev, when the company was on tour in Kazan, a local Party boss appeared at the theatre and ordered them to remove *I Want a Baby* from the proposed repertoire. I am glad to say Rozovsky refused.

To him, therefore, I would like to record my gratitude for providing me with the opportunity to gain some 'inside knowledge' of the workings of Russian theatre which I hope informs this book. Perhaps with the demise of Communism, more Russian theatre leaders will be able to emulate his intellectual daring. To the members of his company who adapted so quickly to my foreign ways, and to my assistant director, Lana Sergienko, as well as to the many other Russian people, especially my hostess, Tamara Garamova, who helped and supported me in so many ways, I wish to record my sincere thanks. The venture would have been impossible without the financial assistance of the incomparable British Council, who also enabled me to return to Moscow in the summer of 1992 to attend the centenary celebrations for Sergei Tretyakov.

I should also like to record my thanks to my colleagues Gerry McCarthy and the late Jocelyn Powell for support and stimulating argument over the years; to Jorg Mihan for inviting me to the Berliner Ensemble when they were presenting *I Want a Baby*; to Richard Taylor for not only supplying me with rare early Soviet film but also pointing me in new and worthwhile directions; to Andrei Molotkov, for acquiring and letting me have copies of obscure film which I would never have discovered for myself; to Richard Gough for wise advice and a lot of his time; to Arch Tait for giving me access especially to his unpublished work on Lunacharsky; to Stephen Holland for hours of agonizing over the precise meanings of obscure Russian phrases; to James Merifield, whose extraordinary imagination has given me rich insights into revolutionary theatre; and to Anne Baird for help with photography. My thinking was stimulated especially by two conferences, 'Eisenstein at Ninety', at Keble College, Oxford, in 1988, and 'Tretyakov, Brecht's Teacher' at the Department of Drama and Theatre Arts, Birmingham University, in 1989. To my former students and actors, amateur and professional, who have worked with me on biomechanics, *commedia dell'arte*, expressive acting and more, and who have appeared in my productions of *The Fairground Booth, A Merry Death, The Suicide, The Bathhouse, Mystery Bouffe, Gas Masks, I Want a Baby, The Nose, Masquerade, Victory Over the Sun, Vladimir Mayakovsky, a Tragedy* and others, I owe an incalculable debt, which I am glad to acknowledge. A special thanks to my three Mildas – Sarah Rose, Vika Zaslavskaya and Caroline Hadley. You were great!

Finally, I wish to record my deepest gratitude to two matchless women: my wife, Anita, without whose support and forbearance the book would never have been written; and Tanya Tretyakova, who acted with Mayakovsky in Eisenstein's production of *The Mexican*, and who has been my inspiration throughout.

TRANSLITERATION

Russian words and names in this book are transliterated according to the usual simplified system, in order to be as quickly and easily comprehensible as possible to the non-Russian-speaking reader. Accepted versions of some names – e.g. 'Meyerhold', rather than 'Meierkhold' – have been adopted throughout the text. However, a more scholarly usage has been adhered to in the Notes.

DRAMATIS PERSONAE

101 names associated with revolutionary theatre

Aksenov, Ivan (1884–1935) Writer, partner of Meyerhold in 1920s.

Andreeva, Maria (1868–1953) Longstanding Bolshevik, actress, wife or mistress to Gorky, governmental organiser of northern theatres after 1917.

Annenkov, Yuri (1889–1973) Painter, stage designer, director, in Petrograd; emigrated 1922.

Arvatov, Boris (1896–1940) Critic, theorist, organiser for Proletkult; liquidated.

Babanova, Maria (1900–1983) Actress at Meyerhold Theatre.

Bebutov, Valery (1885–1961) Theatre director, closely associated with Meyerhold, especially at RSFSR Theatre No 1.

Blok, Alexander (1880–1921) Poet and playwright; initially a Symbolist, who came to accept the Bolshevik revolution.

Blyum, Vladimir (1877–1941) Influential theatre critic.

Bogdanov, Alexander (1873–1928) Marxist theorist opposed to Lenin, supporter of Proletkult.

Chagall, Marc (1887–1985) Painter and stage designer with TEREVSAT; emigrated.

Dmitriev, Vladimir (1900–1948) Stage designer in Petrograd.

Dobuzhinsky, Mstislav (1875–1957) Artist and stage designer at Ancient Theatre; emigrated.

Duncan, Isadora (1878–1927) American dancer, established own school in Moscow in 1922, married Russian poet, Esenin.

Eisenstein, Sergei (1898–1948) Student of Meyerhold, stage designer with Proletkult and Foregger, director with Proletkult; later, film director.

Erdman, Nikolai (1902–1970) Playwright for TEREVSAT and Meyerhold Theatre, whose last play, *The Suicide*, was banned.

Evreinov, Nikolai (1879–1953) Playwright and theatre director at Ancient Theatre, Distorting Mirror, mass spectacles, etc; emigrated 1925.

Ferdinandov, Boris (1889–1959) Stage designer and actor for Tairov, leader of Experimental-Heroic Theatre.

Fevralsky, Alexander (1901–1984) Literary manager at Meyerhold Theatre; theatre historian.

Foregger, Nikolai (1892–1939) Theatre director and choreographer, at Theatre of Four Masks, then MastFor (Foregger Workshop).

Gan, Alexei (1889–1942) Constructivist designer and polemicist, organiser of mass spectacles in Moscow; liquidated.

Garin, Erast (1902–1980) Actor at Meyerhold Theatre.

Glizer, Judith (1904–1968) Actress with Proletkult.

Gorky, Maxim (1869–1936) Playwright and novelist; Bolshevik who emigrated 1921, then returned in 1933; 'Father' of Socialist Realism.

Gorodetsky, Sergei (1884–1967) Poet, playwright and translator.

Gripich, Alexei (1891–1985) Theatre director, student of Meyerhold, succeeded him as leader of Theatre of Revolution.

Gumilev, Nikolai (1886–1921) Poet, playwright; shot as traitor.

Gutman, David (1884–1946) Theatre director with TEREVSAT.

Ignatov, Vasily (1884–1938) Actor, director, secretary of Proletkult; liquidated.

Ilinsky, Igor (1901–1989) Actor for Foregger, Meyerhold, etc.

Ivanov, Vyacheslav (1866–1949) Symbolist poet who embraced the revolution, but later emigrated and became a Catholic priest.

Jacques-Dalcroze, Emile (1865–1950) French inventor and propagator of 'eurhythmics', a system of free movement.

Kameneva, Olga (1881–1936) Sister of Trotsky, Bolshevik organiser of theatres and theatre organisations; liquidated.

Kamensky, Vasily (1884–1961) Futurist poet and playwright.

Kerensky, Alexander (1881–1970) Leader of the second Provisional Government overthrown by the Bolsheviks.

Kerzhentsev, Platon (1881–1940) Theatrical theorist in *The Creative Theatre*; later, Party scourge of revolutionary theatre.

Khlebnikov, Velimir (1885–1922) Futurist playwright and poet.

Khodasevich, Valentina (1894–1970) Stage designer in Petrograd; emigrated.

Komissarzhevsky, Fedor ((1882–1954) Theatre director, emigrated 1919.

Kozintsev, Grigori (1905–1973) Co-founder and director of FEKS, later film director.

Kruchenykh, Aleksei (1886–1969) Futurist playwright and poet.

Kugel, Alexander (1864–1928) Critic, director at Distorting Mirror and of mass spectacles.

Kuleshov, Lev (1899–1970) Film director, who also staged 'films without film'.

Kuzmin, Mikhail (1875–1936) Poet, playwright and composer.

Lazarenko, Vitaly (1890–1939) Satirical clown.

Lebedev-Polyansky, Pavel (1881–1948) President of Proletkult, 1917–1920.

Lenin, Vladimir Ilich (1870–1924) Bolshevik leader, formed first government after revolution.

Lissitzky, El (1890–1944) Painter and stage designer.

Loiter, Naum (1890–1966) Student of Meyerhold, theatre director.

London, Jack (1876–1916) American socialist writer whose stories inspired several revolutionary theatre practitioners.

Lunacharsky, Anatoly (1875–1933) Playwright and People's Commissar of Enlightenment.

Lyutse, Vladimir (1903–1970) Student of Meyerhold, theatre director.

Maeterlinck, Maurice (1862–1949) Belgian poet and playwright, much admired by radical and progressive Russian theatre practitioners up to about 1920.

Malevich, Kasimir (1878–1935) Suprematist painter and stage designer.

Mardzhanov, Konstantin (1872–1933) Theatre director of mass spectacles, at Bi-Ba-Bo and Limping Joe cabarets and in theatres.

Margolin, Samuil ((1893–1953) Critic, historian of Proletkult.

Mass, Vladimir (1896–1984) Playwright, especially with Foregger Workshop.

Mayakovsky, Vladimir (1893–1930) Poet and playwright; committed suicide.

Meyerhold, Vsevolod (1872–1940) Theatre director; shot in prison.

Mgebrov, Alexander (1884–1966) Actor with Ancient Theatre, theatre director for Proletkult.

Miklashevsky, Konstantin (1886–1944) Student of Meyerhold pre-1917, actor, historian of *commedia dell'arte.*

Nikulin, Lev (1891–1967) Writer with TEREVSAT.

Parnakh, Valentin (1891–1951) Actor and dancer.

Petrov, Nikolai (1890–1964) Director, based in Petrograd.

Pletnev, Valerian (1886–1942) Playwright and President of Proletkult, 1920–1932.

Popova, Lyubov (1889–1924) Painter, stage designer, especially for Meyerhold, 1921–24.

Prosvetov, Evgeny (1896–1958) Theatre director with Proletkult, leader of Ton-Plas Studio.

Pudovkin, Vsevolod (1893–1953) Actor, director with Kuleshov, TEREVSAT, etc; later, film director.

Pustynin, Mikhail ((1884–1966) Poet and playwright for TEREVSAT.

Radlov, Sergei (1892–1958) Theatre director, studied under Meyerhold, led Theatre of Popular Comedy.

Raikh, Zinaida (1894–1930) Actress with Meyerhold Theatre; married to the poet, Esenin, then to Meyerhold; murdered by State agents, 1939.

Razin, Stenka (d. 1671) Cossack outlaw who rebelled against the tsar, apparently in the name of social justice; regarded by many revolutionaries as a hero figure.

Razumny, Mikhail (1892–1945) Actor, director for TEREVSAT.

Rolland, Romain (1866–1944) French dramatist and theorist of popular theatre.

Sakhnovsky, Vasily (1886–1945) Theatre director, partner of Fedor Komissarzhevsky before 1917, and at Moscow Art Theatre later.

Savinkov, Boris (1879–1925) Novelist, cultural organiser for Kerensky's Provisional Government.

Serafimovich, Alexander (1863–1949) Playwright, especially with Proletkult.

'Serge' (Alexander Alexandrov) (1892–1966) Circus and theatre performer.

Shershenevich, Vadim (1893–1942) Poet and playwright with Experimental-Heroic Theatre.

Shimanovsky, Viktor (1890–1954) Actor, director of railway workers' Central Dramatic Studio.

Shtraukh, Maxim (1900–1974) Actor at Proletkult.

Sidelnikov, Nikolai (1898–1921) Actor with Proletkult, killed in suppression of Kronstadt rising.

Smyshlyaev, Valentin (1891–1936) Actor, director, left Moscow Art Theatre to work with Proletkult.

Sokolovsky, Mikhail (1901–1941) Founder, leader of TRAM.

Soloviev, Vladimir (1887–1941) Playwright, director, Meyerhold's partner before 1919.

Sosnovsky, Lev (1886–1937) Party *apparatchik*, with Trotskyist affiliations and cultural interests.

Stanislavsky, Konstantin (1863–1938) Actor and director, founder of Moscow Art Theatre.

Tairov, Alexander (1885–1950) Theatre director, Kamerny Theatre.

Tatlin, Vladimir (1885–1953) Artist and stage designer.

Terentiev, Igor (1891–1941) Theatre director in Petrograd; liquidated.

Tikhonovich, Valentin (1880–1951) Theatre director and administrator for TEO and Proletkult.

Trauberg, Leonid (1902–1990) Co-founder, actor and director with FEKS; later film director.

Tretyakov, Sergei (1892–1937) Poet, playwright and theorist of revolutionary culture; liquidated.

Trotsky, Leon (1879–1940) Prominent revolutionary, second to Lenin in Bolshevik government; ousted by Stalin, exiled and murdered.

Verhaeren, Emile (1855–1916) Belgian poet and playwright, whose works were popular with the early revolutionary theatre practitioners.

Vrangel, Baron Petr (1878–1928) Leader of White forces in Russian Civil War, defeated at Perekop.

Yazykanov, Ivan (1898–1974) Actor with Proletkult.

Yutkevich, Sergei (1904–1985) Theatre director, member of FEKS; later, film director.

Yuzhanin, Boris (1895–?1948) Founder and director of the Blue Blouse.

Yuzhin, Alexander (1857–1927) Actor, leader of the Maly Theatre.

Zhemchuzhny, Vitaly (1898–1966) Theatre director for Red Army Workshop.

Zonov, Arkady (1875–1922) Theatre director, worked with Meyerhold before 1917.

1

BEFORE THE REVOLUTION

THE POPULAR THEATRE

Revolutionary theatre's deepest root is embedded in the popular games and plays of traditional peasant life. The folk culture of the Russian empire was as rich and diverse as any, and included a strong strand of folk drama. In the early Middle Ages, at crucial times, Russian peasants performed folk plays which were probably really pagan rituals dealing with the 'mystery' of the earth, sowing and reaping, summer and winter, or the marriage dramas, a Caucasian version of which is described in Lermontov's *A Hero of Our Time*:

> First the mullah reads a piece out of the *Koran*, then the young couple and their relations are given presents. They eat, they drink *buza*. Then there's the trick-riding, (and) when it gets dark they have what we'd call a ball . . . The girls and young chaps form up in two lines facing each other and clap their hands and sing. Then one girl and a man come into the middle and sing bits of rhyme at each other, anything that comes into their head, and the others join in the chorus.[1]

Each part of Russia had its own marriage rituals, and these were always regarded as entertainment as well as ceremony: *Les Noces* is one response to this by artists of the revolutionary period, the marriage sequence in Tretyakov and Eisenstein's *A Wise Man* is another.

The marriage ritual was largely directed by a sort of Master of Ceremonies, who would probably be a *skomorokh*, a professional entertainer. *Skomorokhi* were frequently condemned by clerics but they were extraordinarily versatile performers – *gusli* players, ballad singers, acrobats, tightrope walkers, jugglers, conjurors, actors in farces and mimes, leaders of all manner of revelries. Most famously they were bear-tamers and puppet showmen.

Tsar Alexei banned the *skomorokhi* in 1648, at a time of increasing hardship and oppression for the peasants, when a series of rebellions

1

broke out, notably those led by Stenka Razin around 1670 and by Pugachev a century later. Razin and Pugachev acquired the status of popular heroes, outlaws whose exploits appealed to the common people and who appeared as characters in new – or rather changed – folk dramas which sought to mix quasi-political, public concerns with more domestic or homely situations. Typical of these were *The Life of Tsar Maximilian*, which included plenty of comic and satirical scenes of low life, and *Lodka*, meaning 'The Ship', which presented the adventures of the crew in a manner not dissimilar to that used by Mayakovsky in his revolutionary play, *Mystery Bouffe*. With songs, set dialogues and appropriate actions (rowing, spying the shore with a token telescope, and so on), the plays were performed by villagers, who were generally welcomed wherever they went.

The burgeoning fairgrounds of the eighteenth and nineteenth centuries were an even more fertile breeding ground for pre-revolutionary popular drama. Here, pleasure-seekers were entertained by all manner of acrobats, clowns, puppet showmen, conjurors, tumblers and performing animals. Russia's traditional glove puppet, Petrushka, featured here, 'a carnival figure: lumpy-bodied and never at a loss for a crude joke. Throughout the nineteenth century, his clowning broke taboos, poked fun at figures of authority, ridiculed morality and decency.'[2] But the most notorious public entertainers for topical comment as well as spectacular effect were the *raek* peepshow men, 'grandads', sometimes with beards made of flax. In their shows, the major attraction was the forthright, hilarious commentary on what was seen in the box. Ivan Danilovich Ryabov was a *raek* man who began life as a serf in Orlov; he was emancipated in 1861, and for thirty or more years lived by his wits in the rumbustious atmosphere of the popular fairgrounds. One of his monologues included lines like:

> Here, just take a look, is the city of Rome,
> The Vatican Palace,
> Of all palaces the giant!
> And in it lives the Roman Pope,
> Quite a greedy guy!
> And here is the city of Paris,
> As soon as you get there,
> You take leave of your senses . . .
> Our eminent aristocrats
> Go there to squander money;
> They ride off with a sackful of gold
> And come home without shoes and on foot.[3]

Ryabov's natural milieu was among the *balagany*, the wooden booths where dramatic performances were given. One lithograph of 1862 depicts such a booth, containing Petrushka 'alongside a pair of acrobats, a barrel organ and a performing dog'.[4] Such 'entertainments' provoked Tolstoy to turn to the drama: he wanted to provide more 'judicious' diversions for the 'wretched starveling factory folk', so composed his temperance play, *The First Distiller*, for such a stage.[5] Earlier Nozdryov referred to the *balagany* in Gogol's *Dead Souls*: 'There must have been fifty booths at the fair, I should think. Fenardi, the clown, turned somersaults for four hours.'[6]

Fenardi might have been an Italian, though equally he might have been a Russian who took an exotic Italian-sounding name. It is difficult to be sure that some apparently traditional Russian scenes do not have their origins in *commedia dell'arte*, such as that of the water nymph tickling a man to death or that of the Harlequin-like Cossack who sells a landowner an automatic whip which only beats liars and deceivers and which turns on him when he tries to correct his serfs. Italian *commedia dell'arte* players certainly visited Russia, most notably the troupe of Antonio Sacchi, who stayed at Tsar Mikhail Romanov's court for well over a year in the 1730s. Alexandre Benois has described a 'harlequin-ade' performance he saw as a boy in an overcrowded and noisy *balagan* in St Petersburg in 1874:

Gradually calm is restored, and the crowd is hushed in expectation. The orchestra, who have managed to get a hot drink between the performances, return and resume their seats; the conductor (he is the first violin as well) raises his baton, the overture starts and the curtain slowly rises . . . Immediately we are plunged into a situation which is at once unusual, disturbing, comical and frightening.

Old Cassandra is going to town, and is giving instructions to his servants. One of them, dressed in white with his face covered in white flour, has a silly, bewildered look: Pierrot . . . Something terrible happens. Pierrot and Harlequin come to blows and, oh, horror! that clumsy lout of a Pierrot kills Harlequin. Worse still, he cuts up his old friend into small pieces and starts to juggle with the head, arms and legs. In the end he is terrified by his crime and tries to bring his victim back to life. He pieces together the separate parts of the body and leans it against the door, after which he takes to his heels. It is then that the first miracle takes place. A fairy, brilliant with gold and precious stones, emerges from the hillock which has become transparent. She approaches the folded corpse of Harlequin, touches it, and in one moment all the members grow together again. Harlequin is alive once more; better still, after a second touch of the magic wand Harlequin's shabby attire falls off and he appears in the guise of a handsome youth shining with spangles.[7]

3

In the nineteenth century, a lower-class 'amateur' theatre, a 'people's theatre', also began to take root, and by the end of the century it had developed into a strong and still rising movement. In 1902 over a hundred theatre groups were attached to 'People's Houses', and by 1909, that number had grown to 420.[8] Though their repertoires were so heavily censored that they were often forbidden to present even Ostrovsky's dramas and thus hardly contributed to the development of the form and content of revolutionary theatre, the involvement of large numbers of non-professionals in theatrical activities is significant. Countess Panina's Ligovsky 'People's House', founded in 1903, for instance, or the St Petersburg Workers' Society group, which called itself grandly 'The Source of Knowledge and Light', both provided theatrical education through practical involvement which was extremely significant. Though some radicals like A. Potresov argued that these organisations oppressed rather than liberated lower-class culture, others like Valerian Pletnev, later chairman of the Proletkult and a noted revolutionary playwright, dissented.[9]

The circus arrived a little earlier than the People's Theatre movement, dating from the arrival in Russia of an English equestrian performer, J. Bates, in 1764. In 1827, J. Tourniare erected the first permanent circus building in St Petersburg, and other circuses followed, acquiring a cross-class popularity which included the fervid admiration of such future *avant gardists* as Nikolai Evreinov, who played circuses as a boy and at the age of fourteen appeared with a tenting circus in his home town of Pskov as the clown Boklaro. Sergei Eisenstein was first taken to the circus by his nurse, but his stern father was an enthusiast also: 'I have adored clowns since I was in my cradle,' Eisenstein wrote. 'My father also adored the circus, but what attracted him most of all was what he used to call "high class equestrianship". So I carefully concealed my passion for clowns and pretended to be wildly interested in horses.'[10] Alexandre Benois remembered:

> the performances of the trained horses – a specialty of the members of the Ciniselli family; the ballerinas who danced on the flat drums that served as saddles to the beautiful snow-white horses, and who jumped through the rings; several remarkable turns, like the acrobat who was fired from a gun and seized a trapeze in his flight, or the Red Indian girl who held a rope in her teeth and flew from one side of the circus hall to the other. She had long, black, flowing hair, and when she reached her destination she nimbly jumped on a velvet pedestal and gave a piercing shriek that rang through the building, adding poignancy to her wild act. I loved the musical clowns, the trained dogs and monkeys,

though what I enjoyed most was the performance of a ventriloquist who manipulated a whole group of large comical dolls.[11]

Russian circuses were unusual in staging 'pantomimes', simple stories dramatised, largely without words, through the circus artists' performances. If someone in the story had to climb a tree, the performer would shin up the greasy pole, or 'perch'; if he had to go on a journey, he might walk the tightrope over the audience's heads. Servants, old men, or other such characters, might be played by the clowns, usually the clumsy red-haired clown and his white-faced superior, who was also elegant, self-confident and musical. It was important to the democratic feel of the circus that this white-faced clever clogs lost out to his lowlier opponent.

As elsewhere, Russian circuses often revolved around famous families, like the Nikitin brothers, who toured for many years, before building a permanent circus on Triumphal Square in Moscow in 1911, and the Durov brothers; Anatoly, who was an acrobat and juggler, as well as an animal trainer with a thoroughly subversive turn, and Vladimir, also a clown and an animal trainer, his pig being particularly famous for its satirical tricks aimed at those in authority. On one occasion in Odessa, he brought his pig on painted bright green: the right-wing mayor was Admiral Zeleny ('green'). On another occasion he 'sent shock waves rippling through an audience during a conjuring trick when he told someone trying to bend a silver rouble, "Don't waste time trying to break a fool." The tsar's face was stamped on the coin.'[12]

Other notable clowns were Bim-Bom, a double act, which revolved around a constantly-updated topical song, conceived and created by 'Bim', Ivan Radunsky. He had a series of 'Boms' through a long career, and the focus of his performance was always some contemporary piece of political chicanery, counterpointed by a slapstick entanglement with some extraordinary or hitherto unseen musical instruments. Vitaly Lazarenko was a tramp clown who was also an acrobat and stilt walker. His instinctive hostility to authority led him to join the Bolshevik Party, and on a professional level to learn the techniques of circus satire from Anatoly Durov. One of his handbills demonstrates how difficult it was to silence him:

BANNED!
BY THE CITY OF ORENBERG
VITALY LAZARENKO
AFTER 5.0 P.M. IS FORBIDDEN TO PERFORM ANY LONGER
BECAUSE OF WORDS HE SPOKE ON 3RD SEPTEMBER
AT THE CIRCUS IN ORENBERG
CONCERNING HIS VIEWS ON THE RUSSIAN CONSTITUTION[13]

1 Vitaly Lazarenko, Futurist, acrobat, clown.

Lazarenko allied himself with the Futurists before the revolution, appearing in the film *I Want to be a Futurist*, but was quite able to mock their leading poet's pretensions:

> Lazarenko wore the costume of an equestrienne with a huge red hat, rhinestones in his ears, and an enormous black radish on his chest. 'Why the black radish?' asked Volodia (Mayakovsky). Lazarenko explains: 'I'm incarnating an equestrienne who is madly in love with Mayakovsky. You are usually wearing radishes in your buttonhole, and she is trying to please you and seduce you by also wearing a radish. Hopelessly in love, she recites your poetry riding in the arena of the circus and, constantly falling off the horse, she presses the radish to her heart and exclaims: "Oh! Mayakovsky, Mayakovsky, why did you make me lose my head?"'[14]

The vibrancy of the circus was coveted by the revolutionary theatre, whose practitioners, dissatisfied with their art's dominant conventions, discerned new dramatic potential in the forms which circus used, especially, perhaps, the kind of pantomimes it produced. Similarly the satirical clown was a character full of latent strength. And the circus performer's ability to create a *persona* rather than a fully-rounded character was highly instructive. Bim, for instance, was recognisable instantly by his costume, his prop (an outlandish musical instrument) and his signature tune, Lazarenko by his walk and his conventional make-up. Yet these characters were continually surprising to their audiences.

Here was a kind of creation which the legitimate theatre neither used nor knew; a creation shared, moreover, by the popular drama of the fairgrounds and even by the more ritualistic folk dramas, for which the audience encircled the action, as they would at a circus. The disposition of people in a circus, fairground show or folk ritual was based on the principle of gathering round, which was fundamentally different and more democratic than the expected spatial relationship found in the formal theatre. In this respect, the traditional and popular theatres could serve as a model for revolutionary theatre. At their best, these theatres were neither ritual nor literary phenomena. They left ritual behind as they developed towards a portrayal of social life, but they never became true-to-life portrayals for audiences simply to watch. Spectators were always encouraged to respond out loud, either in repartee provoked by a performer, or in singing an appropriate song, or in being appealed to by a character in the play. One or more actors came quite frequently among them, and even from the stage no one pretended that the words were not spoken for the benefit of the audience. There was a kind of informality about the proceedings, deriving from the fact that everyone present, whether performer or spectator, knew they were at a play, and the concrete actuality of the actor-audience relationship was the play's *raison d'être*.

THE NEW THEATRE

If one foot of the revolutionary theatre stood firmly in popular theatre and circus, the other was placed firmly in the work of the radical intelligentsia, who, after the removal of the Imperial theatres' monopoly in 1882, were at last given the opportunity to develop alternative forms. In the following decades these proliferated extraordinarily, in Stanislavsky and Nemirovich-Danchenko's Moscow Art Theatre, in Diaghilev's *World of Art* group which became the 'Ballet Russe', in the theatres of entrepreneurs like Mamontov and Korsch, and in the whole Symbolist theatre movement.

Some early seeds of revolutionary theatre were planted when Stanislavsky set up a Theatre Studio to search for appropriate methods for the staging of Symbolist drama under his erstwhile friend and *protégé*, Vsevolod Emilievich Meyerhold. In the summer of 1905, this new group began work on plays by Ibsen, Przybyszewski and Hauptmann, as well as on Maeterlinck's medieval *The Death of Tintagiles*, and even though Stanislavsky terminated the experiment after a few months, Meyerhold made some important first discoveries during the months the Studio was in existence. He found that just as Wagner revealed 'inner dialogue' through orchestral colouring, so the actor could achieve something of the same through plasticity of movement: 'The essence of human relationships,' Meyerhold wrote, 'is determined by gestures, poses, glances and silences. Words alone cannot say everything. Hence there must be a *pattern of movement* on the stage to transform the spectator into a vigilant observer.'[15] This 'pattern of movement', which constitutes the dramatic rhythm, frees the actor from the need to create character in the conventional sense, and the stage itself from the need to have footlights, curtains and realistic scenery. The stage can be on a level with the auditorium, and the actor can face the spectator in a truly creative relationship. 'We intend the audience not merely to observe,' Meyerhold wrote, 'but to participate in a *corporate* creative act'.[16] Stanislavsky objected, but Meyerhold was appointed director of Vera Komissarzhevskaya's Dramatic Theatre, which was to be devoted to 'the new drama'.

His most successful and influential productions here were of Maeterlinck's *Sister Beatrice* and *The Fairground Booth* by Alexander Blok. *Sister Beatrice* was the archetypal Symbolist play, soaked in medievalism and telling the story of a nun who 'leaps over the wall' to go with her lover. The play was presented by Meyerhold against 'a Gothic wall in which the green and lilac-tinted stone blends with the grey tones of tapestries and glimmers faintly with pale silver and old gold.'[17] The backcloth was so close to the footlights that the performers were forced onto the forestage and there was no possibility of illusionism. The performance was a subtly-modulated chiaroscuro of pauses, whispers and rustling movements, with the actors grouping and regrouping almost like an unfolding series of bas-relief frescos against the backcloth. Everything was aimed to strengthen the mystical union with the audience which the Symbolists yearned for, and indeed the production may be regarded as the high point in Symbolist performance.

But *The Fairground Booth*, performed a mere five weeks later, undermined everything *Sister Beatrice* seemed to have achieved. This story of the love of Harlequin, Columbine and Pierrot was set amidst mystics and medieval lovers who were unmistakably figures of the Symbolist pantheon but who were here held up for unbridled mockery. The mystics, who Blok based deliberately on his Symbolist friends, were a group of cardboard cut-outs, mere silhouettes against a stylised background. The lovers, too, were parodies of Maeterlinckian knights and ladies, and their court jester fell when struck by a wooden sword, bleeding 'real cranberry juice'. The rapid, swirling crowd movements or still moments of apparent mystery were punctuated by unwarranted entrances by the exasperated author, protesting that his play was being maltreated. And every so often Harlequin would appear, Pierrot would laugh mockingly, or the beautiful Columbine would stand in such a way that the mystics mistook her chignon for the scythe of Death. Through masks, movement and all manner of anti-illusionist devices, *The Fairgound Booth* was a stirring affirmation of concrete life, and a rejection of the self-indulgence of unnecessary symbols. No wonder that at the end of the performance, the audience erupted in cheering, booing, catcalls, laughter and shouted demands for the author, the designer, the composer, and above all the director. No wonder, either, that the production became to young iconoclastic and revolutionary artists 'as the Church of Spas Neriditsa was to ancient Russia',[18] for it effectively put an end to the pretensions of the Symbolists and forced those who wanted a conventional rather than a naturalistic theatre to look elsewhere.

They turned their attention in the first instance to cabaret, which reached Russia in February 1908, when the Bat opened in the basement of a fabulous Moscow mansion, Pertsov House. A few months later the Distorting Mirror was founded in St Petersburg by the actress Zinaida Kholmskaya and her critic husband, Alexander Kugel, and other cabarets, or 'theatres of miniature dramas', followed. In 1910 Kugel invited Nikolai Evreinov to become artistic director of the Distorting Mirror, which moved to the Ekaterinsky Theatre, and became perhaps the outstanding cabaret theatre in the tsarist capital. This stemmed at least in part from the juxtapositioning created by Kholmskaya's method of programming, and seen too at the Bat: 'several songs in costume or in character with slight but eloquent backgrounds; a farce or two played with the earnestness of all good farce; a moment with marionettes; a scene or a short play from Pushkin or Gogol or Gorky.'[19] Such a programme's random variety seems to break down the traditional forms of theatre, deconstructing the apparent equivalence of 'going to a play' and 'going to the theatre', and creating the space for 'a new, original phenomenon', which might become the revolutionary theatre.

At this time the Bat was 'a snug and cosy little auditorium with capacious and bizarre refreshment rooms and a homelike foyer opening off it where the long intermissions seem all too short.'[20] Meyerhold's House of Interludes had a similar intimate arrangement so that its most significant production, *Columbine's Scarf*, was staged in and among the spectators' tables. In *The Transfigured Prince* by the chess grandmaster, Evgeny Znosko-Borovsky, not only was there dancing in the auditorium, but at one point an actor jumped off stage and hid under one of the tables. In a more cabaret-like 'turn' at the Stray Dog, Tamara Karsavina danced not on the stage, but among the spectators seated round the tables. The Stray Dog was situated in the cellar of a mansion and was decorated with pictures of Smeraldina, Pantalone, Brighella and other *commedia* characters (as well as a portrait of Carlo Gozzi), painted by artists such as Sapunov and Sudeikin, and there was an overwhelming air of informality:

> For the most part the entertainments were unrehearsed . . . an actor would come forward and give of what his mood suggested . . . the poets recited their new poems . . . the host would take a guitar and sing, and when he came to a favourite song all joined in the refrain: 'Oh, Maria, oh, Maria, how sweet is this world.'[21] Here the piano improvisations of Ilya Sats and the verses of Mikhail Kuzmin were heard . . . [and] Romanov staged and performed dances 'with a touch of an orgiastic bouquet, slightly immoral and a tiny bit pornographic.'[22]

The miniature drama developed in the Russian cabaret was iconoclastic and stimulating, though hardly revolutionary. Evreinov's most famous work in this genre was probably *The Government Inspector* in which the opening scene of Gogol's masterpiece was presented several times by a thoroughly pedantic caricature of Evreinov himself. We see the scene as it might be produced by students of Stanislavsky, Reinhardt, Craig and a director from the silent films. In *The Fourth Wall*, Evreinov mocked the excesses of Stanislavskian naturalism by showing a rehearsal of Gounod's *Faust* in which the 'unreal' elements are progressively eliminated. First, the music goes, then the poetry, then audible speech, then the 'unbelievable' characters such as Mephistopheles. Finally a fourth wall is built between stage and auditorium, and the actor playing Faust has to drink real poison![23] A second writer associated with the Distorting Mirror whose work was almost as ingenious as Evreinov's was Boris Geyer, whose *Aqua Vitae*, for instance, showed empathetically how the perception of a bar-room changes as the customers become progressively drunker. The lights grow brighter, and the characters smarter; then the talk becomes more animated, and then more flirtatious; finally, the room grows dim again, the music becomes funereal, and the characters maudlin as they snivel into their cups. Highly original and provocative, the plays of Evreinov and Geyer, like Blok's *The Fairground Booth*, demonstrate both the effectiveness of the short form, especially in a 'mixed' programme alongside dance, recitation and other items; they also show its special strength as a tool for cracking open the seeming indestructibility of fixed forms, whether these be dramatic forms or the forms of social life as they appear at any given time.

THE ANCIENT THEATRE

The Fairground Booth's medievalism, and its *commedia* characters, led theatre practitioners towards the roots of popular drama. The medieval theatre was explored most notably by Nikolai Evreinov, who, together with Baron Nikolai Drizen, the censor of the Imperial theatres, and editor of their influential Year Book, created the Ancient Theatre in 1907. Evreinov's main choreographer was Mikhail Fokin: Ivan Bilibin, Mstislav Dobuzhinsky and Nikolai Roerich were among the designers. Ilya Sats and Alexander Glazunov both composed music for the company, and the texts were prepared by, among others, Alexander Blok, Konstantin Balmont and Sergei Gorodetsky.

In the autumn of 1907, the company began rehearsals with dauntless enthusiasm: unable to enter the Kononovsky Hall, where they were to perform, until after the show that was running there had finished, they rehearsed from midnight to 8.0 a.m. each night and in the afternoon as well if necessary. The method chosen for the presentation was called 'artistic reconstruction', and involved the recreation of the whole theatrical and dramatic event, including the contemporary audience. It was essential to the experiment that actors dressed and behaved as spectators. The aim was to tap the strengths of the medieval theatre while simultaneously allowing the modern director (who had studied the period and the theatrical form) the freedom of the contemporary artist.

The Ancient Theatre opened on 7 December 1907 with *The Three Magi*, an eleventh-century liturgical drama for which Evreinov wrote a special prologue, and the thirteenth-century French play, *The Miracle of*

11

Theophilus, translated by Alexander Blok. The story of *The Three Magi* was almost submerged in Evreinov's 'prologue' which opened with the crowd waiting in the cathedral square for the drama, talking, discussing the coming play, sobbing with anxiety. A group of flagellants arrived, adding to the disquiet. Then the scenery was set in front of the cathedral, church dignitaries appeared to watch, and only then did the play finally begin. It was played entirely in Latin, and the main interest lay in the convulsive and passionate responses of the crowd, who, as Herod called for the death of all the first born at the end of the play, rose up with one voice, swarmed towards him in religious frenzy, and drove him out in frightful disorder. The effect was thrilling, and thoroughly 'theatrical'. The second presentation, *The Miracle of Theophilus*, was more naïve, and Dobuzhinsky designed a setting on three levels – heaven, earth and hell – which was placed flat and parallel with the front of the stage in a manner somewhat reminiscent of Meyerhold's setting for *Sister Beatrice*. It was charming, stylised and 'theatrical', but not on the scale of *The Three Magi*,

The second programme of medieval drama consisted of later secular plays, first *The Present-Day Brothers*, a morality story, translated by Gorodetsky, concerning two boys who attempt to drown their younger brother, which used placards to inform the audience of salient information; Adam de la Halle's *The Play of Robin and Marion*, the next part of the programme, was set in a theatricalised context, a supper in a knight's castle, with a Master of Ceremonies who introduced the play to the 'spectators', and laid out the props and furniture. The evening concluded with two short farces, one *About a Tub*, the other *About a Cuckold's Hat*, set in 'a medieval fairground booth with two boxes on either side of the stage'. Two traditional fools, 'fantastically costumed and made up', sat in these boxes to 'deliver their humorous commentary on the action. From time to time they leap from the boxes to disrupt the action.'[24] It made a lively ending to the medieval experiments of the Ancient Theatre, which had revealed some of the potential inherent in naïve staging, interrupted action and audience response.

The first inheritor to this legacy was probably the Moscow Literary Circle, who produced Boris Tomashevsky's rewritten version of the traditional Russian drama, *Tsar Maximilian and his Unruly Son Adolf*, with designs by Vladimir Tatlin, in 1911. The same year the Ancient Theatre was revived, and presented a season of classical Spanish plays, commencing with Lope da Vega's *Fuente Ovejuna*. Evreinov's production, surprisingly for such an overtly non-political person, concentrated on the political implications of the peasant uprising, though the ending was changed to allow a reconciliation between the king and his people, and it was presented on a trestle stage, apparently by a band of strolling players. The traditional popular style was further reinforced in the intervals between the acts: in the first, a troupe of girls danced, making comments to the audience and peeling and eating oranges, whose pips they spat out, before ending with the *guarda-infantes*, a deliberately erotic dance in which the girls 'excited the imagination of the audience with their suggestive costumes, featuring flesh coloured stockings that rose to a little above the knee, exposing bare thighs.'[25] The second interval contained a performance of *Los Habladores* by Cervantes, of small enough importance in itself, but worth noticing for the same reason as the girls' dancing: both are deliberate interruptions of the progress and mood of the main piece.

The remaining productions of the Spanish season, Tirso de Molina's *Martha the Devotee*, Lope da Vega's *The Grand Duke of Muscovy* and *The Purgatory of St Patrick* by Calderon de la Barca, were less significant, but still contributed to the gains from the two seasons of the Ancient Theatre. A third season centred on *commedia dell'arte* was planned, but the First World War prevented its accomplishment. While this was undoubtedly a loss, there was already plenty of experimentation in *commedia* techniques proceeding in *avant-garde* studios and workshops.

Meyerhold's production of *The Fairground Booth* was in a certain measure responsible for attention being turned to this, though Evreinov bitterly disputed his contribution.[26] Nevertheless, the acrid tone within which its whimsy was cloaked, its layers of identity confounded in layers of meaning, its use of irony coupled with virtuoso theatricality, the way in which it addressed the problems of illusion and disillusion, made it an endlessly fruitful text and Meyerhold staged it at least three times. Boris Pronin, formerly a director at Komissarzhevskaya's theatre, tried to establish a theatre devoted to *commedia dell'arte*, though the venture quickly transformed into the Stray Dog cabaret. S. M. Ratov hoped to mount a series of 'Harlequin' plays,[27] the most important result of which was Evreinov's *The Death of Harlequin*, later called *A Merry Death* which the author considered his 'greatest one act play'.[28] Evreinov's *commedia* credentials went back to his teenage days, when he busked in the streets of the Sokol district of Moscow dressed as Pierrot, playing on a comb covered with tissue paper, and waggling his ears for the passers-by. Mikhail Kuzmin, Meyerhold's composer for *The Fairground Booth*, also drew upon *commedia dell'arte* in *The Venetian Madcaps*, first performed by a group of talented and socially influential St Petersburg amateurs in February 1914. This play develops the genre's potential for ambiguity and uses the device of the play-within-the-play to create something of the effect of a hall of mirrors, exploring forbidden sexuality almost frivolously, until the moment of murder abruptly stops the fun.

However, the relationship of these plays to the real *commedia dell'arte* is dubious. Scenarios such as those created for production by Meyerhold under his pseudonym, Doctor Dapertutto, may be truer to the tradition. The first of these was *Columbine's Scarf*, after a play by Schnitzler, presented in October 1910 at the House of Interludes. The tragic triangle of Harlequin, Columbine and Pierrot is depicted here with a sinister intensity which those who saw it found almost unforgettable, especially the nightmare scene in the ballroom where the music is played by a grotesque band and the dancers swirl in ever more rapid circles, while Pierrot's sleeve is glimpsed, haunting the guilty Columbine. Probably more like the *balagan* Harlequinade Benois saw in 1874 was Meyerhold's production of Soloviev's *Harlequin, the Marriage Broker*, in which:

> the actor is given the general outline of the plot and in the intervals between the various key moments he is free to act *ex improviso*. However, the actor's freedom is only relative because he is subject to the discipline of the musical score. The actor in a harlequinade needs to possess an acute sense of rhythm, plus great agility and self-control. He must develop the equilibrist skills of an acrobat, because only an acrobat can master the problems posed by the grotesque style inherent in the fundamental conception of the harlequinade.[29]

Evreinov, too, tried his hand at this sort of pantomime, most successfully in *A Columbine of Today*, the story of a woman's progression from innocence through love to her final embrace in the arms of Death, which he produced at the Distorting Mirror in November 1915. Nevertheless, it was not so much the acting which was so memorable, as the delicately romantic set and Evreinov's music, which combined 'primitive one-hundred-year-old forms with contemporary rhythms of American tap-dance and the two-step'.[30]

The ballet, *Carnaval*, also explored the world of *commedia dell'arte*. It was created in three days in January 1910 by Mikhail Fokin for a charity performance at the Pavlova Hall, St Petersburg. The cast included Tamara Karsavina as Columbine and Bronislava Nijinskaya as Papillon, the giddy girl whom Pierrot hopes to win. Pierrot in this first production was danced by Vsevolod Meyerhold, who, according to Fokin 'gave a marvellous image of the melancholy dreamer Pierrot'.[31] He had of course played Pierrot in the first production of *The Fairground Booth*, when he 'stood like a stork with one leg behind the other and played on a thin reed pipe,'[32] and in February 1914 he was to play him a third time in Boris Romanov's *Pierrot and the Masks* on the stage of the Aeroclub in St Petersburg. But Fokin believed *Carnaval* was Meyerhold's 'first contact with the art of rhythmic gesture set to music'.[33]

These experiments were relevant in all the areas of Meyerhold's work. He called his theatrical journal *The Love of Three Oranges* after Gozzi's scenario of 1761, and he included practical study of *commedia*

2 Sketch for the set design for *A Columbine of Today* by Nikolai Evreinov, November 1915.

techniques in the syllabus of his Studio. His collaborators included Konstantin Miklashevsky, author of a history of the *commedia dell'arte*, and Vladimir Soloviev, whose practical classes explored conventional poses, such as Harlequin's stance with one hand on hip and one toe cocked, traditional gags, including slapstick and clowning, and theatricalised 'set scenes', such as 'the challenge', 'the duel' and so on. At other Studios, too, such as those of Fedor Komissarzhevsky,[34] Maria Rigler (who had played Marion in the Ancient Theatre's production of *The Play of Robin and Marion*) and Samuil Matveevich Vermel, *commedia* and allied techniques were taught, so that gradually but clearly, a new understanding of the place of movement, dance and mime in drama arose. Its attraction lay initially in its challenge to the actor to integrate stylised movement, or even dance, into his performance. Harlequin's individuality resides in his stylised pose and springy movements, but he is also a character type, whose identity is generalised in the mask he wears. He embodies not so much a contradiction as a series of echoes. Meyerhold commented on Harlequin as being simultaneously a buffoon and a 'wizard'. He suggested that the 'mask', in its physical reality and in its intangible quality of a 'character', leads to the root of the actor's art.[35] However, for all its potential, *commedia dell'arte* could be nothing

15

more than a staging post on the way to a more pertinent form. For *commedia* was out of both its time and its place. It needed radical adaptation before it could address the realities of contemporary Russian life.

THE FUTURIST THEATRE

Futurism was the most shocking artistic movement in the immediate pre-revolutionary period in Russia. Futurist poets, Mayakovsky in his yellow shirt with a wooden spoon or a radish in his buttonhole or Burlyuk with his face painted, scandalised their audiences, but also created genuine excitement about performance. According to one critic:

> the idea behind the Futurist 'evenings', in which the Futurists declaimed their verses, read manifestos and lectures, performed concerts of 'noises', and exchanged verbal and even physical abuse with the audience . . . was to expand the stage, to go beyond the boundaries of the artificially limited performing space, to turn the whole city into a stage and life into a performance.[36]

Perhaps the most challenging Futurist poet was Velimir Khlebnikov, who wrote several almost unstageable plays, and also a prologue to Alexei Kruchenykh's opera, *Victory Over the Sun*. This was produced in a double bill with Mayakovsky's *Vladimir Mayakovsky, a Tragedy* in December 1913 at the Luna Park Theatre, formerly Vera Komissarzhevskaya's theatre, in St Petersburg. To get performers, Mayakovsky advertised in the popular newspaper, *Rech*, and the two pieces played to capacity audiences, who reacted vociferously: 'There was boisterous shouting at the top of their lungs from half the spectators: "Out! Down with the Futurists!" and from the other half: "Bravo! Don't disturb us! Down with the brawlers!"'[37]

Victory Over the Sun is, according to Kruchenykh, 'an attempt to destroy one of the greatest artistic conventions, the sun in the given instance . . . The Futurists wish to free themselves from this ordering of the world.'[38] The first step in this process came in Khlebnikov's prologue, which suggested the need for a change in the way we 'see', and the potential of the artist to create such a change. However, it is only certain artists, presumably Futurists, who can effect it, and then only by a fusion of artist, spectator and subject:

> Lookers painted by an artist, will create change in the look of
>   nature.[39]

The old art is part of the conventional way of seeing, and it is with the destruction of all previous art that *Victory Over the Sun* is primarily concerned.

The opera begins with the Strong Men tearing the curtain apart. This is not only a deliberate defiance of the old decorous raising of the curtain, it is also a physical destruction of the most cherished symbol of the traditional theatre. The Strong Men are determined to put an end to the old culture in typical Futurist verse:

> We will lock the fat beauties
> In the house
> Letting these various drunkards
> Walk stark naked there

and disavow any stake in the conventional culture:

> We don't have the songs
> Sighs of prizes
> That amused the moldiness
> Of rotten naiads!

The sun was responsible for the old ideas, and Nero-and-Caligula 'combined in one person' is its first representative, the rich amateur artist and patron. Nero-and-Caligula drives away the Strong Men, adopts a 'noble' pose and boasts of his mindless, destructive consumerism in the arts. But when the Time Traveller arrives, he panics. He can no longer 'trust old measurements' – 'It should be forbidden to treat elders this way!' he shouts. He then takes his boots off and leaves. After more extraordinary confrontations, the Aviator's plane finally crashes, but he strides from the wreckage with loping steps. 'I am alive', he says, and bursts into a strong, joyful, trans-sense song:

> everything is good that
> has a good beginning
>   and doesn't have an end
> the world will die but for us there is no
>   end!
>   [*Curtain.*

Victory Over the Sun affirms a future through the use of deliberately contemporary images. For Matyushin, the composer, the production effected a 'breakdown' of the old, the boring and the literal.[40] His music, though it may seem rather naïve in comparison with what Stravinsky or Schoenberg were doing in Europe at this time, is curiously effective, aware of grand opera, which it often parodies, but then sliding off-pitch capriciously or employing strange intervals and dissonances. Kasimir Malevich created a visual style for the production which re-inforced Kruchenykh's dialectical structuring of the text, with dynamic bustle being set against aggressively geometrical simplicity. The costumes were 'trans-real' cardboard-and-wire contrivances which were

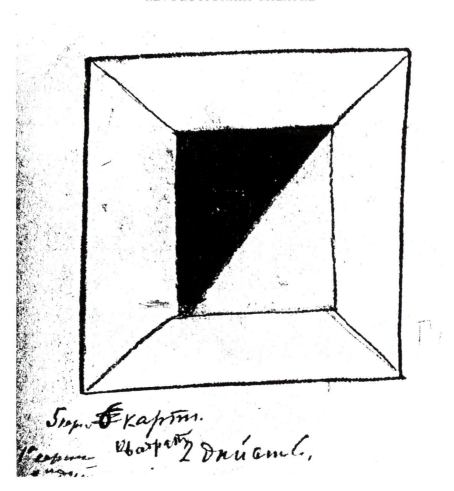

3 Sketch by Kasimir Malevich for *Victory Over the Sun*, December 1913.

highly original in conception even if they were not always realised in practice. Kruchenykh applauded the masks' machine-like qualities, as well as the fact that the costumes 'transformed the human anatomy'[41] and dictated the rhythm of the actors' movements and poses. The backcloths were equally striking, dynamic and Futurist, like the house in the second act, and the black-and-white diagonally divided square which was created for the opening scene, and which has been hailed as the first example of Suprematist art.[42] The stage was lit by brilliant projector beams which roamed seemingly at random over the stage and backdrops, and cast unexpected shadows, thus showing up Malevich's designs to weird and novel effect. If he had not been as rushed as everyone else connected with the production – according to Matyushin he 'created twenty large pieces of decor in four days'[43] – the results might have been even more spectacular.

The second half of the double bill, Mayakovsky's *Vladimir Mayakovsky, a Tragedy*, created an even greater effect.

> The lights went down and the curtain rose. The show began. A mysterious half-light illumined an area closed in with heavy cloth or calico and a tall backdrop made of black cardboard, which was all the stage set consisted of. The cardboard was covered with weird drawings. What it was I couldn't attempt to say: a kind of tube, turned upside down, houses, inscriptions going up and slanting, bright leaves and colours. What was it supposed to represent? Neither I nor anyone else understood, but strangely enough, it created an impression: there was life and energy in it. It was in turmoil . . . it alienated and attracted, it was incomprehensible and simple . . .
>
> From behind the curtain the *dramatis personae* filed out one after another: cardboard, living puppets. The public tried to laugh, but the laughter stopped in their throats. Why? Because it just wasn't funny – it was terrifying. Few of those sitting in the auditorium could understand or explain it. If I had come demanding an extremely funny spectacle, extremely amusing, if I had come to hoot at a clown, and suddenly this clown began to talk very seriously about me – the laughter would freeze on my lips. And in that first instant of stopped laughter – at that very moment, the audience was caught and troubled. They wanted to laugh – that's what they'd all come for. But they waited, and gazed avidly at the stage.[44]

Vladimir Mayakovsky, a Tragedy concerns love, both in its public aspect, the love of the revolutionary for the people whose lives he is impatient to improve, and in its private aspect, the passion of man for woman. Socially, the play deals with the possibility of liberation from the constraints imposed by the past and social convention. This is indicated by the opening beggar's carnival, when the poor indulge in riotous dreams. But their dreams remain dreams without Mayakovsky to realise them for them. The stage is dominated from the outset by a huge figure, draped in dust-sheets, which at the climactic moment are removed to reveal the awesome figure of the Enormous Woman. She is the 'red meat' which, when it is eaten by the downtrodden (that is, when she is unveiled) makes them become revolutionary: they raise her high, then at the climax of the frenzy, drop her as the Man with One Eye and One Leg announces the complete overthrow of the old world:

19

on the foreheads of cities
anger swelled up into rivers
of thousand-mile-long veins.
Slowly,
in terror,
arrows of hair
rose up on the bald pate of Time.[45]

On the level of personal emotional life, the play concerns the seething ungovernable feelings of passionate love. The unveiling of the Woman changes the 'jolly holiday' into the 'joyous madness' of fulfilled love. But love is selfless. It motivates Mayakovsky to set the Enormous Woman, the 'red meat', before the people, for they must eat her. They do so, that is to say, they carry the image shoulder high, but in their intoxication they mistake the giver for the gift. 'We'll raise a monument to red meat,' they cry, drop the Enormous Woman and drape Maya-kovsky in a toga: he is now as the Enormous Woman was at the beginning. On the personal plane, the raising of the monument, the draping of Mayakovsky in the toga stands for conventional respectability, and spells doom to the passionate spontaneity of love.

The play is thus a tragedy, for the protagonist's heroic attempts to make his selfless love productive have come to grief. The object of his love raised a monument instead of continuing the fury of carnival whose fantasies turned the world upside down. At the start of Act Two, significantly labelled 'depressing', the poet has become a monument, institutionalised in a toga and crowned with laurels. The revolution, the grand passion, has failed. He sinks down, exhausted and in despair, then rises up again, finally resolved:

But no! . . .
I'll go out through the city,
leaving
shred after shred of my tattered soul
on the spears of houses.

Institutionalised love – revolutionary or sexual – is a 'bestial faith' and Mayakovsky rejects it decisively.

Unfortunately, Futurism never properly harvested what was planted here: Mayakovsky did not write another play until after the Bolshevik revolution, and until then his and Kruchenykh's work tended to be parodied and mocked rather than faced squarely. Thus Zhdarsky's *Futurists' Cabaret* of 1914 was described by its author as 'A Performance for the Mentally Ill'. The opera, *Song of Universal Growth* by Pavel Filonov, who designed Mayakovsky's play, turned out to be a poor imitation of Kruchenykh's work, and Yuri Degen's play, *Death and the*

Bourgeois, which managed to pick up something of Mayakovsky's anti-bourgeois tone, lacked his passionate intensity. Even the promising Vadim Shershenevich's play, *Swifthood*, rarely achieves the dynamism through montage promised in his radical 1914 manifesto, *A Declaration about Futurist Theatre*. Only Ilya Zdanevich, who between 1916 and 1920 wrote a group of five plays largely in trans-sense language, comes near the earlier achievement. Described by the author as *vertep*, or rod puppet shows, the plays feature a Puppet Master who 'interprets' the action for the audience, and exhibit an intriguing medley of jokes, songs, *double entendres* and spectacular action, aiming to combine thereby the intellectual and the popular.

Despite the apparent poverty of their achievement, the Futurists' theatre work suggested genuinely different possibilities: intellectually tough, but preferring cabaret or circus tricks to psychology, abstract or functional settings to decorative realism, and actors who had more in common with acrobats and clowns than orators or makers of fine phrases. Sergei Tretyakov best expressed what they aimed to do: 'From the very first Futurist performances, it was already clear that Futurism aimed not so much at the establishment of an aesthetic dogma . . . as at exciting the human psyche in its entirety.'[46]

2

PETROGRAD 1917–1920

AN ENTIRELY NEW WORLD

In 1917 the old tsarist empire cracked, split and broke apart, and by the end of the year Lenin and his comrades had seized power, determined to create an entirely new society based on entirely new principles. For ten years or more, every aspect of social life was – or seemed to be – open not only to questioning but to reordering. The proletarian and the radical intellectual found common cause, especially in the theatre, which became a 'laboratory' for new ideas and a 'factory' for the production of the new man: debate about the function and forms of theatre became part of the process of remaking the whole of society.

The most influential theoretician associated with the debate was Alexander Alexandrovich Bogdanov, a doctor of medicine and a revolutionary, who was exiled in 1907. With Gorky, Lunacharsky (who married his sister) and others, he formed the *Vpered* group who opposed Lenin in 1909, especially concerning the part culture played within the building of socialism. For Bogdanov, revolution rested on three legs: through politics, the Party gained and wielded power; economically, the trade unions controlled property and the means of production; and culturally, an independent organisation, the cultural equivalent of the trade unions or the party, would create the *mores* for the new society. After 1917, the third leg of Bogdanov's tripod was the Proletkult ('PROLETarian CULTural and Educational Organisation'), within which Bogdanov wielded great influence for a few years. His ideas, disseminated partly through his popular and readable novels, *Red Star* and *Engineer Menni*, were subtler and more flexible than Lenin's, but Bogdanov lacked the latter's ruthless will to gain power.

Proletarian art was characterised, according to Bogdanov, by a *collectivist* spirit. Arguing that 'there is not and cannot be a strict delineation between creation and ordinary labour,' and that 'labour has always relied on collective experience,' Bogdanov was able to conclude that '(artistic) creation is the highest, most complex form of labour,' and that 'its methods derive from the methods of labour.'[1] Collectivism, he said, unified the spiritual and the physical, and unlike bourgeois individualism it fostered *comradely cooperation* – 'a conscious comradely organisation in the present and a socialist organisation of all of society in the future – these are different moments of one and the same process.'[2] It was through education that one 'moment' would give way to the other, for only education could enable the proletariat to produce the new culture. For Lenin, experience of revolution was enough to create socialist consciousness. Bogdanov, for his part, believed that education was needed to analyse, interpret and use that experience. Thus, Bogdanov suggested the typical workshop pattern which revolutionary artists created, most especially in the theatre, and most notably in his Proletkult organisation. Even after Bogdanov was elbowed off the Proletkult's governing body in 1921, he was still regarded as dangerous enough to be the object of a vitriolic denunciation in *Pravda* in January 1923, and later that year he was arrested on suspicion of involvement with the Left Opposition. He was released after a month of imprisonment. In 1926 he became director of the Institute for Blood Transfusion and, typically enough, died two years later when conducting an experiment on himself.

The application of Bogdanov's ideas to the theatre was attempted most assiduously by Platon Mikhailovich Kerzhentsev, another Bolshevik who returned from emigration in 1917 and ran the ROSTA agency as soon as it was set up. His greatest contribution to the cultural debate was his book, *The Creative Theatre*, which ran into several editions after it was first published in 1918. In it, he accepted Tolstoy's notion that great art 'infects' its audience, and Wagner's idea of a mystic union between artist and spectator. But after Bogdanov, the most important influence on his work was Romain Rolland, whose *The People's Theatre* was published in Moscow in 1919. Rolland's three key ideas for a people's theatre were: first, that theatre should be a recreation, which would give 'joy' and 'a sort of physical and moral rest' to the spectator after a day's work; second, that it should provide the spectator with a source of energy; and third, that it should be 'a guiding light to the intelligence'.[3] For Rolland, the *content* of the play was less important than the emotions evoked and 'shared' by the audience: drama, he said, should avoid 'moral pedagogy'.

Kerzhentsev himself had seen and admired community pageants in England and USA and believed such 'folk' or 'democratic' performances, based on collective creativity, could provide the new form of theatre needed in the new society. Drama which took the crises of class struggle – strikes, upheavals, insurrections, revolts – for its subject matter, such as Kerzhentsev's own *Amid the Flames*[4], could be performed by a proletarian 'actor-creator', part of 'a permanent workshop . . . where stars and extras are unknown.' This meant the theatre being open to all who wanted to participate. As for the specialist craft or art of acting, 'technique is necessary, but in the revolutionary epoch, it is not the centre of our concerns. A correct theoretical line, precise slogans, and burning enthusiasm are just as important.'[5] Professional theatre instructors, the kind of intellectual educators Bogdanov envisaged as necessary, were therefore viewed with some suspicion. Kerzhentsev's 'collectivism' involved all the people of a neighbourhood, so that plays were to be created in 'neighbourhood theatres'. However, they were also collective because each participant was to be involved in all areas of the creation, the actor in the sewing of costumes, the props maker in the scene direction, the stage-hand in the choice of play. Only then could the play properly express the collective consciousness, which was the special feature of the new revolutionary society. The pageant and the mass spectacle were likely to be the most fruitful forms of such drama, beause they encouraged the use of new spaces. 'Why confine theatre to the proscenium arch when it can have the freedom of the public square?' Kerzhentsev asked,[6] echoing Rolland. Moreover, situated beyond the conventional theatre, the mass pageant began to create a new audience-performer relationship, wherein the spectator might be transformed into a participant, and a new sense of community would be forged.

These ideals were difficult to achieve. The Proletkult's most perceptive critic suggests that 'while some local groups accepted (these) ideas as difficult but laudable goals, others ignored them altogether and tried to find their own guidelines.'[7] But Kerzhentsev's more specifically dramatic ideas, including the actor-creator (whether amateur or professional), the mass spectacle, the permanent workshop, the unconventional theatre space, and the new actor-spectator relationship, all clearly informed revolutionary theatre practice, and most obviously in the Proletkult. Its first President, Pavel Lebedev-Polyansky, an old member of the *Vpered* group, argued that 'the principle of collective labour must always be [Proletkult's] foundation,'[8] while Vasily Ignatov, its secretary, insisted on its independence from government. He also boasted that 'in Petrograd we call actors fighters and doers,'[9] an image taken up by N. I. Goncharko of the Saratov Proletkult, who talked of the theatre as 'a weapon of socialism'.[10] Another Proletkultist, Stefan Krivtsov, in January 1919, noted: 'The Proletkult is striving to create a new proletarian culture, not just new songs, new music, new theatre, but rather a whole new mode of life; we must create an entirely new world from top to bottom'.[11] Maxim Gorky, before he emigrated, advanced a plan for a new epic theatre dedicated to 'staging the history of human culture' in a circus arena.[12] Vyacheslav Ivanov, who in the early years of the century had been a leading advocate of Symbolist theatre, and who eventually emigrated to Rome and became a Cardinal in the Catholic church, wrote the introduction to the 1919 Russian edition of Rolland's *The People's Theatre*, and advocated 'song festivals with theatrical elements; the development of mass festivals into grand dramas involving the active participation of all; open-air theatre presenting monumental, allegorical scenes from the past'.[13]

The Commissar responsible, Anatoly Lunacharsky, remained nervous of these ideas. He believed in the autonomy of art, and the need to keep it free from state interference. Like Bogdanov, he saw culture as a crucial area for communism to conquer. He developed a theory of Man as God, whose deification would be reached in the Communist form of social organisation. For Lunacharsky:

> the essence of socialism was 'religious atheism', since people, striving to triumph over the finality of death, could experience immortality by merging with the collective, submerging the finite 'I' in the infinite 'We', and sharing in the great deeds and heroic acts of collectivised humanity.[14]

The theatre was an obvious vehicle for this, though whether this was the 'old' theatre or the new, revolutionary theatre was not immediately clear: 'We are dealing with a *new* public,' he wrote. 'They have almost never seen the theatre. They must see it and reorient its values.'[15] Hidden underneath this statement is the typical Bolshevik desire to organise 'them'. Perhaps there was civil war and famine, foreign intervention, transport and communication breakdown, or gangs of children roaming the streets, no electricity or fuel for warmth, assassinations, attempts at assassinations and the institution of 'red terror'. The burgeoning new theatre movement must be organised.

In January 1918 Lunacharsky's Commissariat of Enlightenment established a Theatre Department (TEO). Stanislavsky was invited to head it, but not surprisingly, he declined. Instead, the chair fell to Olga Davidovna Kameneva, sister of Leon Trotsky and wife of Lev Kamenev, the Moscow Party Chief. She took her responsibilities very seriously and became a familiar figure, arriving at many theatres before curtain up in her large and comfortable chauffeur-driven car. The Board consisted of Vsevolod Meyerhold, I. M. Lapitsky (artistic director of the Petrograd Theatre of Opera and Drama, and later head of the theatre inspectorate of TEO), Vera Menzhinskaya (a revolutionary schoolteacher who was to go on to head the whole TEO operation), Vasily Ignatov (the secretary of Proletkult), an obscure party functionary by the name of Rink, David Petrovich Shterenberg (the avant-garde artist who was also Head of the Commissariat's Fine Arts Department), and Donat Khristoforovich Pashkovsky (an actor at the former imperial theatres who was on the committee for their reorganisation into state institutions).

Meyerhold, whose more radical notions had been constantly thwarted at the Imperial theatres, proposed a single centralised structure for the administration of theatre. His designs to 'save the theatre' had earlier interested the Provisional Government of 1917, whose responsible minister, Boris Savinkov, later a virulently anti-Bolshevik fighter, promised support, but the second revolution overtook his good intentions.[16] Meyerhold argued that the Imperial theatres needed nothing less than a clean sweep from top to bottom, a new repertoire as well as new styles, while the private theatres should be taken over by the state so that they too could be brought into line. He formed a strategic alliance with Olga Kameneva, but Lunacharsky, fearing that artistic autonomy would be infringed by such a programme, published 'Statutes for the Autonomous State Theatres' on 11 March 1918, thus guaranteeing their position.

Kameneva and Meyerhold realised the need for a workable organisation to support their plans. These plans were not helped by Lunacharsky's appointment of the actress Maria Fedorovna Andreeva, a long-time Bolshevik who was totally opposed to 'leftist' trends in the theatre, as head of the TEO covering the 'northern oblast' (a vast area of northern Russia). But they made some progress. In August, a Moscow Department of TEO opened, and the following month Kameneva transferred the central organisation there; the Commissariat of Enlightenment had already moved there in March. She believed this would put her in a better position to argue for the centralisation of theatrical control, thus bringing the great former Imperial theatres into her department's responsibilities. She set up a new section in Petrograd, with Meyerhold (who had now joined the Bolshevik Party), in charge. Lunacharsky, despite wishing for a *rapprochement* with Stanislavsky, Alexander Yuzhin and others, found himself promising 'radical reform' and the 'centralisation' of the theatre in a single department, though it is not clear what he meant by this.

Control and centralisation, if Lunacharsky meant it seriously, was threatened by the 'chaotic' but extraordinary growth of the Proletkult, an organisation intended for anyone wanting to try their hand at art forms they found interesting. Theatrically, Platon Kerzhentsev articulated Proletkult's demands: to create cadres of proletarian actors; to continue to use professional instructors; and to work towards a new dramatic repertoire. To create a truly proletarian company, Kerzhentsev demanded that while Proletkult retained autonomy, the state should take control of the 'bourgeois theatre'.[17] The organisation's apparently inexorable rise was crowned on the first anniversary of the revolution, when Lenin attended their concert of music, poetry, drama and dance.

Perhaps in a measure to counter Proletkult's advance, Olga Kameneva created a new Workers and Peasants Section of TEO, with Valentin Tikhonovich at its head, aiming to monitor developments across the country, while she and Meyerhold moved towards their main objective. They had become convinced that Lunacharsky's previous proposal to 'centralise' the theatre had to be implemented, but their plan, to put the whole management, administration, repertoire and artistic style under their control at TEO went considerably further than the Commissar's original idea. But Meyerhold's determination to 'tame' them had hardened after his experience of trying to mount a production of Mayakovsky's *Mystery Bouffe* in the autumn of 1918. The actors at the Alexandrinsky Theatre, where Meyerhold was still a director, simply refused to perform it, and he was forced to find another, private venue. In February 1919, he and Kameneva therefore actively began to consider ways to achieve nationalisation. A meeting of various representatives in Moscow on 3 February, however, expressed considerable dissent, and after further rumination, the department's magazine, *The Theatre Herald*, invited correspondents to submit their opinions on the matter to the editor. Many contributions were forthcoming, including offerings from Kerzhentsev and Lunacharsky. Meetings continued also: in the actors union, in the Commissariat and elsewhere, and by the end of April Kameneva had drafted a plan which essentially put all professional theatres under the control of an expanded and more powerful TEO.

At the beginning of May 1919, Maly Sovnarkom (the cabinet office) discussed Kameneva's proposals with TEO's board, and then held a further detailed meeting to discuss it on 18 May, at which Meyerhold, Elena Malinovskaya (who was to be director of the Bolshoi Theatre in 1920) and others were present. On 6 June the results of these deliberations were passed to the cabinet in the form of a draft decree on the nationalisation of theatre and circus art. The essential features of Kameneva's proposal, that theatres should be organisationally unified under TEO, remained intact. However, events then took an unexpected turn, for in May, Meyerhold had fallen ill with tuberculosis, and had been compelled to retire to Yalta to recuperate. Maria Andreeva, head of the theatre section for the Northern Oblast, took his place in Petrograd, and her implacable opposition to TEO's plan, stemming perhaps from her personal antipathy to Kameneva, changed the course of the reorganisation.

Olga Kameneva and Maria Andreeva, for a short period the most powerful people in the Soviet theatre, make a fascinating contrast. Kameneva's background was entirely political, and her work in TEO was 'a cross' which she bore because 'I serve the Workers' and Peasants' government with complete devotion.'[18] She was not interested in the contending artistic schools and groups, though for a time she hosted a literary *salon* where impoverished writers came for hospitality and debate. And she must have been, in some measure, a 'Trotskyist'. One student of her career remarks that she was 'a thorn in Lunacharsky's flesh.'[19] Maria Andreeva, Gorky's second or common-law wife, by contrast, had a wholly theatrical background, even though Gorky nicknamed her, not inappropriately, 'the Commissar'. She had been a founding member of the Moscow Art Theatre, where she had allied herself with Meyerhold in his early struggles against Stanislavsky and Nemirovich-Danchenko, who said she was a 'big troublemaker'.[20] She left the Art Theatre in 1904, partly to be free to act elsewhere – she was at the Nezlobin Theatre for some years – but partly also to pursue revolutionary activities with Gorky. After the revolution she struggled mightily against 'decadent' artistic trends, which entailed (among other things) protecting the established theatres against what she regarded as over-eager empire-builders. She was a main instigator of mass revolutionary spectacles, but her contribution to building a new theatre was the co-founding of the conventional Bolshoi Dramatic Theatre of Petrograd with Gorky, Lunacharsky, Alexander Blok, Yuri Yurev and Nikolai Monokhov. She also there acted frequently, including playing the parts of Lady Macbeth and Desdemona.

Perhaps it was she who alerted the theatrical establishment to Kameneva's proposals. At any rate, Stanislavsky, Nemirovich-Danchenko, Yuzhin, Tairov and others whom Lunacharsky held in awe at last began to mobilise, and on 16 June 1919 they met to discuss ways in which Maly Sovnarkom's plan could be torpedoed. In the chair that day was Yakov Novomirsky, head of the All-Russian Central Trade Union Council. He went on to meet Lenin, and suggested to him that the current plan should be dropped. He also recommended that a new framework for the future organisation of the theatre should be devised by a different, less radical group of theatre workers, involving Stanislavsky and Yuzhin in particular. Lenin agreed, and Kameneva's plan was dropped.

Seeing her attempt to put the major theatres under TEO control defeated, Kameneva vented her fury in an article, published in *Izvestiya*, 'Why the Theatres Must Be Nationalised.' Ten days later, however, Lenin met Lunacharsky, Fedor Chalyapin, the opera singer, and the theatre adminstrator, Ivan Ekskuzovich, to begin to work out a new kind of reorganisation. Kameneva, ignored and powerless, resigned. (At her leaving party Vyacheslav Ivanov read a poem he had written to her!) With Trotsky's formidable sister out of the way, Lunacharsky took over the chair of TEO himself, and prepared an entirely new scheme which was ready by the beginning of August. It envisaged the nationalisation of all theatre property, and the financial supervision of all theatrical operations, but almost total artistic autonomy for theatres not regarded as subversive. Private theatres would have to accept a government nominee on their boards, but they could aspire to the autonomy of the established theatres as they developed. The administration of the former imperial and allied theatres and that of the others which were the responsibility of TEO, were to be united, as Kameneva had advocated, but in a new organisation, Tsentroteatr, to which TEO would be subordinate, and its president would be the Commissar himself. On 14 August Maly Sovnarkom passed this plan forward to the cabinet with few changes, and after some further discussions it was accepted by Lenin and his colleagues and published as a decree on 26 August 1919.

Ironically, almost the first action of Tsentroteatr was thoroughly 'Leftist': it abolished all theatre charges as from 1 September 1919. But a month later the favoured former Imperial theatres and a few others were designated 'academic'. This effectively guaranteed their continuing subsidy, perhaps to the exclusion of other theatres, and thus created a two-tier system, with the academic theatres (or 'accies' as they soon came to be called) on top. Tsentroteatr's desire to demonstrate its power and pre-eminence focused first on the small cabarets and theatres of miniatures which had sprung up with the abolition of censorship after the February revolution. Less like the pre-revolutionary Distorting Mirror than indoor *balagany*, the atmosphere at many of these places of entertainment was acrid with cheap tobacco smoke, and patrons drank coarse vodka or beer, watching singers, dancers and comedians perform their 'numbers' above a continuous hubbub of talking and laughter. Often housed in small rooms holding fewer than a hundred spectators, with a tinny piano as the only musical accompaniment, the performances were not, however, without interest. The *chanteuse* with her street songs, the singer dressed as Maxim Gorky with his chorus of 'If you know the vodka taste, You won't think what I do is base!' and the actress who undercut propaganda catch-phrases with gypsy music, all have a place in the development of revolutionary theatre, in which irreverence plays a vital part. The performance which most offended the Bolsheviks may stand as an example of the work of these theatres: a barefoot dancer, *à la* Isadora Duncan (whom the Bolsheviks admired), performed a 'dance of the dying revolutionary' as a kind of belly-dance!

In October Lunacharsky brought these iconoclastic performances to the attention of Tsentroteatr's board, though his remedy – to create sketches and a repertoire for these theatres acceptable to Tsentoteatr's board – seems either Utopian or ridiculous! In December, all except about half a dozen were closed down in Petrograd, pending further discussion. On 19 February 1920, the Moscow Soviet closed fourteen cabaret theatres, 'in view of their intolerable character', and confiscated their property,[21] and the following day, 20 February, the Petrograd Soviet of Art Workers passed a motion calling for the closure of all such institutions in their city. On 17 March Maria Andreeva signed the order for their closure.

In a sense, the treatment of the cabaret theatres was a rehearsal for the more arduous business of bringing Proletkult to heel. In February 1920, as part of a reorganisation of the whole Commissariat of Enlightenment, Tsentroteatr was absorbed into the ministry, the weakened Theatre Department (TEO) was put in the charge of the placid Vera Menzhinskaya, and Proletkult was officially moved into the Commissariat's extra-mural department. The move, however, had little practical effect, and throughout the summer Proletkult continued to prosper: so much so in fact that in August an International branch was established, and Lunacharsky accepted the office of President. But Lenin's removal of the autonomy of the trade unions, making them subservient to the Party, exposed Proletkult's weakness. Now he instructed Lunacharsky that at the forthcoming conference of Proletkult a decision to subordinate the organisation to the Commissariat of Enlightenment must be taken, as intended in February. But on 7 October, at the conference, Lunacharsky reiterated with new force that Proletkult's autonomy was absolute and must be completely protected. Lenin's fury was boundless. It was, he exploded, 'theoretically wrong and practically harmful [to attempt] to invent a special culture . . . or to establish the Proletkult as an "autonomous" organisation.' He went on to insist that 'all organisations of the Proletkult [had] the absolute duty of regarding themselves as being entirely auxiliary organs in the . . . People's Commissariat . . . under the general guidance of the Soviet government.'[22]

Consequently a group of Party members in the Proletkult, led by Valerian Pletnev and his wife Anna Dodonova, were dragooned into pressing Lenin's resolution, which was then accepted. The Party's Central Committee now set up a sub-committee to consider Proletkult's position while reforming the extra-mural department of the Commissariat of Enlightenment, partly in order to get a closer grip on the organisation. On 1 December 1920, *Pravda* published the Central Committee's final damnation of Proletkult:

> Proletkult had a purpose up till the October revolution. It was proclaimed an 'independent' workers' organisation, independent of Kerensky's Ministry of Education. The October revolution altered that perspective. The Proletkult continued to be 'independent', but now this was 'independent' of Soviet power. Thanks to this, and for a number of other reasons, there flowed into Proletkult elements which were socially alien to us, petty bourgeois elements, who sometimes actually took the leadership of the Proletkult into their own hands. Futurists, decadents,

advocates of idealistic philosophies hostile to Marxism and finally just dropouts from bourgeois journalism or philosophy began to appear all over the place in Proletkult. Behind the appearance of 'proletarian culture' the workers were presented with opinions drawn from the philosophy of Machism. And in the sphere of art, they were inculcated with absurdities and distortions in the style of Futurism.[23]

When *Pravda* refused to print Proletkult's reply, Lebedev-Polyansky resigned the Presidency and Pletnev of the 'Party faction' was elected to his place.

The attempts by the Party hierarchy to control and dampen *avant-garde* and working class theatre, however, were not yet successful. Krivtsev's 'entirely new world' did not turn out quite as any of the participants planned or expected.

'STAND AND MARVEL'

The first play to attempt to address the revolution's 'entirely new world' was Vladimir Mayakovsky's *Mystery Bouffe*, 'the first Soviet play',[24] which received its première at the theatre of the Petrograd Music and Drama Conservatory on 7 November 1918, in a production by Vsevolod Meyerhold. In it, a group of the so-called Unclean stood on the stage and declaimed:

> Our turn!
> Today, over the dust of theatres,
> scathing,
> our motto begins to burn:
> 'Renovate the world!'
> Stand and marvel, spectators!
> Curtain,
> unfurl![25]

This was not how the new authorities had planned it. A Repertoire Section of TEO had been set to work by Olga Kameneva when she began to argue for the centralisation of the theatre in the summer of 1918, but at the Proletkult Conference in September of that year, one of Kerzhentsev's resolutions stated flatly that 'the repertoire of the proletarian theatre has yet to be created, and urgent attention is to be paid to this in the theatrical and literary departments of Proletkult.'[26] Three months later, at the special meeting of TEO and after the first performances of *Mystery Bouffe*, Meyerhold was urging that 'TEO's first duty is to reform the repertoire'.[27] Olga Kameneva reported that the Repertoire Section had looked through an (almost unbelievable) total of 50,000 plays, and was now compiling a list of scripts to publish. However, because of the lack of specifically revolutionary drama this would also include work by Molière, Ibsen, Bernard Shaw and others. She suggested that potential playwrights should be encouraged to test their skills in practical workshops. The section also intended to sponsor competitions, to encourage new playwrights to submit their work for consideration.

The demand was acute but there was a lack of unanimity about the kind of drama the new situation required. Lunacharsky and Gorky favoured melodrama, since its high passions and emotional shocks enabled inexperienced spectators to respond quickly. Kerzhentsev, Pletnev and others in the proletarian movement all pushed the case for history plays drawn from significant moments in the class struggle. Others advocated 'literary montage'.[28] The idea of an 'Heroic, Epic and Satiric Portrayal of Our Epoch', as Mayakovsky described *Mystery Bouffe*, was not proposed. Even by April 1919 Alexander Blok, who headed the Repertoire Section of TEO, could still only recommend classic drama, and he suggested ways in which plays could be modified to express the correct revolutionary attitude. Plays which were endorsed, all more or less contemporary to each other, included Verhaeren's *The Dawns*, Heijermans' *The Death of 'Hope'*, Mirbeau's *The Power of Money* and Mérimée's *The Discontented* – all almost entirely forgotten today and none of them Russian. As head of Petrograd TEO, Meyerhold proposed a rather more subtle list, including Gogol's *Marriage* and *The Gamblers*, Aeschylus' *Agamemnon*, Byron's *Cain*, Maeterlinck's *The Miracle of Saint Anthony* and Oscar Wilde's *Salomé*. What is interesting about this list is its relationship to 'mystery': each of the plays tries to penetrate beyond social consciousness into less tangible areas of experience, relying as much on the form of the play as on its content. And this is a quality immediately noticeable in Mayakovsky's tellingly entitled *Mystery Bouffe*.

This play was Mayakovsky's dramatisation in largely symbolic terms of the 'highway of the revolution'. Revolution's flood sweeps the world. A few (carefully representative) people have managed to reach the last dry place on earth, the North Pole, where they decide to build an ark to escape. Of course, the Workers, the Unclean, build the vessel, while the Clean encourage them. On board, the Negus of Abyssinia is made tsar, and the Unclean fetch food, which the Negus eats alone, to the fury of the other Clean characters, who imagined they would get some too. They decide to overthrow him and institute a 'bourgeois democracy': the Unclean still fetch the food, but all the Clean can now eat it. It is the Unclean's turn to be outraged, and they overthrow the democracy, but are unsure where to go without leaders. A vision of 'Simply a Man' advises them to trust their own strength, and they go on, through hell and heaven, to the Promised Land. This Promised Land turns out to be their own homes, but, in the new workers' state, the tools, the things and the food are freely theirs.

Mayakovsky obtained a cast for *Mystery Bouffe* as he had for his first play, by advertising in the Petrograd newspapers:

> Comrade Actors! You are under obligation to celebrate the great anniversary of the Revolution with a revolutionary production. You must present the play *Mystery Bouffe*, a heroic, epic and satiric portrait of our era, written by Vladimir Mayakovsky . . . To work, everyone! Time is precious.[29]

The company he recruited was extremely mixed and lack of time prevented their being welded into much of a unit. Mayakovsky assisted Meyerhold in rehearsals, 'diligently explaining the laws of putting verses together to the actors', as Vladimir Soloviev, who also assisted, remembered:

> Sitting on a chair, slightly rocking his head and tapping on the chair with his pencil, Mayakovsky gradually got carried away, stood up, broke away from his place, jumped up on a chair and began to conduct like an experienced choirmaster, infecting the actors with his enthusiasm.[30]

Meanwhile, the theatre of the Music and Drama Conservatory was commandeered for the show, though the staff tried to lock the company out, hid items like nails, and refused to display the printed playtext at the Box Office. 'They brought the posters only on the day the show was due to open, and then it was just an unpainted outline. Then they announced that no-one was allowed to stick it up.'[31]

Mystery Bouffe is heavily reminiscent of a medieval mystery play, having characters escaping the flood in an ark, the harrowing of hell, the quest for the Promised Land and more. It was staged in a manner which recalled the Ancient Theatre's staging of *The Miracle of Theophilus*, primitive and emblematic in conception, but a little more sophisticated in practice. Using a vast globe (five metres in diameter) as the centre-piece, Kasimir Malevich created a series of striking, dissonant settings in gaudy colours, which were memorable though repellent to many. Perhaps the most successful item was the velvet curtain where posters of pre-revolutionary plays were pinned: at the appropriate point in the Prologue these posters were torn down.

In performance, something of the jagged rhythms of the play was perceived, because Meyerhold broke the action of the play down into a series of 'numbers'. These numbers included the Italian and the German catching of the Unclean in a rope as they emerged from below decks; the chucking overboard of the Negus; the moment when the Unclean realise they have been duped:

> CARPENTER. It's a knife in our backs!
> VOICES. And a fork, too!

The American roared on stage on a motorbike, while the Merchant fell off-stage as a clown: 'his tilted head weighs over, and he tumbles overboard, head-over-heels.' There are many such moments. The use of *balagan* conventions – 'Night. The moon skims across the sky, then goes down. Daybreak.' – and the ancient folk dream of the Land of Cockagne, now adapted to the Soviet situation, reinforce the achievement:

> In my heaven furniture fills sumptuous halls,
> electricity serves you in stylish rooms.
> Sweet work there will never callous your hand,
> but bloom in your palm like roses luscious.

The highlight was the appearance of the author as 'Simply a Man', an amazing 'number' in its own right:

> He climbed unseen by the audience up an iron fire-escape to the left of the stage onto a gantry four or five metres high, and there he fixed round himself a broad leather safety belt, and at the right moment he somehow fell off the gantry, soaring above the crowd of the 'Unclean', crowded on the deck of the ark . . . In this position, he minted the rattling verse of his monologue.[32]

The play unashamedly resorts frequently to popular devices, which it mixes with spectacular and conventional effects. It provides a 'mass meeting basis'[33] for the drama, uses 'distorting mirror' techniques and relies on unexpected 'turns' rather than seeking consistency of tone. Mayakovsky himself summed up his achievement succinctly:

> The mystery is the greatness of the revolution, the bouffe, the laughter in it. The verse of *Mystery Bouffe* is found in the slogans of meetings, the cries of street sellers, the language of newspapers. The action of *Mystery Bouffe* is the action of the crowd, the conflict between classes, the struggle of ideas – the world in little within the walls of a circus.[34]

The production aroused strong, if mixed, reactions. The unpredictable Lunacharsky described it as 'impassioned, audacious, high-spirited, challenging', and plenty of spectators 'laughed freely and with pleasure', but others 'greeted *Mystery Bouffe* with fixed bayonets, writing and speaking of "a profanation of art"'.[35]

In Moscow, the first anniversary of the revolution was marked by the première of Vasily Kamensky's *Stenka Razin*. It was one of five plays, as well as an opera and a ballet, about the popular rebel staged around this time: his picture decorated revolutionary posters and he even made his appearance in the circus. Kamensky's play was probably the pick of this glut, displaying a vitality and excitement appropriate to the occasion. Largely overlooked in western accounts of Russian drama,[36] it nevertheless achieved its energising aim, even if some scenes were less successful than others. Kamensky, Futurist poet, early aviator and biographer of Evreinov, treated the life of the seventeenth-century outlaw in several forms, including a novel, a long poem and this play which was rewritten more than once. But this, the most convincing version, created a very strong impression when it was presented at the Vvedensky People's House, Moscow. The company was rather better than that which Mayakovsky and Meyerhold had managed to assemble for *Mystery Bouffe*, with Alicia Koonen (wife of the Kamerny Theatre director, Alexander Tairov) as the Persian Princess, and Anatoly Ktorov from the Korsh Theatre as her consort. Stenka Razin was played by Nikolai Znamensky from the Moscow Art Theatre, the play was designed in an attractive childish-primitive style by Pavel Kuznetsov and directed by Meyerhold's former pupil, Arkady Zonov, and Vasily Sakhnovsky, formerly Komissarzhevsky's partner at the theatre named after Vera Komissarzhevskaya. It was, wrote one critic, an 'enormous success', partly at least, it should be noted, because it 'reeked of streets and circus'.[37]

Kamensky was a countryman, whose best work previously had been a novel, *The Mud Hut*, which is suffused with a 'love of nature and feeling of comradeship with animals'.[38] This is Stenka Razin's background – he is a village hero rather like Robin Hood. And just as in the best Robin Hood stories, where the hero acts under a moral compulsion to right oppressive social wrongs, so Stenka Razin in this play feels morally obliged to take up arms against a cruel system. The play employs an utterly direct and simple style, with plenty of clowning but a minimum of Futurist mannerisms, and achieves something of the spirit of the folk-tale. The play's 'irrepressible spirit' showed 'a very Russian and very talented work where historical truth is blended with poetic invention and authenticity of legend is interwoven with unrestrained fantasy'.[39] In fact, Stenka Razin, who is on one level a well-rounded 'character' with a wife and family, attains a 'mythic' status through Kamensky's treatment and the play as a whole, beyond its buffooneries, becomes a kind of 'mystery'.

Thus the theatre celebrated a year of revolution with two memorable plays by prominent Futurists, both designed to make their audiences 'stand and marvel'. They were markers for a future which was still to be won.

THE THEATRE EPIDEMIC

The political struggles to control the theatres were unpredictable partly because of the 'theatre epidemic', the frenzied enthusiasm for theatre which overran Russia after 1917. In conditions of enormous hardship, of starvation and cold, during the dislocation of society and the dangers of lawlessness, the demand for plays and for dramatic activity was almost insatiable. 'There was not a village where some barn had not been converted into a theatre'[40] and drama circles were 'multiplying more rapidly than protozoa. Not the lack of fuel, nor the lack of food, nor the Entente – no, nothing can stop their growth.'[41]

Even the most conventional theatres found a new audience crowding their doors:

> The Moscow plutocracy of bald merchants and bejewelled fat wives had gone. Gone with them were evening dresses and white shirt fronts. The whole audience was in the monotone of everyday clothes . . . There were many soldiers, and numbers of men who had obviously come straight from their work. There were a good many grey and brown woollen jerseys about, and people were sitting in overcoats of all kinds and ages, for the theatre was very cold . . . Looking from face to face that night I thought there were very few people who had had anything like a good dinner to digest. But, as for their keenness, I can imagine few audiences to which, from the actor's point of view, it would be better worth-while to play.[42]

But these people not only wanted to watch but to participate themselves. Street parades and demonstrations, modernisations of traditional Russian forms of celebration, perhaps, were the first primitive manifestations of the urge to theatricalise. Huntly Carter, describing a May Day parade in Moscow, found himself using theatrical imagery almost willy-nilly:

> It is overwhelming in form, colour, movement and sound . . . It is a mixture of old and new medieval pageantry on a vast scale . . . There is the parade of the army partly in the glory of the old Russian uniform and partly in the livery of King Machine, who commands the new services, air, tank corps, etc, and is served by battalions of young workers. The parade is followed by the gay procession of children – children in white – children like flowers amid bowers of evergreen. And then comes the merry trades procession, and you see emblematic cars, theatrical cars, industrial cars, exhibiting the occupations and recreations of the workers and peasants. Then there is the play of satire, the interchange of wit, the merry andrewism of clowns and buffoons, and above all

the response of a great crowd of spectators ready to let themselves go in the true spirit of street pageantry and revelry.[43]

Such events provided the impetus for the many strange, almost unique forms of theatre, or theatricalised life, which characterised so much in the immediate post-revolutionary years in Russia – agit-prop theatre, living newspapers, mock tribunals, mass spectacles and so on. Most of these forms found their beginnings here, and were carried across the country by 'red amateurs' and quasi-professional troupes, through government agencies such as TEO, under Olga Kameneva, and ROSTA, headed by Platon Kerzhentsev, through PUR, the Red Army's political-educational arm, through agit trains and agit ships, through the activities of Proletkult, and through the movement and dispersal of enthusiastic individuals, both amateur and professional.

One of Gorky's suggestions was almost executed: Mikhail Mordkin presented his ballet *Aziade* in the Nikitin Circus ring, with 200 'extras', while *Macbeth* was performed in the arena of Ciniselli's circus with 'mass scenes' staged by the choreographer, Boris Romanov, who also co-directed a new production of Kamensky's *Stenka Razin* at the Theatre of the Baltic Fleet with Sergei Radlov, on the second anniversary of the revolution. Even Petrushka became 'sovietised', either with sly subversiveness, as in his greeting, 'Best wishes for the 'oliday, the Sov-iet 'oliday, not the Cadet 'oliday', or in a form more acceptable to the authorities: in *Crack on the Nut*, Petrushka:

> hits a variety of undesirables over the head with his club (including Denikin, Vrangel and a Bourgeois), and is saved by a Teacher and a Red Army Officer from falling into the jaws of the traditional Barbos, here in a new incarnation as the Cur of Illiteracy.[44]

The typical drama of the 'theatre epidemic' was the one-act play, geared to propaganda purposes. Usually known as *agitki* (agit-prop playlets), these sometimes took the form of a simple 'slice of life', probably framed by a Prologue or Epilogue (or both) explaining the message, but more often the playlets treated – or deformed – reality for political purposes, perhaps through melodramatic action ('red guignol'), or through distorted decor or acting styles. The play *How They Caught the Spirit* is typical enough. Printed in a collection published by TEO in 1920, the play concerns Vasily, a worker in a scythe factory, and Andrei, a peasant. In four short balancing tableaux, each learns that he cannot survive without the other, for Andrei needs Vasily's scythes and Vasily needs Andrei's grain. What is interesting in the play is its use of 'non-naturalistic' elements. The Musician is a sort of Narrator, who accompanies the action with popular tunes played on the balalaika or accordion. The *impasse* is only broken when audience 'plants', a Worker and a Peasant, come on stage to point the way to the main characters. The stage is split in half with each half representing one character's base and during the play, the costumes become more threadbare, and the characters 'grow thin'! These transitions are apparently 'very abrupt and very visible'.[45]

Innumerable plays like this were hastily duplicated and sent for performance to different parts of the country. The official publication, *Red Shirt*, named after the basic costume of many of the groups, published suitable material for shows and suggested methods of staging. Groups were particularly encouraged to perform in rural areas, which were more cut off from developing events, and 'dramas' like *The Plots of the Counter-Revolution* and *October*, (embryonic living newspapers) were performed in many parts of Russia. There were also mock trials, such as described by Kerzhentsev in *The Creative Theatre*: *The Trial of Gabon*, performed with 'great success' by large numbers of participants, the trial of the assassins of Karl Liebknecht, a 'trial of illiteracy', and so on. In these, the spectators became the jury, and had to pass judgment on the action, thereby forcing them to articulate their attitudes. This was collective creativity of a special and effective sort. A variation on the mock trial was the trial of a character from a play which had occupied the first half of the evening. Thus, in Kharkov on 7 December 1919, a performance of I. Sambuyrov's *The Revenge of Destiny* was followed by a trial of the protagonist's wife, an essentially good woman driven to murder by a brutal husband. The trial was a highly animated affair, at the end of which the accused was acquitted. Such an event, the reporter remarked, was 'worth ten meetings on the same theme.'[46]

This entertainment was presented by a Red Army group for an audience of soldiers. The troops also received visits from civilian theatre groups: Valentin Smyshlyaev's extremely successful Moscow Proletkult production of Verhaeren's *The Insurrection*, for example, was shown at many front-line posts. Although the Civil War constantly disrupted the many clubs (which included drama circles and theatre groups) because it so frequently called up their working-class members, it appeared that nothing could actually stop their phenomenal growth. By 1920, Proletkult's many branches had over 500,000 members, and there were many other theatre clubs besides, especially factory and trade union clubs. In 1919 there were nineteen Proletkult theatre studios in Moscow alone, drawing members from all over the city. For some, such as Platon Kerzhentsev and Valerian Pletnev, the amateurism of the proletarian participants in these clubs was important, for professionalism tended to contrive drama 'which may be brilliant technically, but is not rooted in the class position of its creator.' Fedor Kalinin (brother of Stalin's future henchman) opposed this, arguing that artistic skills must be developed by proletarian artists, and that to do this the would-be artists required time, concentration and technique.

The experience of the Petrograd railwaymen's theatre group, known as the Central Dramatic Studio, went far to prove Kalinin's point. This troupe was founded on 31 August 1918 by Viktor Shimanovsky and Elizaveta Golovinskaya, formerly members of the Touring Theatre of Pavel Gaideburov and Nadezhda Skarskaya, which was splitting apart under the pressures of post-revolutionary life. Starting as amateur activists of precisely the kind Kerzhentsev believed in, the Central Studio aimed to create a popular demand for high quality drama, and presented the classics to other railway workers as well as in clubs and barracks. They were so popular that in January 1919 they were invited to tour northwestern railway depots, and the following month the Red Army invited them to tour the troops in the same area. Their very success forced them away from an everyday working life, and by September 1919 they were fully professional. That winter they performed three times a week in their own theatre, and in other venues on other days. They also organised conferences, concerts, readings and debates on matters of artistic interest.

One advantage of amateurism, however, was its usual lack of prejudice about how drama was created. Groups often did not simply put on amateur versions of the standard professional repertoire: 'In the remote villages where there were no standard plays, the peasants who had no "instructors" at all staged Russian songs. They themselves wrote plays, and – what is more interesting – they frequently wrote plays collectively.'[47] In one club:

> a group of workers took a picture and tried to 'produce' it. The picture was hanging on the wall of the club room. Someone suggested that they should take its subject, a woman and man holding a barricade, and dramatise it. They proceeded to analyse the picture. They inquired why the woman was at the barricade. This led to a discussion of the social relations of man and woman, the questions of labour, and the many questions arising therefrom. When they had fully analysed it, unfolded it, as it were, they arrived at the material for a play. First they produced the play without words. Then words were introduced. Thus collectively they built up the play, altering it here and there as they did so, till finally they gave it a fixed form. By this time it had ceased to resemble the picture. This play is called, 'Don't Go.' It has passed into the proletcult repertory.[48]

Don't Go was one of those plays sent to other groups and performed all over Russia. At Rybinsk, the local reviewer suggested that the play demonstrated how 'Proletkult theatrical technique will be completely independent and will not be created according to methods borrowed from the old theatre.'[49]

Theatre groups frequently learned through practical classes such as those held 'in the former merchant Savva Morozov's private residence, [where] Proletkult . . . improvised études, sought a new repertoire, and discussed the meeting-points of politics, economics and art',[50] a syllabus Bogdanov would have approved of. Proletkult's teaching staff included Sergei Volkonsky, teaching 'expressive speech' and 'expressive gesture', Nikolai Alexandrov, teaching movement, Mikhail Chekhov, with his version of Stanislavsky's 'system', Smyshlyaev, Nikolai Foregger and others. In Petrograd, Meyerhold and Leonid Vivien held classes which, despite relying on material developed in his pre-1917 studio, was still remarkable in range and breadth:

> The meaning of the 'refusal'; the value of the gesture in itself; the self-admiration of the actor in the process of acting; the technique of using two stages, the stage and the forestage; the role of the outcry in the moment of strained acting; the elegant costume of the actor as a decorative ornament and not a utilitarian need; the headgear as a motive for the stage bow; little canes, lances, small rugs, lanterns, shawls, mantles, weapons, flowers, masks, noses, etc, as apparatus for the exercise of the hands . . . large and small curtains (permanent and sliding, curtains in the sense of 'sails') as the simplest method of changes . . . parade as a necessary and independent part of the theatrical appearance.[51]

All these areas were covered by their classes, and much more besides.

But all this did not produce a distinctively 'revolutionary' theatre. The mass of theatrical activity was much more haphazard than the would-be organisers would have liked. Petrograd Proletkult, for example, created a theatre structure focused on a central theatre, under the leadership of Alexander Mgebrov, who had learned in Vera Komissarzhevskaya's Symbolist Theatre, and had worked successfully with Nikolai Evreinov at the Ancient Theatre. His early successes, especially with the Russian première of Romain Rolland's *The Storming of the Bastille*, gradually gave way to increasingly abstract and Symbolist works with a narrowing appeal to non-specialist audiences. Moscow's Proletkult theatre, on the other hand, was structurally much more diffuse. It was led by Valentin Smyshlaev, whose earlier career had been at the Moscow Art Theatre under Konstantin Stanislavsky. Thus, in answer to the question of what proletarian or revolutionary theatre should be in practice, no agreement was reached.

Plays which aspired to contribute to the development of a specifically revolutionary theatre were similarly diverse. Huntly Carter records self-made dramas such as *Don't Go*, and others like *The Mangy Dog*, which dealt largely with recruitment for the imperialist army, and involved getting people, probably 'plants', out of the audience, and ended with the red Soviet star rising above the burning Stock Exchange and a show whose name seems to have been lost which started at midnight on May Day and included such emblematic devices as a character carrying a large bottle full of the tears shed by big business over the Bolshevik revolution, and the unravelling of a ball of red tape, signifying the bureaucracy's contribution to society.[52] Most of these rather naive dramas nevertheless exhibit in full Romain Rolland's essential attributes – energy, joy, and intellectual stimulation – for the proletarian actors and spectators involved.

Proletkult groups also presented improvisations based on ideas shouted out by the audience, and staged plays by local authors or playwrights from their literary groups. Poetry readings, more or less dramatised by the group were also frequent, one of the best of these being Smyshlyaev's production of *The Insurrection* by Emile Verhaeren, already alluded to. Using basically Stanislavskian techniques of 'emotional recall' and 'affective memory', the performers were encouraged to invent a biography for their 'Voice', thereby creating an overwhelming impression from a mass of carefully-wrought details. 'In separate cries was heard the heroic pathos', wrote a critic. 'In the separate flashes of passion was heard a significance greater than ordinary experience.' Smyshlyaev thought that 'only thus is it possible to make a collective, for then each member feels as if his word stands for the words of all, his throat, which throws out a sound, is the colossal throat of the heroic collective.'[53] Mgebrov, the Petrograd Proletkult Theatre's director, also tried to stage poetry, but apparently less successfully, since one of his authors, Vladimir Kirillov, wrote after the production of his *We*: 'The collective reading is permeated from start to finish with a strained and unnatural drum-major's attitude to action. Hysterical and noisy bathos is not proletarian at all, but purely of the intelligentsia.'[54]

More conventional plays which tried to capture the spirit of the revolution included *For the Red Soviet* by Pavel Arsky, which Mgebrov presented on 7 November 1919 in Petrograd, where the author was a member of the Proletkult Studio, besides being a soldier in the Red Army; Pavel Bessalko's *The Mason*, a not very convincing descendant of Ibsen's *The Master Builder*, now proletarianised and owing a debt to *Mystery Bouffe*; and P. Kozlov's *Legend of a Communard*, even more overtly symbolic, with characters who have names like 'Wisdom' and 'Truth'. Better received was Moscow Proletkult's production of *Mariana* by Alexander Serafimovich, dealing with a woman's change of allegiance to the Reds when her soldier husband is fighting for the Whites. Smyshlyaev's production of this play was generally admired, but its dramaturgy was essentially conservative and its style predictable. A better play is *The Red Truth*, written by another Red Army man, Alexander Vermishev, who, like Arsky, was to die in the Civil War. However exciting this play was, it is basically realist in form and thoroughly predictable; so although its popularity was enormous at the time, it hardly moved revolutionary drama forward.

This disappointing list of plays, all that remains in effect from the proletarian theatre epidemic, suggests that the people's enthusiasm needed to combine with the skills of the intellectuals if something more lasting was to be created.

THEATRE OF A NEW SCALE

The period of the Civil War produced drama which mixed mystery and buffoonery in unpredictable combinations, and the apotheosis of this phase was reached in spectacular, highly public performances on the city streets. The first group specifically dedicated to bringing theatre onto the streets was the Red Army Theatre Workshop, directed by Nikolai Vinogradov, who on 12 March 1919 presented *The Red Year* for the Petrograd Soviet, followed by several open-air performances in the city and at the war front. The production used a poster style, depicting the enemies of the proletariat in coarse caricature and the workers as heroic and steadfast. It revolved round the battles of the revolution from February to October, culminating in the storming of the Winter Palace. The play was received enthusiastically by most Petrograd workers, who sometimes joined in singing the revolutionary songs, shouted appropriate slogans during the action, and even, at one or two performances, attacked the actors playing the parts of the bourgeois. Their next productions, *The Third International* and *Bloody Sunday*, were characterised by the same spirit and in some ways were still more like demonstrations than theatrical performances, using placards, crude costume and make-up, and sometimes even floats depicting scenes relevant to the subject.

It was only a short step from such performances to the open-air mass spectacles, the craze for which reached its height in Petrograd in 1920. These shows were similar to the medieval mystery cycles in presentation, in that they dealt with an event or a series of episodes which provided a celebration and a justification: not of the Christian faith, but of the revolution. Performances were often given on May Day or 7 November, marking the importance of these dates in the same way that the medieval Church marked Corpus Christi Day and the ancient peasantry its days of harvest or procreation. There is a strong sense in the performances of a new mythology being created to enable the community to understand and celebrate its new identity, just as the mystery play explicated and celebrated the identity of the Christian community. Alexei Gan, supervisor of Moscow's mass spectacles, forecast the replacement of the theatre by a new form of dramatic interventionism in life itself, perhaps growing out of this form: this might also seem to reinforce Lunacharsky's 'god-building' socialism as 'religious atheism'. Here, if anywhere, 'I' melted into 'We' and shared 'in the great deeds and heroic acts of collectivised humanity'.[55]

The particularly spectacular series of mass spectacles staged in Petrograd began on May Day 1920 with *The Mystery of Freed Labour*, directed by Yuri Annenkov and Alexander Kugel, with S. D. Maslovskaya, a mezzo-soprano and director at the Maryinsky Theatre. Annenkov was a close friend of Nikolai Evreinov, for whom he had designed sets at the Distorting Mirror, where Kugel's wife was proprietor. Naturally a strong flavour of the satirical-grotesque was evident in the performance which took place in front of the Stock Exchange. The huge flight of steps up to its imposing frontage formed the stage and supplied the driving symbolism of the production: at the top were the exploiters, at the foot the exploited, and on the steps themselves the drama of the class struggle was played out. The symbolism was strengthened by the fact that the huge crowds of workers at the foot of the steps were formally grouped, and performed in unison so that the effect was somewhat like a gigantic gymnastic display, while the exploiters at the top of the steps were played by performers with clowning and acrobatic skills – some of them, indeed, being professional circus artists. The symbolism was deliberately naïve, and was enhanced by the backcloth: a feudal castle with a golden door, reminiscent of the fairytale giant's castle which is so frequently penetrated and despoiled by the poor but honest hero. In *The Mystery of Freed Labour*, when the Red Army finally appears to overthrow the age-old rulers, the cloth depicting the castle falls to the ground, revealing a second backcloth of the Tree of Freedom. Here is a symbol functioning in popular, rather than intellectual, terms, and as unselfconscious in its meaning as in its exuberance.

The Mystery of Freed Labour was a huge success, watched, it was reported, by some 35,000 people, and its performance gave rise to a demand for new mass spectacles which Maria Andreeva was disposed to meet. Consequently, Sergei Radlov staged *The Blockade of Russia* on Stone Island, Petrograd, on 20 June. The show was designed by Valentina Khodasevich and Ivan Fomin, who created a massive amphitheatre at the bottom of which was a stretch of water eight or ten metres wide separating the audience from the stage. On this a fleet of boats, led by Lord Curzon, attempted to enforce the blockade, while the heroic blockade-runners tried to breach the cordon. Later, over the arched bridge across the water, the invading hordes of Poland tried to reach Russia, the stage. Sergei Yutkevich recalled years later how:

at the end of Red Dawn Street, a vast amphitheatre had been created, and beyond . . . a fantastic spectacle was presented, rather like the classical spectacles, with the participation of boats, warships, military detachments, the whole concluding with an immense fireworks display.[56]

A month later, on 19 July, during the second congress of the Third International, Radlov was involved in another mass spectacle, *In Favour of a World Commune*, which was again performed in front of the Stock Exchange, before delegates to the International who watched from a specially built gallery. The new spectacle was under the overall direction of Konstantin Mardzhanov, whom Ilya Ehrenburg described at this time as 'a man bursting with excitement, with bold plans, a man of gentle but uncompromising spirit'.[57] He was assisted by Radlov, Nikolai Petrov, a friend of Nikolai Evreinov, who had worked in children's theatre but was now directing the Free Comedy Theatre, Vladimir Soloviev, Meyerhold's erstwhile partner, and Adrian Piotrovsky, a theatre critic and historian, who was also co-author with Sergei Radlov of a number of plays, including *The Battle of Salamis*, directed by Radlov in April of the previous year, and a succesful adaptation of *Lysistrata* by Aristophanes. The Cubo-Futurist painter, Nathan Altman, was responsible for the decor and settings.

The heavy walls of the building were hung with bunting and flags, and huge banners greeted delegates to the congress in many languages. Though it is doubtful whether the comparison occurred to many of those present, the likeness to fairground decor was striking, especially when lit by searchlights hung on columns, on the Saints Peter and Paul Fortress and on warships on the River Neva. Mardzhanov's production introduced two important new features to the staging of mass spectacles. First, the whole square, not just the steps up to the Stock Exchange, were used by the performers. And second, the performance was organised and directed in a new, more efficient, way. Whereas in earlier spectacles the directors had been participants and had 'directed' from within the action, in *In Favour of a World Commune*, the directors stayed outside the action, and gave the signal for the start of each of the 110 episodes at the appropriate moment. As a result, the whole presentation became not only much bigger but much more precisely executed. *In Favour of a World Commune* dramatised the events of the specifically Communist struggle for power, from the publication of *The Communist Manifesto* in 1848 to the time of its performance (summer 1920), using a kind of realism – Radlov called it 'naïve realism'[58] – especially in bringing the action out onto the square. The spectacle used some 4,000 participants who played to an estimated audience of 45,000, and provoked an almost religious ecstacy in Radlov himself:

4 Scene from *In Favour of a World Commune*, directed by Konstantin Mardzhanov, July 1920.

'What perfect bliss – to feel, carry, watch over stage time! To be master of the theatrical minutes! To wave the conductor's baton!'[59] Parts of this show formed the core of the next, *International Festival in the Red Countryside*, directed by Adrian Piotrovsky, but more significantly it led into the most impressive of all the mass theatre spectacles, *The Storming of the Winter Palace*.

This show, which took place on 7 November 1920 (the third anniversary of the October revolution, and of the actual storming of the Winter Palace), may have been the most literal theatricalisation of a historical event ever staged. It was presented in and around the real Winter Palace in Petrograd, and those who had been participants in the events three years before were actively sought out and asked to play themselves – and many did. There were over 8000 participants in the action, and over 500 musicians in the orchestra. The spectacle was watched by more than 100,000 spectators, who huddled wide-eyed and cloudy-breathed in the history-laden square outside the old tsarist palace. The whole event was co-ordinated and directed by nine men: five assistant directors, three directors all by now familiar with this sort of work – Yuri Annenkov and Alexander Kugel, who had co-directed *The Mystery of Freed Labour*, and Nikolai Petrov, who had been an assistant on *In Favour of a World Commune* – and one overall directorial supremo, Nikolai Evreinov.

This mass spectacle seems in some ways to be the natural culmination of Evreinov's career, being a theatricalisation of life without previous parallel, such as he had called for in his book, *Theatre for Oneself.* Others, Sergei Radlov, for instance, had begun to doubt the new interpenetration of the real and the dramatic, and was rather testily reasserting the distinction between the reality of demonstrations, parades and other 'real' events, and the non-reality of a theatrical reincarnation of such an event.[60]

The Storming of the Winter Palace began before the curved frontage of the General Staff building on Palace Square. Platforms to the left and right of the central archway were used by the Reds and Whites respectively. The White platform had two stages, each fifty metres long and fifteen metres deep, connected by a wide gangway, and behind them hung a huge backcloth depicting a crumbling medieval castle. On the Whites' side, there were 2,685 participants, including 125 ballet dancers and a hundred circus artists. There were many more than that on the Reds' side, which had similar platforms and a backdrop of brick walls, factory chimneys and so on. The two sides were linked by a bridgeway running in front of the General Staff building's arch. In the square itself the spectators were divided into two groups, separated by a wide aisle. The Alexander column, hung with arc lights, stood in the middle of this aisle, and Evreinov and one assistant were situated here, on a raised platform. Facing the General Staff building was the Winter Palace itself, with projectors and lights concealed inside it, and a huge pile of logs in front. In the side streets and around the square, army lorries, trucks, cars and vast numbers of participants awaited their cues, and the crusier, *Aurora* was anchored nearby on the Neva.

The performance began at 10.0 p.m. with a single gunshot in the night. This was the signal for the orchestra, on the bridge between the two platforms, to begin 'The Marseillaise', anthem of the Provisional Government. The White platform was illuminated: the Provisional Government was deciding to continue the war. The White platform dimmed, the Red was lit up. 'The Internationale' was played hesitantly, and proletarians in working clothes were seen staggering home tired, while soldiers wearily reformed ranks. The Red platform faded, and on the White platform Kerensky was seen making a speech, which was highly applauded by the Whites. Then petitioners approached, and humbly bowed before giving in their petitions. Resplendent aristocrats brought gifts, huge sacks of money which matched their vast pot bellies. The Red platform, illuminated again, was now buzzing with meetings and agitations. Gradually the cry 'Lenin!' was voiced and raised and brought to a climax. On the White platform, 'The Marseillaise' was by now slightly out of tune. Kerensky was orating again, but desperately, and his audience, a long row of listeners, jerked in unison: first left, then right, their movements gradually becoming more ragged and chaotic. On the Red platform, more people appeared from behind the scenery. With hurrying, busy movement they crowded round a gigantic raised red flag and began to sing 'The Internationale' loudly. These alternating scenes, depicting emblematically the movement of the events of 1917, continued until the Red platform attacked the White across the bridge. As the Reds gained the upper hand, scattered Whites were seen to defect.

At this point, two cars appeared from a side street and sped to the White platform. Kerensky and his ministers toppled over each other in their absurd haste to clamber aboard, and the cars drove at speed through the crowd across the square to the Winter Palace. The remnants of the White Army followed and took up positions behind the pile of logs. Now, lorry loads of soldiers and workers entered through the archway in the General Staff building and headed for the Winter Palace. When they were checked by the White defenders, more lorries poured into the square from the side roads. The Whites, defeated, rushed into the Winter Palace, followed by the Reds. Suddenly the Winter Palace itself was illuminated, and white blinds drawn over the windows were lit from behind to show shadow fights going on. The *Aurora* fired her guns, signalling a deafening roar of artillery and machine gun fire which lasted for two or three minutes. A huge rocket streaked to the sky. Victory. Silence. Then, massed voices began 'The Internationale'. The windows of the Winter Palace, which had gone dark, were now each lit with red stars projected onto the blinds, and a huge red banner was raised over the building. At this moment, Kerensky, recognisable although now in woman's clothes, came out, jumped into a car and drove off. As he disappeared, a firework display began.

The whole performance was clinically worked out and directed. 'As a matter of fact, it was better organised than the actual storming of the Winter Palace, which was full of confusion.'[61] All the participants in the spectacle were strictly controlled by the directors. Each director and assistant director controlled one group, and each group was divided into subgroups, each with its own leader. These leaders were rehearsed in the evenings for three weeks before the performance at the Gervovy Hall. The other participants were told the plan of action in advance and they had to follow the leader. Evreinov, on his raised platform in the centre of the square, co-ordinated and orchestrated the performance by field telephone, light signals and motorcycle couriers. Considering the fact that the evening was cold and damp, and the ground slushy, it is remarkable that the only hitch during the show came when the telephone link to the *Aurora* was broken, and a motorbike despatch rider had to be sent to tell the cruiser to stop firing.

The performance juxtaposed buffoonery on the White platform with mystery on the Red platform, reality on the square itself with mystery heightened to apotheosis in the Palace. Archive film of a dress rehearsal still exists,[62] and gives a strong indication of what the show was like. The chief impression is one of activity and bustle, large clumps of people swarming up or down the steps, coming together, parting, running, raising their arms, marching. The images are created through spatial relationships and groupings in which the participants are never arranged haphazardly or 'like life'. The movement, too, is very precisely choreographed and characterised, as the characters strut, bow, march, wave their handkerchiefs or lean forward to point to a new arrival. Wounded soldiers hobble and limp, workers in a dense crowd trudge with bent backs, and all the government members *plié* or shake their heads in unison. The choreographed movements of the vast crowds enable the director to make patterns with his actors. A line of people climbs the broad steps diagonally from the bottom corner to the opposite top corner, the Red soldiers enter confidently through the archway in a curving line, a vast troop marches in in greatcoats and puttees, their sloped rifles like a forest of leaning needles.

More complex are moments when, for example, one group runs up the steps while another wearily descends; some are in a confused melée, while others cheer and charge. The size of the groups creates an extraordinarily powerful and energising effect, a collective dynamism crystallised in moments, such as the time when all the workers are smiting with their mallets, or when the soldiers are entering: on horseback, in cars, with gun carriages, on motorbikes with sidecars, on bicycles or simply marching. Set against these are frozen, or nearly frozen, silhouettes – flags and fists upraised; the fighting men on the bridge poised, about to strike; the puppet-like heads of the government ministers seen like coconuts in a coconut shy above the canvas walls. Simultaneous contradictory movement, such as lines of people walking in opposite directions on the two stages of the same platform, creates a sort of *moiré* effect. Kerensky, the only individualised character, is curiously like Buster Keaton when unsure what to do next, and just as funny.

The division of the stage into positive and negative sides, already used in the theatre by Evreinov and others, was enhanced by the use of bright white searchlights carving through the night. As for the costumes, even on archive film they are flamboyant and striking, while the props are an unexpected mixture of the real (Kerensky's car) and the fantastic (the bankers' briefcases). The armoured cars, and indeed Kerensky's car, and the huge banners, ruffled gracefully by the breeze, remind the watcher that this is a show, not reality, with every movement sharp and decisive, every image grotesque but recognisable. *The Storming of the Winter Palace* was an awesome and elating experience for the people in Palace Square that night. Evreinov's 'acted' spectators at the Ancient Theatre were now real. But the scale, as Zamyatin noted, was altogether different, possibly unique:

> The play mattered little, what mattered were the scale and size of the theatre. Instead of the gong at the beginning of the performance – a six-inch gun, instead of the footlights – search-lights, instead of scenery – tremendous white columns, with the silky blackness of the sky as a background. The crowds of many thousands on the shore of the Neva – formed the audience of the stalls, and those on the ships at the shore – the audience in the boxes. This was indeed a great theatrical spectacle . . . perhaps the beginning of a new road, a road which will lead across the square to the theatre of the future, and which may lead us back to the long forgotten Greek 'αγορα.[63]

Unfortunately, the form developed no further: after *The Storming of the Winter Palace* it faded, partly at least because it was so expensive at a time of great hunger and hardship. The only fee Evreinov received was a fox fur coat, and his assistants were paid a dozen eggs and half a pound of tobacco each.

Nevertheless, the mass spectacle clarified several elements of revolutionary theatre. In terms of content, political tendentiousness was now not only acceptable but became a generating force, especially in its use of popular heroes. The spatial distinction between performance area and auditorium was typically blurred, and conventional and spectacular elements were mixed apparently indiscriminately in front of emblematic settings. It was simple but energetic, schematic but vivid, and, especially in *The Storming of the Winter Palace*, rhythmically staccato, though with an immensely dynamic climax. Furthermore, the mass spectacles convinced many theatre workers that they could contribute to the building of the new society through their profession. The theatre's potential for social intervention was established.

CIRCUSISATION

The 'mystery' of the revolution found its first sustained expression in mass spectacles, especially those of Petrograd, and that city, too, saw the first deliberately constructed series of experiments to try to penetrate the laughter of liberation. For Soviet Communists, circus provided a 'healthy' alternative to cabaret: it is characterised by the strength and concentration of the performer, and by a democratic disposition of those involved. Moreover, the circus ring, like the open public square used by the mass spectacle, provides 'real' space for the action, as opposed to the 'false' space behind the proscenium arch of a conventional theatre. The circus is neither drama nor reality, but has something of both contained in it. Yet its potential for satire remained even after the revolution. Thus, the popular clown Bom entered the ring carrying a great sack. To Bim's question, 'Have you been getting wood?' Bom replied, 'No, here is the wood,' and he held up a match. 'Then what is in the sack?' inquired Bim. 'The necessary permits,' replied Bom.[64]

Meyerhold admired the fact that while the circus artist has the 'solitude' necessary for any great performance, he is simultaneously intensely aware of the audience. In the second version of *Mystery Bouffe* he was to employ the acrobat-clown, Vitaly Lazarenko, whose work (he later asserted) led to 'the transformation of the abstract show [circus] into an agitational theatrical performance'.[65] Yet in February 1919, he wrote that 'there is not and cannot be a theatre-circus . . . circus art and theatrical art can develop along parallel, not intersecting, lines.'[66] Other revolutionary theatre practitioners dissented, however, and cited 'Eccentrism' in their own support. Eccentrism derives from the Auguste of the circus and from the solo music-hall comedian, and mixes grotesquery with artistic brilliance. The slapstick clown Grock, for instance, also played beautifully on various absurd or outsize instruments. Little Tich, who sang 'character songs' and did a peculiar, but not ugly, dance in long wooden boots (known as an 'eccentric' dance), was a dwarf with a manic stare and six fingers on each hand. The combination of beauty and the beast made the performance eccentric.

Probably the first person to try to bring eccentrism to the infant Soviet stage was Nikolai Foregger, judging from Meyerhold's disparaging side-swipe of February 1919 that merging theatre and circus would only produce the amateurishness of 'a Foreggeresque theatre-circus spectacle.'[67] The Russified Austrian Baron Foregger von Greiffen-turn had graduated in Philology in 1915 from the University of Kiev, where he had created the Intimate Theatre with Sergei Sudeikin and Alexander Deich. He had come to Moscow, where he worked briefly with Fokin and at Tairov's Kamerny Theatre. His interest in theatre history, however, led him to pantomime and *commedia dell'arte*, whose gestures and poses especially excited him. Consequently, in Moscow, he gathered a scratch company from among friends and acquaintances. His enthusiasm inspired them sufficiently for many to work under false names in order to prevent the directors who employed them from finding out where they were. He then set up the Theatre of Four Masks.

His stage was in the living room of his own flat, which was filled with rare books, engravings and old furniture. He and his family moved into one small room, and the family helped the wardrobe mistress create the deliberately primitive costumes while the tiny company painted the hall-foyer and the auditorium as well as the scenery, and pinned little bells onto the curtains to tinkle as each scene was revealed. The auditorium held fewer than forty people when it opened with Tabarin's seventeenth-century farce, *Karataka and Karataké*. Following productions included the medieval *Farce of the Worthy Master Pierre Pathelin*, some of Cervantes's interludes and *Mandragora* by Machiavelli. Foregger sought a popular acting style for these plays – modern but unmistakably descended from that of the histrions and *skomorokhi* of the time when the plays were written – the 'eccentric' style now found in music-hall and circus. The little company on its meagre stage used acrobatic tricks, rapid rhythms, and plenty of song, music and dance to create something which may have seemed primitive, but which was also charming and surprising: 'The old French farce was pretty archaic and naive,' wrote Igor Ilinsky, one of Foregger's actors, 'but it was played amusingly and freshly, the theatre aroused some curiosity, and 30–40 people always came. Therefore, "the house was full".'[68] Foregger was invited by Valery Bebutov to direct Plautus's *Menaechmi* at the New Theatre, which he did with some panache. But the Theatre of Four Masks was impossibly poverty-stricken. After rehearsals, the actors were often reduced to scouring the neighbourhood for fence posts, bits of old shed, boards, anything to burn in the Foregger family stove. Foregger himself was eventually forced to leave Moscow, moving to Voronezh and working on an agit-train, his ideas still barely hatched.

Meanwhile, Meyerhold's *protégés* in Petrograd were making a more sustained attempt at the circusisation of the theatre. In June 1918, he encouraged the formation of the First Communal Theatre Troupe, also called the Experimental Theatre, to be directed by Sergei Radlov. This theatre aimed to perform in the People's Houses, and in clubs and halls round the city. They began with two plays recommended by the Repertoire Section of TEO, Yakov Knyazhnin's eighteenth-century comedy, *The Hot Drinks Seller*, followed by Plautus's *Menaechmi* in which the characters appeared masked. But despite Radlov's attempt to make them into 'grotesque buffoonades', the productions failed and the troupe disbanded before the end of the year.

More ambitious was the Theatre Studio, established shortly after Meyerhold took over the running of the Petrograd TEO in September 1918. Again the aim was to tour productions, this time of three kinds: live performances for children and for adults, and specially-created puppet shows. *The Life of Art* noted that the new company wanted to work out 'a genuine people's repertoire, new methods for actors' techniques, new directorial and design concepts.'[69] The new ways would include 'experiments in pantomime and verbal improvisation', probably at the behest of Radlov, who was a member of the board, along with Mikhail Kuzmin, Yuri Bondi, Konstantin Tverskoi and other Meyerhold associates. Their first show was *The Tree of Metamorphoses*, a children's play by Anna Akhmatova's former husband, Nikolai Gumilev, which opened on 6 February 1919. The story, set in India, concerns a fakir who controls the reincarnation of animals into humans; when they come to kill him, he himself metamorphoses into an angel, while the would-be murderers are claimed by a demon. Valentina Khodasevich, who was to design Radlov's spectacle, *The Blockade of Russia*, created a luxuriously impossible tree in front of a brilliant yellow backdrop, on which was painted a black sun. The effect was startling, and the whole production highly original and successful. *The Tree of Metamorphoses* was followed by two adult plays, one by the Distorting Mirror dramatist, Sergei Antimonov, the other Macchiavelli's *Mandragora*, but these did not fare so well, and the group was amalgamated with Nikolai Petrov's and reorganised into the Little Dramatic Theatre.

A third theatre set in motion by Meyerhold during his time at Petrograd TEO was the State Exemplary Theatre, based at the Hermitage, which also aimed to be an experimental 'people's' theatre. It was for this theatre that Meyerhold's repertoire[70] was drawn up. Although it was not followed, the flavour he imparted was to some extent retained. The first production was Molière's *The Doctor In Spite of Himself*, performed in the Armaments Room of the Winter Palace on 12 July 1919, followed by Schiller's *Love and Intrigue*, Molière's *Tartuffe*, Tolstoy's *The First Distiller* and *A Northern Story* by Viktor Rappaport. This theatre caused something of a furore, for at last some of the unorthodoxies which accompanied the search by *avant-garde* artists for popular forms achieved a proper impact, and the productions considerably unsettled the critics. There is some evidence, however, that the popular audiences were not so upset, and the company played every Saturday through August exclusively for Red soldiers and sailors. The production of *The First Distiller* by Yuri Annenkov, whose previous intrusions into theatre had been designs done mostly for cabarets, caused a particular sensation, since it was the first deliberate piece of 'circusisation' (that is, if *Mystery Bouffe* is excluded) on an important public stage.

Annenkov's aims were set out in an article published in 1919 in *The Life of Art* under the title 'The Merry Sanatorium'. If the theatre was a sanatorium for the 'tired city-dweller', ministering to his exhausted spirit, then the circus was a *merry* sanatorium. Where the earnest Tolstoy, in *The First Distiller*, had hoped to liberate the peasants from the demon drink by the content of his message, Annenkov attempted to free them through the 'subtle and magnificent art' of circus.[71] Annenkov's non-specific, even anarchistic, position was a provocative alternative to Meyerhold's attempt to yoke together the forces of popular theatre and the social and political energies unleashed by the revolution. Meyerhold's favoured forms – *balagan* shows, variety and the like – also fed into Annenkov's theatrical eccentrism: 'The art of variety,' he wrote, 'is by its nature genuinely a people's art, brought to the city with the lower classes, from fools and *skomorokhi*, from saints' days holidays, in *chastushkas* and jokes.'[72] But Annenkov totally lacked the desire to link his work to the developments of contemporary politics, and a few years later he emigrated.

The First Distiller concerns a lumpish peasant who refuses to curse a devil who steals his lunch, and instead wishes him well. After desperate plotting by the Chief Devil and others, the idea of giving the peasant alcohol is agreed upon, and with this temptation, the devil reduces the peasant, his family, and indeed the whole village, to swinish ruin. Annenkov freely adapted the text, and he structured the performance through the use of an unconventional mixture of traditional and futuristic music. Inserting several professional circus performers into the cast, notably George Delvari, a clown and ground acrobat, and Alexander Karloni, an 'india rubber man', Annenkov created a 'hell' which was a frantic and distorted image of the world – beside the circus turns, the 'straight' actors moved grotesquely, the lighting changed weirdly and fell at unexpected angles, and the setting was a kind of nightmare circus ring, making no reference to the fields and village of Tolstoy's drama. Trapezes swung, ropes dangled, odd-shaped platforms were suspended from the flies, tubs and steps gave actors height but led nowhere. There were no stage curtains and the performance consisted of a series of circus-like turns.

The peasant was played by Konstantin Gibshman who managed to combine hesitant speech and naturalistic gestures (such as scratching the back of his head when puzzled) with an ability to suddenly transform into an eccentric variety number. His synthesis of drama and eccentricity was, however, unique among the cast, so that the whole remained a slightly uneasy mixture. Annenkov's acknowledged debt to Marinetti, the Italian Futurist then forging an alliance with Mussolini's Fascists, did not make acceptance any easier. Nevertheless, as a liberating force for the 'circusisation' of theatre, *The First Distiller* was influential, notably in the work of another Petrograd experimental director, Sergei Radlov.

Radlov's classics course at St Petersburg University had given him an interest in the Roman comedies of Terence and Plautus, and as a member of Meyerhold's Studio from 1913 to 1916, he had studied practically pantomime and the techniques of *commedia dell'arte*, and had also worked with Evreinov before 1917. Two days after the closure of the Exemplary Theatre, Radlov and his friends founded the Theatre of Artistic Divertissements, soon renamed the Theatre of Popular Comedy, in the Iron Room in the Petrograd House of the People. Here Valentina Khodasevich designed a stage across the back wall which consisted of three acting areas side by side, and behind each of these 'stages' a three-storey construction, so that there were nine acting areas in all. The company included many of Meyerhold's former collaborators – Miklashevsky, Soloviev, Tverskoi, Kuzmin, and others, including Alexander Blok's wife, Lyubov – together with a group of circus performers – Delvari and Karloni again, the trapeze artists Ivan Taureg and Alexander Sergeivich Alexandrov, better known as 'Serge' from Ciniselli's circus, the musical eccentric clown, Bob (Boris Kozyukov), the conjuror Ernani, the Japanese juggler Takoshimo, the ballad singer Stepan Nefedov, and others.

This combination began work under the influence of Meyerhold's *commedia dell'arte* experiments. Stock situations with titles like 'Night' and 'Love' formed the basis of their early experiments in improvisation, but Serge as a Deburau-derived Pierrot added the influence of the Théâtre des Funambules. Radlov's first show, *The Corpse's Bride*, which opened on 8 January 1920, was the story of a sailor who falls in love with the daughter of J. Pierpoint Morgan, the banker, and is driven off by the girl's grandmother. With Morgan an updated Pantalone, and the sailor and the girl traditional *commedia* lovers, the grandmother, played by Serge, became the focus of the circusisation, as he swung across the stage and leaped off springboards dressed as a traditional travesty 'dame'. The top-hatted Morgan sang:

5 Stage designed by Valentina Khodasevich for Sergei Radlov's Theatre of Popular Comedy at the Petrograd People's House.

In Vienna, New York and Rome,
My bulging purse is known;
Far has spread my fame,
And Pierpoint Morgan is my name.
   On the Stock Exchange today
   I will win and you will pay –
   All those baubles that I gave
   Will more than pay for a new black slave.[73]

When the doctor, who covets Morgan's wealth, proposes for his daughter, Morgan-Pantalone interrupts his declarations of love with: 'Do you earn enough from your work to accumulate any capital?' This kind of satirical humour in a theatre of buffoonery and grotesque traditional comedy, descended from the fairground *balagany*, was elaborated into the main line of revolutionary satire.

Other shows continued on the same path, so that Konstantin Derzhavin was constrained to disagree with his erstwhile teacher, Meyerhold, and declare that Radlov had 'sought out' a third art between circus and theatre, called 'theatre-circus'.[74] *The Monkey Who Was an Informer* had Serge as the monkey climbing up to the roof of the hall and swinging like Tarzan from beam to beam, over the heads of the audience, while jokes with a contemporary flavour exploded from the stage: '"Show us how the Whites advanced on Petrograd?" I (Serge as the monkey) marched putting on the airs of a great bear. "But how did they run away?" I ran holding my beaten backside.'[75] In *The Adopted Son*, Serge was entrusted with valuable revolutionary documents which the capitalist police wanted. He was chased all over the theatre, through the audience, up Khodasevich's three-storey set, and across a long tightrope. Finally he was rescued by an imaginary aeroplane: a rope appeared through a hole in the ceiling, and Serge climbed up and out.

The fast rhythms, the use of machines, skyscrapers and so on, suggested that Radlov was moving away from traditional *commedia dell' arte* and towards something closer to Futurism. 'The spirit of 1921,' he wrote, consisted of:

> express trains, aeroplanes, avalanches of people and side cars, silk and fur, concerts and variety, electric lights and lamps, arches and light and thousands of lights and more silk and silken slippers and silk hats, telegrams and radios, top hats, cigars and tennis rackets, leather book bindings, mathematical treatises . . . [76]

He conjured it up with scenes played simultaneously on different stages, two actors playing a single part, thereby allowing for apparently impossible entrances and exits, and sudden unexpected addresses to the audience. Khodasevich's sets were done in the bright, primitive but challenging style described earlier, and her costumes and props were notable for their starkness and economy:

> She had a gift for picking a central prop – like a striped hatbox – and making the whole design of the set come out of it. As for her costumes, which were particularly admired, the theatrical historian Stefan Mokulsky considered her a pioneer in the way she integrated makeup and hairdo into the concept of the costume as a whole.[77]

The style of the Theatre of Popular Comedy was that of 'a Russian *lubok* passed through the prism of Futurism'.[78] The key, according to Radlov, was 'verbal improvisation' which effected the transition from 'the irritating pettiness of realism to the expression of the real'.[79] The method of creation involved taking a story line which was reduced to a scenario by the author-director. Then during the rehearsal process the story was filled out by the actors, tricks and spectacular feats were introduced by the circus artists, and snatches of dialogue or whole monologues were devised and even written down. Thus improvisation was in no way immediate or *impromptu*, but gave the actor a new responsibility for his work. In fact, the technique is extremely difficult, and Radlov's actors barely mastered it. But, by backchat, questions, challenges and direct appeals, it brought the audience into the creation of the show. Though the critics were never certain of their opinions of the Theatre of Popular Comedy, one significant achievement was indisputable:

> The audience was largely composed of what were ironically known as 'cigarette merchants'. These were youngsters who sold cigarettes singly or as tab-ends – the 'gamins' of revolutionary Leningrad. Naturally the theatre was equally patronized by intellectuals, writers, artists . . . but there were also the workers and soldiers. It really was a popular audience.[80]

In June 1920 the Theatre performed a scenario composed by Maxim Gorky, *The Workaholic Mr Slovotekov*. It concerned an inexhaustibly verbose bureaucrat, who was quite unable to make a decision about anything, till the roof finally fell in on him – but he went on talking in party slogans regardless. After a few performances, to Gorky's dismay, the play was banned. Soviet apologists suggest this was because of the 'feckless slapstick' which carried the actors 'away from satire to farce',[81] but this unlikely reason is flatly contradicted by Valentina Khodasevich, who concluded exactly the opposite – that George Delvari's bureaucrat was too close to the truth for comfort. At any rate, the ban effectively marked the end of the theatre's experiments with original material. Radlov, no rebel, began to play safer with accepted classic texts, the circus performers drifted back to Ciniselli's, and by February 1922, the Theatre of Popular Comedy was disbanded.

In December 1922 Radlov founded a Laboratory for Theatre Research to reflect on his experience. In 1923 he still defended 'verbal improvisation', asserting that the actor was 'the main thing in the theatre, the playwright's basic material', and that the word was only one weapon in the actor's armoury.[82] Since it is the actor who creates the spectacle for the audience to watch, Radlov suggested that true theatre was to be found in the conjunction of actor and spectacle. The actor had at his command sound, movement and emotion; by 'emotion', Radlov meant the added ingredient communicated by the actor which is beyond sound or movement. And since theatrical art alone can communicate through both time and space, the actor's art lies in the deployment of sound, movement and emotion in time and space. The art of the actor in its highest form combines dance and music, both of which are thoroughly non-realistic. Radlov's conclusion, that realism stultifies the art of theatre, though it remained rather abstract in his theory, was in fact a crucial article of principle for the revolutionary theatre. Yutkevich neatly sums up the apparent contradiction in this product of the circusisation of theatre: 'Radlov, refined aesthete though he was, offered the public an extraordinarily interesting experience – the first experience of a popular theatre.'[83]

MOSCOW 1920–1921

OCTOBER IN THE THEATRE

At the start of the 1920–21 theatre season, A. V. Lunacharsky spoke at the Moscow House of the Press on 'Hopes and Problems for the Forthcoming Winter'. His main hope was a rather bland one: 'In the current year it is necessary to intensify the *rapprochement* between the *avant-garde* of the proletariat – the Russian Communist Party – and the *avant-garde* of the intelligentsia – the workers in the sphere of culture.'[1] He did not add that such a *rapprochement* might not be altogether smooth.

While Petrograd had produced some useful beginnings for a revolutionary theatre, comparatively little had happened in Moscow. Kamensky's *Stenka Razin* was produced on 7 November 1918 by Vasily Sakhnovsky, who the following year became director of the newly established Exemplary Theatre, subsidised by and responsible to Tsentroteatr. It took over the Hermitage Theatre from the Moscow Dramatic Theatre (which had occupied it since 1917) and had had some success with experimental work of its own – a production of *The Death of Tarelkin*, for instance, had achieved a degree of brilliance by presenting this usually dark satire as farce. Sakhnovsky declared that his new 'academic' theatre would be one of 'new forms and bold aspirations'[2] and Lunacharsky wanted 'a style which would answer demands for a genuinely popular theatre'.[3] He pencilled in Meyerhold as co-director, but Meyerhold had by now become ill and had moved south to recuperate. Still, Arkady Zonov and Sergei Radlov were among those associated with the theatre and a number of excellent actors participated in the venture, which opened on 4 November 1919 with a production of Maeterlinck's *Ariana and Blue Beard*. In the following spring it toured the Civil War front with productions of Goldoni's *Pamela the Maid* and Kleist's *The Broken Jug*, classical comedies which indicate the company's direction. Even Lunacharsky had to admit his disappointment, and the theatre, having failed to live up to its ideals, ceased to exist in October 1920. Sakhnovsky went on to become a director at the Moscow Art Theatre and a People's artist of the RSFSR.

The Moscow City Cultural Department (MONO) started its own theatre in October 1918 probably known most often as the Zamoskvoretsky Theatre after the the the south central district of the city where it was situated, at the former cabaret theatre of P. P. Struisky. Never a large company, it won a good reputation on the basis of productions by V. V. Obratsov and E. A. Belyaev which appealed to the local public – soldiers and workers and their families. Its repertoire, however – which included *The Beaver Coat* by Gerhardt Hauptmann, *The Dawns* by Verhaeren, and works by Molière, Lope da Vega, Gogol and Ostrovsky – showed little commitment to new drama. Before its opening performance (the Russian première of Hauptmann's *The Beaver Coat* on 10 October 1918), Platon Kerzhentsev made a short speech, calling on the audience members to be not just passive watchers, but active participants in the creation of the first specifically Soviet theatre. He saw it as a 'neighbourhood theatre', the first of what he hoped would grow into a new network, and it took the task of spreading theatre culture among its hitherto deprived audiences very seriously. But though its nurturing of the new audience was significant, its theatre practice was not, and hopes for a spread of such 'neighbourhood theatres' went wholly unfulfilled.

Also in Moscow were the remnants of Komissarzhevsky's theatre and the small but not insignificant Free Theatre. On 1 September 1918 Fedor Komissarzhevsky, having parted on bad terms with Sakhnovsky, reformed his theatre with trade union subsidy as the KPSRO Studio Theatre[4] at the run-down and echoey Zon Theatre on Triumphal Square, with the aim of creating a 'synthesis' of drama, opera and ballet. But Komissarzhevsky's work came to seem increasingly self-indulgent, even extravagant, in war-torn and starving Moscow, and in the late spring of 1919 he emigrated, leaving his embattled troupe to sort out their own futures. Elena Malinovskaya took most of his opera singers into the Bolshoi Theatre, while the actors, now calling themselves the 'New Theatre of KPSRO', or simply the New Theatre, reformed under the auspices of MONO, who put Valery Bebutov in charge. Bebutov commissioned productions of *Menaechmi* by Plautus from Nikolai Foregger and *The Seducer of Seville* by Tirso de Molina from Alexei Chabrov, an actor at the Kamerny Theatre. Bebutov himself directed an evening of works by Schiller, including his own adaptation of *William Tell*. The work was promising, but the extreme fuel shortage in the winter of 1919–1920 forced the theatre to close temporarily.

The actors continued to rehearse new shows, and indeed managed to open again for a few performances, but Tsentroteatr closed them down on 2 February 1920, and passed the Zon to the Free Theatre. This

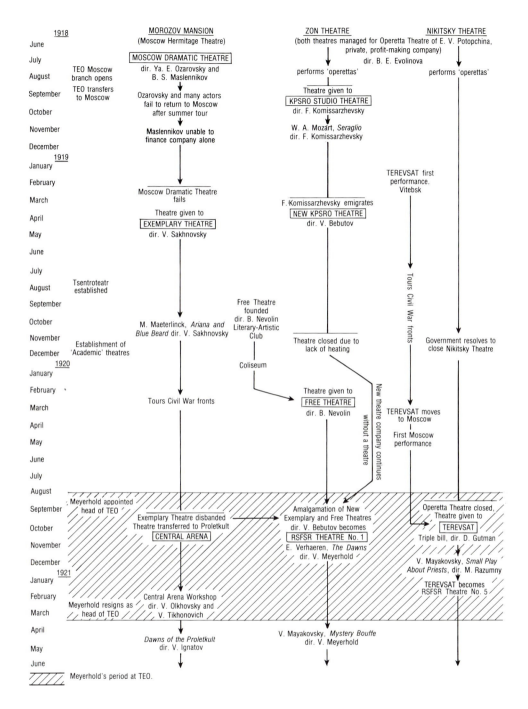

Figure 1 Moscow's Revolutionary Theatres, 1918–1921. How Proletkult, RSFSR Theatre No. 1 and TEREVSAT acquired the Morozov mansion (Hermitage Theatre), Zon Theatre and Nikitsky Theatre during Meyerhold's period at TEO.

company, founded by the entrepreneurial director Boris Nevolin, opened in October 1919 at the Literary-Artistic Club on Dmitrovsky Boulevard with a production by David Gutman of *Fuente Ovejuna* by Lope da Vega. The company aimed to be a theatre of melodrama and pantomime, and its next production was a melodrama, *Behind the Monastery Walls.* However, the informal space was thought to be unsuitable, and the company moved to the former cinema, the Coliseum. By now the company, like the New, had come under the control of MONO, who in late summer 1920 amalgamated the two groups and in October added Sakhnovsky's former Exemplary Theatre troupe to them, putting Valery Bebutov in charge of the whole combination and once more handing him the Zon Theatre.

Meanwhile Meyerhold had left Petrograd in the summer of 1919 for Yalta where he received sanatorium treatment for tuberculosis. When the Whites took Crimea, Meyerhold managed to reach Novorossisk, further east on the Black Sea, but he was arrested by Denikin's counter-intelligence agents. Saved when the Reds retook the area, he met Lunacharsky at Rostov-on-Don in August 1920 where the Commissar had come with an agit-train. The two talked, and the upshot was an invitation to Meyerhold to replace the ineffectual Vera Menzhinskaya as head of the Commissariat's entire Theatre Department (TEO). He accepted, thereby becoming the third 'Leftist' head of an arts department: Shterenberg was head of fine art and Lourié head of music. But the natural anarchism of these men, as well as their Russian predilection for absolutism, prevented them from collaborating to usher in what might have been a genuinely dynamic and democratic regime in matters artistic and cultural. Political realities would probably have stifled any such attempt at co-operation, but the fact is that it was never tried.

Once returned to the capital, Meyerhold made a tour of inspection of TEO's theatres like Napoleon surveying his dispositions.

> He was in a soldier's coat, and on his slightly tilted head he had a peaked cap with a badge with a portrait of Lenin on it . . . [His] clothes were deliberately poor and apparently uncared for, but actually they were expensive, and they gave him a kind of new, fresh, proletarian appearance.[5]

He called on the actors:

> not only to take our art to the people, to our spectators, workers and peasants, but also to create a theatre in which the idea of communism would reverberate, to create a theatre, in keeping with our epoch, in keeping with the Great October revolution. He called for contemporary themes, themes near to our own day,

themes which would excite the people, all the people, who had accomplished such great things in Russia.[6]

Noting that the 'crisis in the repertoire' had still not been solved, Meyerhold advocated working from scenarios, groups making 'theatrical compositions' of their own.[7]

> Let [the spectator] in our theatre acquire that dynamic which he does not acquire in other theatres, that strong-willed effort towards construction which he needs. Our task comes down to bringing onto the stage good, healthy laughter, and if something moves the spectator, he should not pull out his handkerchief, but shake his fist at his neighbour . . . In our epoch, tears are not for us, but we do need the occasional whiff of gunpowder.[8]

He even suggested making a play 'In Praise of Electrification'. 'Here is our theatrical programme,' he said at the end of October. 'Plenty of light, plenty of high spirits, plenty of grandeur, plenty of infectious enthusiasm, unlaboured creativity, the participation of the audience in the corporate creative act of the performance . . .'[9]

To achieve this state of revolutionary beatitude, Meyerhold launched a theatrical campaign comparable to that of the Bolshevik shock troops who in 1918 and 1919 had raided the countryside and requisitioned grain for the starving urban proletariat. 'October in the Countryside', Lenin called it. 'October in the Theatre' was announced by Meyerhold and Olga Kameneva in an article in *Izvestiya* on 27 October, and not only would it involve introducing a new revolutionary repertoire and developing new staging and presentational techniques, but also entailed a reorganisation of the theatres under a single authority, their authority. Meyerhold and Kameneva set their sights on the Bolshoi and the Alexandrinsky, just as Lenin and Trotsky had set their sights on the Kremlin and the Winter Palace. It was a bid for total, unashamed hegemony.

In a sense, Lunacharsky had no-one but himself to blame for the assault. He had called Meyerhold to Moscow to create 'an exemplary theatre, imbued with a revolutionary spirit and making revolutionary agitation in new . . . forms'.[10] Meyerhold's first chance to stage a drama to conform to these ideas came when Valery Bebutov invited him to direct Verhaeren's *The Dawns* which he, Bebutov, was planning for his new theatre combination. Meyerhold accepted, having cherished a desire to present the play since at least 1905, and shortly afterwards took over the whole amalgamated company. A structure for it was worked out: Meyerhold was artistic director, with Bebutov his deputy. Head of the literary department was Mikhail Zagorsky, and Alexander Orlov became head of music halfway through the season. Olga Kameneva was chair of the Board, which included Mayakovsky, the actor Alexander Zakushnyak, one member of the technical staff and others. The management committee consisted of Meyerhold, Bebutov, Boris Nevolin, who acted as administrator at the beginning of the year, Zakushnyak, Zagorsky and Alexander Mgebrov, formerly of the Petrograd Proletkult, now an actor in the company. Nevolin led the opposition to Meyerhold, especially after Meyerhold put a stop to Nevolin's rehearsals for a revival of Gutman's production of *Fuente Ovejuna*. Nevolin's group wanted to transfer power from the management to the board, and when this failed, he resigned. The administration was then made the responsibility of yet another committee, until its inefficiency led to the appointment of Semyon Brailovsky as administrator. Meanwhile Meyerhold allowed Zakushnyak to continue in Kommissarzhevsky's production of *The Marriage of Figaro* by Beaumarchais for a few performances, while trying to build a new young company on the basis of his pre-revolutionary experiments. It was all rather piecemeal.

Nevertheless, for Meyerhold it was a start and he called his theatre RSFSR Theatre No 1. He saw it as the first of a series of theatres which would combine the 'factory' and the 'laboratory' functions on, respectively, a main stage and a studio stage, and include a training school as well. There were to be four sections, 'artistic agitation' to be headed by Alexander Serafimovich, a 'neoclassical section', headed by Valery Bryussov, a section for 'socialist plays', headed by Mikhail Reisner and a section for 'new art forms', under Mayakovsky. When in November two companies, the Red Army theatre and the former Nezlobin, came separately to Meyerhold (as Head of TEO) to discuss their future, he suggested they unite to form RSFSR Theatre No 2. When Nezlobin demurred, Meyerhold encouraged the Red Army group to seize their theatre in a night raid. Next morning the second RSFSR Theatre was in place, and Meyerhold invited Nikolai Evreinov to become its director. Evreinov refused, partly because he was vainly trying to revive the Ancient Theatre in order to stage plays of the eighteenth century.

Companies disrupted by the revolution, or the defection or dispossession of their leaders, saw which way the wind was blowing and the RSFSR Theatres multiplied. The company of the Korsh Theatre passed a resolution on 1 December 1920 stating that:

> at this time when RSFSR Theatre No 1 is creating a theatre of revolutionary tragedy and buffoonade, and RSFSR Theatre No 2 (formerly Nezlobin) is bringing about a largely romantic drama, the former Korsh Theatre is creating a theatre of revolutionary comedy and it is appropriate that it should call itself RSFSR Theatre No 3.[11]

The former Studio of Fedor Chalyapin became RSFSR Theatre No 4, though this was disputed by a theatre in Nizhni Novgorod which claimed to be RSFSR Theatre No 4, and the Moscow TEREVSAT (ThEatre of REVolutionary SATire) No 5.[12] Meyerhold then divided the country into districts and aimed to send the various RSFSR Theatres, like military detachments, out to them.

For a time Lunacharsky appeared mesmerised by all this. His task, he said in October, was 'to diffuse the revolutionary image of ideas, sensations and actions throughout the country'.[13] But a series of events intervened to erode Lunacharsky's apparent support, beginning on the third anniversary of the revolution, when Meyerhold's production of *The Dawns* opened at the Zon.

The Dawns is a curious play, half mystical, half naïvely down to earth. Hérénien, the dreamy populist leader who is at the centre of the drama, is extraordinarily gullible politically. He loses his father early in the play, then his small son's life, as well as his own, later on in the play, to create a kind of formal pattern. In between there are scenes of great strength of emotion, besides political argument, sexual excitement and mob demagogy.[14] Kerzhentsev had suggested adapting the play in September 1918, and Meyerhold and Bebutov now made Hérénien a Bolshevik and shuffled the events to permit the story's application to contemporary Soviet reality. Though the cast was uneven, and Meyerhold's monumentalism deemed by some to be static, he asked for and sometimes obtained an unusual degree of passionate intensity from his actors, as with the 'solitary voice' described by Ilinsky:

'But why did the war flare up?' The actor who had to say this proved flaccid and expressionless. Suddenly Meyerhold himself, from the auditorium, like lightning, cut through the rehearsal with a wild, emotional cry, which can be represented on paper only thus: '*But why???!!! did the war! – flare up???!!!*'[15]

Perhaps to atone for some of the acting, Meyerhold had 'plants' in the audience, less obtrusive but functionally similar to Evreinov's on-stage audience in *The Three Magi*, and he tried desperately to achieve the enthusiasm of the revolutionary meeting, succeeding most notably on the night Perekop fell to the Red Army. Meyerhold, 'in a flash of inspired genius', handed the news to the Herald in the play to announce:

It is difficult to describe what happened in the theatre when this historic telegram was read. Such an explosion of shouts, exclamations, applause, such a universal, delighted, I would say furious, roar never was heard within the walls of a theatre. The impression was strengthened because the news of the defeat of the enemy solidly and organically fit into the fabric of the entire show, as though supplementing it with a bright episode dictated by life itself. A greater merging of art with reality I have never seen in theatre, either before or since.[16]

This strength, however, sat rather uneasily with the abstract set designed by Vladimir Dmitriev, a student of Meyerhold's from 1918 in Petrograd, when he had made the original designs. In front of a velvet backdrop was an intrusive and threatening arrangement of geometrical shapes in red, silver and gold, hanging or angled ropes and metallic objects. Similarly unspecific costumes of silvery-grey sackcloth and what was an unprecedented absence of make-up and wigs, contributed to the overall impression which was 'disturbing and exciting' even for so formidable a spectator as Nadezhda Krupskaya, Lenin's wife.[17]

Krupskaya, however, was not pleased, and demanded changes, also attacking Lunacharsky for supporting the project. Lunacharsky, feeling his position threatened, thought it prudent to reaffirm the special status of the academic theatres on 20 November. The Left's response came in a series of public debates, when Ehrenburg, Mgebrov, Mayakovsky and others defended the production and Kerzhentsev went onto the offensive by attacking Lunacharsky's plays as ideologically suspect. Four days later, Lunacharsky announced the death of Futurism – 'it already stinks'[18] – to which Mayakovsky retorted by reminding Lunacharsky of his enthusiasm for *Mystery Bouffe*. On 1 December the Central Committee's statement 'On the Proletkults' obliquely attacked Meyerhold, and Lunacharsky's Commissariat for supporting him. Two weeks later Lunacharsky, in full retreat, asserted that Meyerhold, though adept at destroying the 'old and bad' and at creating 'new and good' work, was not to be trusted with the 'old and good' embodied in the true traditions of Russian theatre.[19] He called 'October in the Theatre' 'a tiny wee thing' and again defended the two-tier organisational structure he had imposed on the theatre.[20] Meyerhold's response was immediate: first, at an official meeting of heads of arts sections of the Commissariat he pushed through a resolution to create an independent Ministry of Art, presumably with some Commissar other than Lunacharsky; then he proposed that theatres be 'unified' under a single authority, presumably his own. At the same time he published an article, 'J'Accuse', in *The Theatre Herald*, stressing that he only opposed 'sham traditions' and reaffirming 'October in the Theatre' – 'and Lunacharsky with us!'[21] One week later the revised *The Dawns* opened, and though controversy still raged, it played without a break till the end of April to constantly packed houses.

The Dawns was a 'bridgehead' for 'October in the Theatre',[22] and the auditorium, which was 'more like an evacuation point or a transit camp,

6 'Monumental art.' Meyerhold's production of *The Dawns*, November 1920

with whirling draughts, bleak and peeling walls and comfortless corridors,'[23] frequently 'bristled with "budyanovkas", the pointed helmets worn by Red Army soldiers'.[24] Afterwards, there were debates, 'The Mondays of *The Dawns*':

> Here the discussion on the problems of the Soviet theatre took its beginning, a discussion which assumed such wide dimensions by taking on diverse forms beginning with 'after show disputes' and ending with the discussion of plays and productions in the present political-art Soviets, of the revolutionizing of the professional theatre.[25]

Ilinsky bears out the popularity of these 'disputes', recalling one arranged for a small theatre when so many people arrived they could not be accommodated. Led by Mayakovsky, they marched to the larger Zon auditorium. On another occasion passions flared so high that Tairov, director of the Kamerny Theatre, refused to shake Meyerhold's hand at the end.

Despite Meyerhold's growing unpopularity in important places, and despite warnings given to him by Lunacharsky to drop his 'October in the Theatre', Meyerhold continued to dream of grandiose schemes. There was, for instance, his attempt to link with Vsevobukh, the institution for military training which all Soviet citizens had to undergo. In the autumn of 1920 Meyerhold was developing a 'theatrical physical culture' which would be applicable to this military training, and as Head of TEO he concluded a formal agreement with Nikolai Podvoisky, head of Military Training. Again, it could be said that Lunacharsky had encouraged such a link by exclaiming in October 1920:

> Just think what character our festive occasions will take on when, by means of General Military Instruction, we create rhythmically moving masses embracing thousands and tens of thousands of people – and not just a crowd, but a strictly regulated, collective, peaceful army sincerely possessed by one definite idea.[26]

Meyerhold demanded the Aquarium gardens and the adjoining site of the former Nikitin Brothers Circus to stage a version of Romain Rolland's *The Storming of the Bastille* as a mass spectacle along the lines of Lunacharsky's suggestion. Nothing came of the request, but Meyerhold's 'Te-Phys-Cult' remained popular for several years.

Meanwhile, the Communist establishment's dissatisfaction with Lunacharsky's performance, especially his apparently over-helpful attitude towards 'Left' artists, had not evaporated and Evgraf Litkens, of the Political Education Department (Glavpolitprosvet) was commissioned to undertake another reorganisation of the Commissariat. Litkens put the whole of the arts directly under the control of Glavpolitprosvet, and on 26 February took powers of censorship, particularly over the theatre. On the same day, he demoted Meyerhold to deputy head of TEO and promoted a professional bureaucrat from the Commissariat of Agriculture, Mikhail Kozyrev, to its head. Simultaneously, TEO's function was downgraded so that it became administrative, not policy-making.

Worse was to come. In March 1921, Lenin dismayed the Left by introducing his 'New Economic Policy' (NEP), which restored a measure of capitalism and threatened most theatre subsidies; then he had the Kronstadt rising forcibly suppressed. In the same month, Meyerhold's theatre was stripped of its rank. Already the RSFSR Theatres Nos 2 and 3 had gone their own way, and both, perhaps seeing their best way forward, were presenting plays by Lunacharsky. Now RSFSR Theatre No 1 was handed to the Moscow Soviet, and became MONO Theatre No 1. On 5 April, in a last act of defiance, Meyerhold, Bebutov and Konstantin Derzhavin published a scathing attack on bureaucracy in theatrical affairs,[27] and three days later Meyerhold resigned from TEO.

DAWNS OF THE PROLETKULT

The Proletkult's theatre work seemed as headily challenging as that of the RSFSR theatres. The actor Maxim Shtraukh wrote:

> We wanted to serve the kind of art which could be a weapon in the revolutionary struggle. That's why we went to Proletkult. We chose this theatre because we young people were burning with the desire to serve not simply art, but a new and revolutionary art.[28]

Thus, although Proletkult was losing ordinary members rapidly from December 1920, it still attracted artists such as David Burlyuk, Nikolai Chuzhak and Sergei Tretyakov in Vladivostok, as well as Boris Arvatov, Sergei Eisenstein and others in Moscow. The usual pattern for theatre work in Proletkult groups consisted of a teacher leading about fifty participants, in classes broadly based on his professional experience. Thus, Mgebrov, in Petrograd, applied what he had learned in the pre-revolutionary Symbolist and Ancient Theatres to the proletarian performers he now had before him, and presented poetic productions which relied greatly on mass movement and choral speech. And in Moscow Valentin Smyshlyaev, formerly an actor with the Art Theatre, relied on Stanislavsky's ideas in his teaching (though Stanislavsky regarded him as 'an inadequate and backward pupil').[29] His productions, such as Verhaeren's poetic *The Insurrection* and Pletnev's adaptation of Claudel's *The Avenger*, as well as the less successful *Woman at the Crossroads*, also by Verhaeren, were much closer to conventional drama. *The Avenger* was criticised by some, including Valentin Tikhonovich, for not employing more revolutionary stage techniques: it could have been presented by the Nezlobin or the Maly, he said. The same criticism was levelled at his production of Serafimovich's *Mariana*, which opened the Second Central Theatre Studio on 22 March 1920.

When Meyerhold took over at TEO in September 1920, Moscow Proletkult had only the First and Second 'permanent' studios. Within two weeks, he had increased that number by fifty per cent by handing over TEO's Tonal-Plastic Department to Proletkult. This had been established after a number of leading Proletkultists, including Valentin Smyshlyaev, Petr Kogan, Valentin Tikhonovich and Evgeny Prosvetov signed a 'Declaration for a Tonal-Plastic Association' on 4 April 1920, proposing an alternative system to Stanislavsky's which would create a 'collectively-synthesised' theatre, bringing together fine art, music and literature. In June, TEO had set up a Tonal-Plastic division under Prosvetov, and it was this which Meyerhold transferred to Proletkult. Developing out of Kerzhentsev's ideas of collective creation, anti-individualism and anti-psychologism, Vyacheslav Ivanov's advocacy of Greek choric dance and song, and Emile Jacques-Dalcroze's ideas of musical awareness through physical movement, the Tonal-Plastic, or 'Ton-Plas', Studio formulated a presentational style based on rhythmic movement and choral speech. The comprehensive curriculum Prosvetov proposed for those workers entering the Ton-Plas Studio divided into three parts: educational-technical, scientific-methodological, and artistic-creative. Members studied the technique and music of speech, choral and solo speaking and singing, the reading of music, solfeggio, the classics, fine arts, 'tonal-plastic synthesis', emotional recall, cultural history, world affairs, and mathematics. It is difficult to realise that the participants were only workers wanting to do amateur dramatics in their spare time.

In the scientific-methodological part, members were tested in tonal performance, eurythmics, gymnastics and the synthesising of these. The artistic-creative element involved rehearsal and performance. The earliest Ton-Plas performances comprised concerts of choral speech, when poems by Verhaeren, by Proletkultists like Vladimir Kirillov, and even collectively-created poems, were declaimed, and demonstrations of movement, often work movements stylised into a kind of free dance, were performed. For example, *The Leader*, the main role of which was originally danced by Nikolai Sidelnikov, killed while helping to crush the Kronstadt rising, and then by Ivan Yazykanov, later a leading actor with the First Workers Theatre of the Proletkult, was a series of études, or *tableaux vivants* accompanied by choral speech. Finally the strands were synthesised, most successfully in a show called *Labour*, choreographed and directed by Prosvetov, which was given its premiere on 16 December 1920, but afterwards effectively presented, like other products of the studio, from the backs of lorries and on mobile stages in the

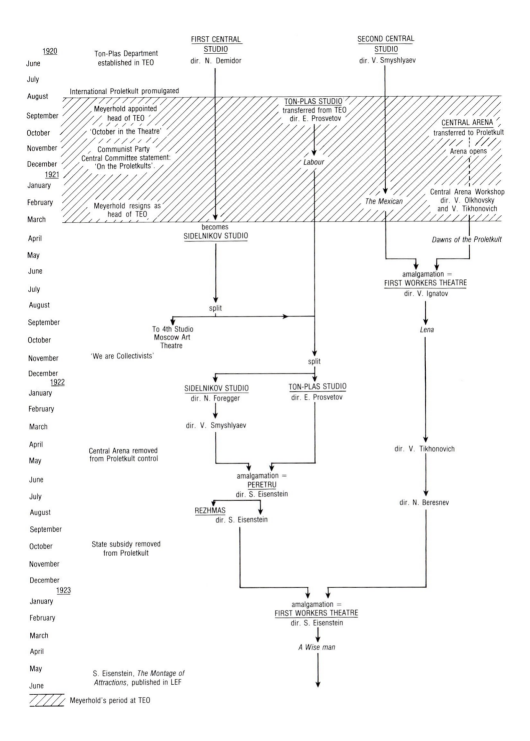

Figure 2 Moscow Proletkult Theatres, 1920–1923

city squares and at workers' clubs. *Labour* began with heavy, resonant music, suggestive of work in a capitalist state. The light blazed on to show a half-naked blacksmith wielding an imaginary hammer, a group of workers performing work movements, and, above, the capitalists scoffing at them 'like a flock of black birds'.[30] There followed what we would now call a dance-drama with *tableaux*, depicting the overthrow of Capital by Labour, notable as one of the first examples of mass movement synchronised for narrative purposes.

Having established the Ton-Plas Studio in Proletkult, Meyerhold next presented it with the magnificent Hermitage Theatre, housed in what had been the millionaire merchant, Savva Morozov's mansion. This became vacant with the failure of Sakhnovsky's Exemplary Theatre, and was now renamed the Proletkult Central Arena, intended as a showplace for the achievements of the various Proletkult studios in all the arts. It opened to the public on 7 November 1920 with a programme which included lectures from Pavel Lebedev-Polyansky and the Arena's 'chief organiser', Vasily Ignatov, and performances of successful Proletkult shows, including *The Avenger, The Leader, The Insurrection* and *The Marseillaise.*

Under this regime, Proletkult's theatres flourished, most remarkably when the Second Central Theatre Studio presented an adaptation of Jack London's story of revolution in central America, *The Mexican* on 10 March 1921. Ostensibly, it was directed by Valentin Smyshlyaev, but Yutkevich and others have testified that the designer, Sergei Eisenstein, was the true begetter of the show,[31] which he redirected when it was revived in August 1923. At this time, Eisenstein's excessive energy was suggested by 'a very thick crop of hair that seemed to vibrate with electricity.'[32] He and Boris Arvatov had joined Proletkult, seeking an 'agitational-dynamic' theatre, which would 'emancipate dynamic action from the demands of subject – that gaoler of theatrical freedom'.[33] While Arvatov roughed out a scenario, Eisenstein designed a fantastic Cubistic set of cones, triangles, cubes and lattice-like strips. The costumes were preposterous and clown-like, and many characters wore fabulous masks – large square ones for capitalists, a parrot's head for the clerk, and so on. The exception was Rivera, the hero, who had no make-up and wore a sombre hat and cloak. At the first rehearsal, London's story was read to the participants, the scenario and the designs were shown to them, and collectively the show was created through improvisation and discussion.

The first act showed the revolutionaries in a gloomy cellar; the second had one of them, Philip Rivera, enter the brassy fairground world of prizefight promotion to challenge Denny Ward, the champion; in the third the boxing match itself occurred, Rivera won, and with his prize purse the revolution was able to begin. The acting style was basically grotesque and exaggerated, until the finale, when Eisenstein staged the boxing match as a 'real event':

> carefully planned in advance but utterly realistic. The playing of our young worker-actors in the fight scene differed radically from their acting elsewhere in the production . . . While the other scenes influenced the audience through intonation, gestures and mimicry, [this] scene employed realistic, even textural means – real fighting, bodies crashing to the ring floor, panting, the shine of sweat on torsos, and finally the unforgettable smacking of gloves against taut skin and strained muscles.[34]

In Eisenstein's phrase, this was 'real doing', though Margolin's description – 'the victory of the puny-looking worker over the hired Hercules'[35] – suggests something more complex. Nevertheless, it contrasted starkly with the 'pictorial imagination' of the other scenes and thereby undermined the audience's expectations. But then the audience was no longer fulfilling the traditional role of passive watchers; they had become part of the action, not just because Rivera came up from among them to the ring itself, but because the ring was thrust out into the stalls area, with on-stage spectators completing the circle. The 'real' space of circus was nudging out the 'false' space of theatre.

The new relationship with the audience was of immense significance to revolutionary theatre: the real world and the world of the drama now overlapped. In *Mystery Bouffe* and Radlov's Popular Comedy, the danger of circus performance intrudes; in the mass spectacles and the Herald's report of the victory at Perekop in *The Dawns*, the intrusion is more direct. *The Mexican* was constructed with the intention of breaking down the conventional barriers, especially in the interludes when the audience was assaulted directly in many ways, as for example by 'sandwich men', shouting: 'Who's coming? He's coming! Denny Ward! The great boxer!'[36] The grotesqueries and clowning of course are there partly to ease this new relationship, for their very theatricality implicitly draws attention to reality, and in *The Mexican* they were worked out with a surprising degree of sophistication, considering the inexperience of Eisenstein and his collaborators.

A circus turn forces the spectator to see the performer as performer, and tiny sequences of clowning, involving characters who appear nowhere else in the play, epitomise this. Between the rounds of the boxing match in *The Mexican*, there were such episodes. One involved an alluring dancer making eyes at a cleric, who was watching with his wife. He began to respond, whereupon the wife flew at the dancer and began beating her about the head with her umbrella. The husband managed to drag her away, to the amusement of the other spectators. The audience's response to this incident and its relationship to the

7 *The Mexican.* (1) Rivera faces Mr Kelly, the boxing promoter, in Eisenstein's fantastic Cubist setting for the Second Central Studio of the Proletkult.

8 *The Mexican.* (2) The Boxing Match. Denny Ward is knocked out.

actual fight which will determine the outcome of the plot, were challenged in the next pause between rounds, when a Japanese docker expressed his support for Rivera and was attacked by a dignified elderly lady for it.

The interlude between Acts One and Two was more complex, because its reference to the theatre audience was more disturbing. Fairy lights lit up the proscenium arch, and the play's revolutionary leaders came forward to harangue the audience about the evils of capitalism, especially in Mexico. Destroying the illusion, they appealed to the spectators not to forget the plight of the real Mexico in their excitement about constructing socialism in the RSFSR. At this moment reality was interrupted by fiction: the speaker was arrested by a policeman. But two clowns bounded on and knocked the policeman down. The revolutionary dashed off through the auditorium, with the policeman in hot pursuit. The clowns began a cross-talk act with topical jokes about Moscow life, interrupted by the appearance of two young girls each on an arm of the impresario of the boxing match. They charmed free tickets from him, then sold them to a lascivious passer-by at a hugely-inflated price. The policeman, having now returned, saw this and a crazy chase ensued all over the theatre, especially through the audience. The theatre director appeared, and ordered them to their places for the next act, the lights dimmed, and the show proper resumed. It was breathless, fast, funny, full of variety and surprises. And by constantly and in unexpected ways undermining the audience's relationship to the presentation, it challenged each spectator's response. By contrast, the heavily symbolic Epilogue failed in this regard: out of the chaos of darkness and confusion at the end of the boxing match, spotlights picked out the triumphant figure of Revolution, ascending from the melée.

The Mexican was hugely successful: it 'turned the Central Workers Studio into a genuine theatre overnight', according to Margolin, for whom the circus episodes stuck in the memory with especial clarity, and who found that the vivid theatricality conveyed an 'impetuous *joie de vivre*'.[37] Of course there were those who regarded the production as incomprehensible and affected, but there is no doubt that the majority of those who watched found it both exciting and absorbing.

In the same month as *The Mexican* opened, a new Central Arena workshop was established under the Maly Theatre's Viktor Olkhovsky and Valentin Tikhonovich. Calling itself an 'educational-creative institution', it aimed to produce 'synthetic performers and director-teachers' as well as 'a new theatrical form'.[38] Its greatest, perhaps only, achievement was Ignatov's *The Dawns of the Proletkult*, a friendly riposte to Meyerhold, premièred on May Day 1921. This presentation used the poetry of Proletkult's best poets to illuminate working-class experience from May Day, through a strike and a revolution, to the sunny uplands of communism. Using mime, eurhythmics and choral speech, and with Maxim Shtraukh taking the leading role, the work nevertheless slithered into proletarian 'furnace and anvil' cliché: Act Two takes place inside a factory, 'old and dark . . . where everything is primitive. A row of furnaces and anvils. Light only from the furnaces. The impression is of total darkness, slaving labourers, and penal conditions.'[39]

By now Meyerhold had left TEO, and his 'October in the Theatre' was in retreat. The Communist Party's denunciation of December 1920,[40] and the reduction in funding were also affecting Proletkult: the First Studio dissolved, some members joining Ton-Plas, others forming the Fourth Studio of the Moscow Art Theatre, while the Second Studio and Tikhonovich's Arena workshop amalgamated to form the First Workers Theatre of the Proletkult.[41] Despite the opposition of the new Party-approved President, Valerian Pletnev, the organisation was forced to stress the specialist functions of its creative and cultural work to survive, thereby virtually ending its mass character.

Pletnev himself had worked as a carpenter for nineteen years, though he had been politically active as a Menshevik, and twice been exiled to Siberia: he was in Lena at the time of the strike in the gold-mines. In 1913 he had argued for the importance of culture in working-class life, and advocated strengthening cultural organisations. He was active in the Civil War, and in February 1921 became head of the arts section of Glavpolitprosvet, though his ideas seem to have been largely frustrated by less radical civil servants. His wife, Anna Dodonova, was an active Communist in the Moscow Party, and also prominent in her own right in Proletkult. After the revolution, Pletnev published two volumes of stories, as well as plays. He remained President of Proletkult until its liquidation in 1932, after which he continued to do educational and editorial work, and even had a play, *The Hat*, successfully performed at the Vakhtangov Theatre in 1936. In April 1942 he was killed in action at the age of 55.

He wrote a number of plays which were popular with local Proletkult studios in the first years after the revolution, including *Incredible, but . . . Possible*, first performed in 1919 but most interestingly-directed in a different production by Alexei Diky in April 1920. The play has a typical Civil War plot, Whites fighting Reds in a remote rural village, where the garrulous mayor arrests a group of protesting workers, who are rescued by an avenging Communist. On this occasion, according to Arvatov, the actors rejected the naturalistic style and decided to turn the play into a satirical buffoonade. The text was radically revised and much of Diky's work was jettisoned; although the result was a hotch-potch of the grotesque, the naturalistic and more, it certainly provided a stimulating evening for many.

Pletnev's best play was probably *Flengo*, first produced by Vladimir Tatarinov, and made into an opera for the tenth anniversary of the revolution in 1927. It is set in the Paris Commune and tells the story of an orphan boy, looked after by the gruff but kindly old soldier, Tiebeau. Flengo's idealism leads him to disobey Tiebeau and join the communards on the barricades as Thiers's forces are overrunning the Commune. At the climactic moment, Flengo stands up and shoots at the soldiers point-blank, wounding their officer, but he is shot dead himself. Pletnev tries in an interlude between scenes to achieve the same undermining of conventional performer-audience relationships which Eisenstein was to achieve in *The Mexican*, though Pletnev's attempt is by no means so convincing;

ENTR' ACTE

From behind the curtain the crackle of gunfire is heard, rifles shooting. Flengo runs through the auditorium.

FLENGO   [*as he runs*]. There's the firing . . . There's the killing . . . Quick, over there! [*He vanishes behind the curtain.*]

WOMAN   [*running from behind the curtain*]. Where's Monsieur Tiebeau? . . . Oh, my God! (*She runs through the auditorium.*) Come quickly, M. Tiebeau. They want to shoot one of your youngsters. It's terrible there. I'm afraid the officer won't be able to hold his men back.
Your youngster was on the barricade.

TIEBEAU   [*runs onto the stage, vanishes behind the curtain. As he goes*]. This cannot be! It cannot be!
[*Blackout. In the blackout, the curtain rises.*][42]

The new First Workers' Theatre of the Proletkult opened on 11 October 1921 with a production by Vasily Ignatov, designed by Sergei Eisenstein and Leonid Nikitin, of *Lena*, Pletnev's play about the strike in the gold-fields of Siberia. The play opens in the St Petersburg offices of Lengold, the company which owns the mines. The bosses learn that the strikers have 'a whole programme'. They want 'an eight hour day, participation in the hiring and firing of workers, a check on the calculations of the work done at the mine face'. Police co-operation is requested and guaranteed. As the Lengold Vice-President remarks:

Over the last three years we have paid out over 1,300,000 pounds sterling to our shareholders, and this has evoked a very favourable response. 1,300,000 pounds. It's not bad. Aren't I right? But it will be very bad if Russian gold starts to wobble because of this.

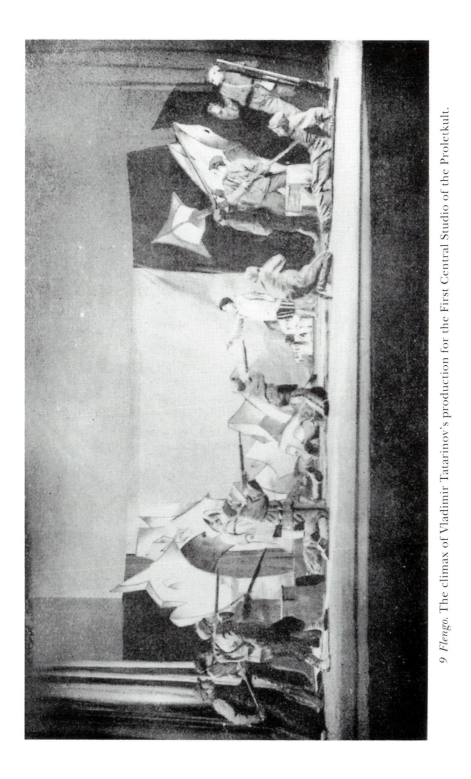

9 *Flengo*. The climax of Vladimir Tatarinov's production for the First Central Studio of the Proletkult.

The rest of the play takes place in the gold-field. The miners refuse to compromise, their leaders are arrested, but when they protest *en masse*, they are ruthlessly gunned down. There is a powerful scene in which some soldiers try to remove the bodies, while others scrub up the blood. At the end, the surviving workers pack up to go when someone brings in a newspaper with news of a wave of sympathy strikes and demonstrations across Russia and even abroad. 'We'll be the masters yet,' says Khrennov at the end.[43]

The play is stark and emotionally well-focused, though the pervasive naturalism is sometimes disappointing, for example in the scenes in the workers' huts and outside near the pithead, as well as in matters such as the persistent sound of a woodchopper offstage in Act Four, before the protesters are mown down. But there is also an original use of emblematic primary colours – snow, blood, the coal in the hoar frost, and a simple symbolism in moments such as when the miners tumble out of bed and the sun's rays shaft through the window. Watchers found the actual production either 'timid' (Margolin) or 'Futurist' (Lunacharsky) depending on their viewpoint.[44] Zagorsky felt that the 'correct path' discovered by *The Mexican* was lost here because history was treated as 'social study'; he found the first act good in its use of the grotesque, but this seemed to have no connection with what followed.[45] But taking his cue from Platon Kerzhentsev, Pletnev argued that *Lena* and his other plays answered aspirations for a new type of history play:

> 'The path of the proletariat's struggle in all centuries and in all places has been marked by immense suffering, and by the highest heroism,' he wrote in his Preface to *Lena*. 'Here should be an ineffable spring of creative work . . . [To] resurrect great images of our struggle . . . will be the most fitting contribution from us to the great future towards which we are going.'[46]

The play, flawed though it is, does achieve something of this, and reminds us again of Lunacharsky's vision of achieving 'immortality by merging with the collective, submerging the finite "I" in the infinite "We", and sharing in the great deeds and heroic acts of collectivised humanity.'[47]

But Proletkult was stumbling towards new crises. In November 1921 an anonymous pamphlet entitled *We Are Collectivists* was circulated at the Proletkult Congress, denouncing NEP, aligning Proletkult with the Workers' Opposition, and asserting Bogdanov's importance. Bukharin denounced the pamphlet in *Pravda* on 22 November and Pletnev and the 'Party faction', disclaiming all knowledge of it, protested their utter orthodoxy as communists. Early the next year, Tikhonovich looked back at Proletkult as one of 'The Mistakes of Youth', to which Pletnev angrily replied with an article entitled 'The Mistakes of Old Age'.[48] In

10 *Lena*. The newspaper tells the apparently-defeated workers of support across the country, in the first production of the First Workers Theatre of the Proletkult, October 1921

May the former Hermitage Theatre, now the Central Arena, was taken from Proletkult. Four months later, Pletnev spelt out his view of proletarian culture, Bogdanovist as it still was, in *Pravda* on 27 September and 17 and 20 October. Lenin's response was one of furious contempt and he set Yakovlev, the Party's Head of Propaganda, to write a riposte, the two parts of which were published in *Pravda* on 24 and 25 October. On 26 October the Politburo voted to remove Proletkult's subsidy entirely.

The organisation had been outmanoeuvred in three successive autumns: in 1920 it had to foreswear its autonomy; in 1921 it had to promise submission to the Party line; and now in 1922 it lost all financial support. Bogdanov's ideas of proletarian culture were made the special target of a further article by Yakovlev in *Pravda* on 4 January 1923, and on 1 October of that year he was arrested as a potential oppositionist, though he was released on 3 November. Paradoxically, however, the Proletkult theatre was to go on to achieve its finest success now that it was wholly autonomous.

THEATRES OF REVOLUTIONARY SATIRE

If Proletkult initially aimed to cater for the enthusiastic amateur, the Theatres of Revolutionary Satire which sprang up through 1919 and 1920 were mainly professional. During the revolution and its aftermath, many theatre practitioners, like people of all trades, were displaced, their lives disrupted, their jobs lost. But in a year or two, wherever they found themselves – Kaluga, Baku, Kiev, Vitebsk – they formed makeshift troupes and began the process of making theatre again.

The first Theatre of Revolutionary Satire (TEREVSAT) was the brainchild of the Vitebsk Director of ROSTA, Mikhail Pustynin, and for a year or more TEREVSAT was closely bound to ROSTA. Pustynin's idea that news could be made more accessible through dramatisation thus brought the Living Newspaper to fruition. Pustynin, a poet who later worked with the Blue Blouse and was also closely involved in the satirical magazine, *Krokodil*, was supported by his assistant at ROSTA, N. P. Abramsky, the local Art Workers Union secretary, A. A. Goldman, the artist Marc Chagall, who was Head of the Vitebsk Art Institute, and the director of the local theatre, Alexander Sumarokov. A former actor of Evreinov's Distorting Mirror, Mikhail Razumny, became director of the troupe, and their first performance was given on 7 February 1919.

That first programme was typical enough of TEREVSAT's shows for the next year or so. It opened with a song, 'The March of TEREVSAT', sung by all the performers to a catchy operetta tune, accompanied on the accordion:

We hope our Terevsat
Is acrid and fun,
And our lively satire
Will sting those who'd run.
We'll vanquish your boredom,
It's all for the cause;
We assure you, when smiling,
We've got teeth in our jaws.[49]

This was followed by *The Shrine of TEREVSAT*, a short 'political satire' by Pustynin, directed by Razumny, designed by Chagall, with only two characters, Lloyd George and Poincaré. Then came an 'agit-play' in one act, *The Blockade*, from the same team, and then a parody of Boris Savinkov's novel *The Pale Horse* directed by Sumarokov, with Razumny as the reader. *An Adventure of the Angel of Peace*, another 'political satire' by Pustynin, was followed by *TEREVSAT's Chastushki*. Then came *A Block of Hell*, a parody of Blok's poetry performed by Razumny, and the show finished with a mass singing of 'The Internationale'.

This revue-like format continued to be used by TEREVSAT, whether the show they were giving was to last thirty minutes or ninety. Often the performance was preceded by a short talk by a professional 'agitator' and 'The March of TEREVSAT' was sung as the performers came through the audience to the stage. Then the actors often swept the performance area, symbolically sweeping away the old regime, and the items followed one another with little pause. As in the Distorting Mirror cabaret, there was no master of ceremonies to link the items. Characters usually wore fairly extravagant costumes, and Chagall designed some strikingly imaginative and figurative backcloths:

Everything was in short supply. No material for the costumes and sets. The night before the theatre opened, people brought me old worn-out suits. I hurriedly painted them . . . I couldn't enter the auditorium, I was so spattered with paint. I even ran onto the stage a few minutes before the curtain went up to paint in the props. I couldn't stand 'naturalism'.[50]

Programmes contained political songs and verses, parodies, *chastushki* and 'tantomoresques', poster-like animated cartoons, made by cutting out the head and arms of a life-size drawing and having the actor stand behind and insert his own head and arms through the holes. Chagall designed a particularly successful 'tantomoresque', *The Cossacks*, in which shaven-headed Cossacks sang, 'The night exhales a voluptuous ecstasy' with comic topical allusions.[51] TEREVSAT also used folk dance and gymnastic group movement, song which fitted topical words to known tunes, animated *lubok*, and *raek*-style ballads. The adaptations of

Petrushka puppet shows, performed by actors with jerky marionette-style movement, may have been more subtle, but they still used the standard TEREVSAT technique of injecting an unexpected political question or aside into basically traditional fun. Petrushka plays using this technique included *Petrushka's Polka*, *Petrushka the Peasant* and *The Search for Truth*, in which Petrushka encountered a parson, a mullah and a rabbi, before finding the truth in revolutionary struggle. Especially successful in the role of Petrushka was the actor, Boris Usynovich, who was unbelievably thin, with large expressive eyes and an extraordinarily long nose.

This was perhaps the Living Newspaper's equivalent of the comic strip, which existed alongside dramatisations of news items, letters to the editor (often as fictional as some of those in printed newspapers), and leading articles. In a montage of brief, unconnected items, structured according to the revue-format already developed, Living Newspapers kept their illiterate audiences in touch with the issues of the day. The subjects were by no means always topical or political, however. Often a Living Newspaper would include an item or two of more general educational content, such as the dramatised *Fight Against Typhus*, and sometimes whole shows were educational rather than concerned with 'news'. Topics such as looking after and breeding hens, and the productive cultivation of the land, were common. Attempts to enlighten the audience in the sphere of personal life were also produced – sketches demonstrating the right way to breathe or explaining basic hygiene, for instance. In 1921 Mayakovsky wrote such a Living Newspaper article called *Yesterday's Exploit*, about the correct distribution of grain, which was directed by Nikolai Foregger at TEREVSAT's Moscow Studio. The form might be expected to appeal to the author of *Mystery Bouffe*, since it is characteristically dynamic and provocative. Much of the work associated with the Blue Blouse groups grew from the early, almost naive, attempts to inform ordinary people.[52] So did the whole documentary tradition, which was adopted by left-wing theatres in Europe, Britain and USA over the decades, and may not be worn out yet.

TEREVSAT began in Vitebsk, but were soon to be seen on tour in the local countryside and at the Civil War front. The style of acting continued the resemblance to the old troupes of strolling players, and was often rooted in improvisation based on character types. Because the news (which made up the content of much of the show) changed day by day, the actors often had only time to agree the form of the sketch before going on stage, and, performing in the open air, they frequently had to cope with interjections and heckling from the audience. On one occasion prefiguring the better-known episode in Meyerhold's *The Dawns*, an agitator interrupted the performance to announce the defeat of Denikin. The audience burst out cheering, and the actors improvised a scene of Denikin dancing, then being chased off by Red Army soldiers.

This was a reinvention of *commedia dell'arte* to fit the times, and though undoubtedly Razumny, Sumarokov and others knew the old form, and must have used what knowledge they had, there is an extraordinary freshness and excitement about this work which only partly results from the people's excitement at liberation; it is also a surge of creative originality.

The performers' pay was minimal, often 'in kind' (potatoes, grain, salt herring), and the discomforts enormous, yet the shows were dynamic and the audiences wildly enthusiastic. Once the actors playing Kolchak, Yudenich and Vrangel were almost lynched, and they retreated to the local canteen while those on stage urgently explained that they were only actors *impersonating* the White generals. Another time, bad roads and foul weather prevented the troupe reaching the village which was expecting them. When the villagers discovered the problem, they went with horses and ropes, and dragged the troupe's vehicle to the village, where the exhausted performers were unable to refuse to give their show. Some audiences were so unfamiliar with the conventions of theatre that they watched in dumb amazement, until the 'agitator' told them they could laugh or clap.

Success breeds success. In late 1919 Ekaterina Khersonskaya of the Party's Agitation and Propaganda Department suggested that TEREVSAT perform in Moscow, and if they were successful, move permanently to the capital, where they would receive regular salaries. In April 1920 this happened, and the company acquired a new director, David Gutman, to share the post with Mikhail Razumny, and a new designer, Vasily Komardenkov, a founder member of the Society of Young Artists (OBMOKhU). In 1912 Gutman had created the Blue Eye cabaret in Ekaterinoslav, then worked at the Distorting Mirror from 1915, and after 1917 had organised a 'revolutionary Petrushka' puppet theatre with which he had toured the front.

On 15 April 1920 the new Moscow TEREVSAT Studio was established with TEO backing. It included twenty-five actors and the same number of students from clubs in and around the city. They were to study the forms and functions of satire of earlier periods, especially the one act play, as well as improvisation and scenography under, among others, Ivan Maly-utin and Isaak Rabinovich. Mayakovsky, enthusiastic and involved from the beginning, wrote a fine trilogy of short plays for them to perform on the forthcoming May Day, which happened to coincide with Easter weekend as well as a 'Communist Saturday', when people were expected to do socially useful work for nothing. But the plays were refused permission for performance, a fate suffered by several other projects of the Studio, and in the autumn, perhaps because of such rebuffs, it closed.

Mayakovsky's plays were later passed by the censor, and the first of them, *And What If . . .?* was performed by the Studio that autumn.

Subtitled 'May Day Dreams in a Bourgeois Armchair', the play shows Ivan Ivanovich falling asleep after a good meal, there being a knock at his door, and two Spivs entering to tell him that Kerensky is back. The Stock Exchange, the expensive restaurants and shops, all the exclusive haunts of the *haute bourgeoisie* are open again. Ivan is delighted, he and the Spivs run off and meet a fearsome tsarist policeman, whom they hug, and bow down to. Swearing to string up all Leftists, they remain on all fours like dogs in a pack. The door knocks, Ivan Ivanovich wakes: he has to come and sweep his patch of the street. The play is extremely vivid and theatrical, employing grotesque effects with great economy and force, the one act form intensifying both the high comedy and the horror.

The second of the plays, *Small Play for Priests Who Do Not Understand What a Public Holiday Is*, which was performed by the main TEREVSAT company on 31 December 1920, is also mordant and fast moving. It concerns a priest ('Father Pighead') and his wife, starving through lack of a congregation to pander to their wants. By hard experience Father Pighead learns that bread must be earned in the new society. But what is striking is the theatricality of the piece. Father Pighead, played by Boris Usynovich, comes home by tumbling through the window, for instance, and when the final curtain has fallen, he bursts through again to thank all those who have taught him the lesson: 'the workers' and peasants' government, comrade Lunacharsky, comrade Mayakovsky, comrade Zonov [who was supposed to direct the play, though in fact Razumny did], comrade Malyutin, and all the masses . . .'[53]

How Some People Spend Their Time on Public Holidays was the weakest of the three plays, and may never have been performed. Nevertheless it includes what is perhaps the most horrifying scene of all, set on Christmas Eve, when the self-absorbed and mawkish parents hang baubles on the tree which drops bits, needles, decorations, on the children, who then drown in the discharge:

CHILDREN.   Papa!
            Mama!
            That's enough,
            I can't breathe.
            We're drowning.
            Papa!
            It's up to our necks!
HUSBAND.   Do be quiet,
            You're not completely buried yet!
            Here's some more for you,
            And some more,
            And some more bits and bobs
            Out of the crackers.

CHILDREN. Oh Goddy, save us!
Oh Guardian Angel, rescue us!
We're going under, poor things,
Drowning in droppings![54]

Unable to present Mayakovsky's dramas, TEREVSAT appeared on May Day on three wagons commandeered by the Party: on the first was a brass band, the second was rigged up with tarpaulin to make a dressing room (though a piano was also on board), and the third was a stage on which the actors performed. Beginning in Red Square, they toured the city, trumpets blaring, and performed at about twenty different locations. On board the wagons with them were Party 'agitators' who made brief speeches – Ivan Skvortsev-Stepanov, Lev Sosnovsky, Rozaliya Zemlyachka – as well as international figures who were in Moscow – the German Spartacist Clara Zetkin, the French Communist Marcel Kashen, and the head of IAH (International Workers' Aid), Willi Muenzenberg.

A fortnight later, TEREVSAT made its proper Moscow debut in front of members of the city Soviet, as well as representatives of the Red Army, the press, social organisations, and others. The programme, beginning with 'The March of TEREVSAT' in a new arrangement by Gutman, followed the familiar pattern, with a tantomoresque and an agit-play by Pustynin, two or three musical numbers, including dance, by Argo, and two political satires by Lev Nikulin. Most were directed by Gutman, though Razumny directed two, and most of them were designed by Komardenkov (Chagall having remained in Vitebsk). The show was well-received, and the company was offered a temporary base in the Moscow Communist Party building. From here they toured the city over the next months, performing in barracks, clubs, hospitals and even in the Taganka prison, as well as beyond, to the Civil War front in Siberia and the Caucasus. One troupe (or 'brigade', as they were called) went on an agit-train with the Red Army to the Crimea, another went along the Volga on the agit-ship 'Red Star', though cholera broke out and several members of this group died. They performed on Lenin's fiftieth birthday, and for the 2nd Congress of the Comintern, and by the end of 1920, the Moscow TEREVSAT had 350 active participants.

On 7 November 1920 they presented a triple bill at the Nikitsky Theatre, formerly a light opera house with an unvirtuous reputation, now their new permanent base: *Rubbish*, a satire by Efim Zozulya, *The Little Peasant*, an agit-play in two acts, by Vyacheslav Shishkov (both these directed by Gutman and designed by Komardenkov), and Gutman's ballet-pantomime, *The Balance*, directed by Razumny. *The Little Peasant*, according to one critic, owed a debt to Mayakovsky's *And What If . . .?*[55] It concerned a kulak whose reactionary attitudes were only overcome when some young workers performed a scene of a return to pre-revolutionary days for him. Housed in a permanent theatre, with an obviously more sophisticated audience, and with the Civil War which had motivated them over, TEREVSAT's role and nature had to change and Meyerhold (who had at least a hand in securing the Nikitsky Theatre for them), and Kameneva now signed them up as RSFSR Theatre No 5, while Razumny, reported to be Kameneva's lover, urged the company to wear 'productivist' clothes and shoes, and tried to institute a 'collective lifestyle', which some actors flatly refused to join.

The repertoire also reflected the concerns of 'October in the Theatre'. Mayakovsky's *Small Play for Priests* had been presented along-side Mark Krinitsky's anti-religious eccentric buffoonade, *At the Gates of Paradise*, and *The New Front*, dealing with the need to increase production. It dramatised both a domestic and a work crisis, precipitated by the return from America of the hero's brother, but remained disappointingly naturalistic, simply stating its point and never seeking a dramatic form to surprise or jolt the spectator. Thus the play opens in:

> a room in Ivan's house. Straight ahead is the outside door, on either side two windows, to the right the door to the kitchen. To the left are two beds along the wall by the window. To the right is the dinner table. The windows have tulle curtains. On the wall hangs a kerosene lamp. By the beds a cradle is suspended from the ceiling.

When the curtain rises, Ivan is 'sawing a wooden board. It is cold.'[56] This seems far from Chagall's figurative backcloths, his Cossacks with shaven heads, or indeed Petrushka's (or Father Pighead's) attention-grabbing grotesqueries.

On 1 December 1920, the same day, ironically, that the Central Committee published their letter against Proletkult, TEREVSAT's Political and Theatre Committees met together to consider their future. Zinovy Daltsev, actor and president of the Theatre Committee, summarised their aims: to deliver theatrically what was usually delivered in pamphlets, speeches and newspaper articles; to do it clearly, but entertainingly; to choose appropriate forms for the work; to encourage a variety of styles in a single programme. This sounded fine. But the plays which apparently followed from this included such dramas as Bernard Shaw's *Great Catherine*, and Lunacharsky's *The Dream of Lloyd George*. Others – Gutman, Argo and Aduyev's *Political Revue* and, perhaps, Ehrenburg's *The End of the World* – offered a more promising means of finding 'striking forms' to 'stir up large masses of workers and peasants who are not in the Party'.[57] But the problem of the repertoire was clear: the agit pieces were too bald for a traditional theatre, and the conventional plays lacked the element of agitation which was TEREVSAT's *raison d'être*.

But while TEREVSAT in Moscow was anguishing about its future, other theatres, calling themselves Theatres of Revolutionary Satire, were springing up across the country, using the methods and indeed the scripts of the original TEREVSAT. Lunacharsky encouraged this, and was closely involved in the establishment of TEREVSATs in Baku, where members of the Bat Theatre who had not followed their leader, Baliev, into exile set up a TEREVSAT in a small cinema; and in Nikolaev, where the Red Pepper Theatre was created by ROSTA under the direction of Boris Glubokovsky, and a second TEREVSAT, the Sverdlov, by Lunacharsky. In Grozny, in the Caucasus, TEREVSAT under Graf Etinghof called itself 'the Commissariat of Laughter',[58] while that of Kaluga, south of Moscow, considered itself 'an orthodox fighter for "October in the Theatre"'.[59]

Also under Lunacharsky's patronage, the Free Comedy opened in Petrograd in the basement of the Palace Theatre, as the northern capital's TEREVSAT on 10 November 1920. The performance began with the actors walking through the audience onto the stage, and a series of sketches developed from a supposed telephone conversation between elegant 'former people', one supposedly in Paris, the other languishing in Petrograd: in fact in the upper boxes on either side of the stage. They were the butt of much humour as well as contempt in Lev Nikulin's *Here and There*, Vladimir Schmidthof's *Parisian Rumour* and others. Meanwhile, the company had declared its allegiance, first, to the tradition of the Distorting Mirror, the repertoire of which, its manifesto added a touch disingenuously, 'ridicules bourgeois ideology', and, second, to contemporary romanticism, found 'in the accomplishment now of the revolution'.[60] Nikolai Petrov was the artistic director, and he was assisted by Nikolai Evreinov and Yuri Annenkov, as chief designer. Maria Andreeva and Konstantin Mardzhanov were on the board. Despite further politically-motivated productions, like Evreinov's of *The Celestial Mechanic*, an anti-religious play by Lev Nikulin and Mikhail Reisner, the theatre's allegiance to the Distorting Mirror proved stronger than its urge to romanticise victorious revolutionism. In February 1921, Petrov presented Evreinov's rather fastidious comedy, *The Main Thing*, a highly theatrical but somewhat abstruse work. It was well-received, but it helped redirect the Free Comedy TEREVSAT away from the original road of these theatres towards what a contemporary commentator called 'a calmer path'.[61]

Meanwhile, on 17 March 1921 the Moscow TEREVSAT, in common with the other RSFSR theatres of Meyerhold's 'October in the Theatre', was handed over to the city's care. Though an apparent downgrading, MONO Theatre No 5 now came under Olga Kameneva's remit, and this probably prolonged its life as a political theatre. Three days earlier, Argo, Aduyev and Gutman's revue, *Bulbus's Journey 1917–21* received its premiere to much acclaim. It was an eccentric review, 'a montage of attractions in the style of music hall',[62] and it included a live jazz band: Its list of characters, including countries – Greece, Rumania, Bulgaria and Serbia – real emigrés – Kerensky, Baliev of the Bat Theatre, and more – and character types, like The Speculator and The Millionaire, indicates its scope, as it reviewed the period since the overthrow of the tsar, making especial fun of the February revolution and the Provisional Government. A week later, Ilya Ehrenburg's satire on the League of Nations, *The End of the World* received its premiere, to less acclaim.

Over that summer, as the New Economic Policy came to take effect TEREVSAT's position became harder. It lost its subsidy, and had to struggle to avoid realigning its work for an audience which would pay better. But on the anniversary of the revolution, it presented *The Town Encircled* by Sergei Minin, a melodramatic chronicle of the revolutionary years set in its author's native Tsaritsyn. Komardenkov designed a set for it which only had what was needed for the action – real doors, lampposts and so on. This 'minimalism', as Komardenkov called it,[63] allowed the play to find its necessary rhythm in a way which is commonplace now, but was original then. The set also included a screen for projection, though whether this was used for film or simply still pictures is unclear. The following month, an adaptation of Jack London's *The Iron Heel* by Vsevolod Pudovkin, the future film director, and his teacher, Vladimir Gardin, was staged, with Pudovkin directing and Komardenkov again designing, and this time film was used with some success.[64] Filmed scenes and live scenes were interspersed, and some of the actors, notably Olga Preobrazhenskaya as Avis, scored a particular success through the juxtapositions. To save production costs, crowd scenes were stolen from American imported films and spliced in, which made for a curiously disjointed feel to some of the film footage, but there was no doubt that when the lights dimmed for the next episode on the big screen, a *frisson* of excitement went through the audience. Unfortunately, the stage action appears to have been rather static, the adaptation rather wooden, and the overall standard of acting extremely uneven.

That same month, TEREVSAT mounted Mikhail Reisner's tantomoresque, *The Nightingale* and a political revue, *An Industrial Harlequinade*. In the spring came a new agit-play by Pustynin, *The Backyard*. But then a scandal erupted when it was discovered Mikhail Razumny, who had earlier been so enthusiastic for collectivised life, had discovered the possibilities of individualistic entrepreneurialism offered by NEP. He was found to be the impresario behind an extremely shady series of entertainments (including gambling tables and various apparently-improper nocturnal presentations), in the garden of the Hermitage. His profits no doubt helped him to bear the loss of his position in the theatre, but it was no help to TEREVSAT. On 22 April 1922 they put on their last genuine programme, which included *ROSTA's Province* by Argo and Aduyev, *Music To Them*, a musical parody, *The Angel of Peace*, a political satire by Demyan Bedny, and *The Entente*, a tantomoresque by Lev Nikulin. Sinking fast, the last show mounted by TEREVSAT was *Russia No 2*, about the decadent Russian emigré society. Out of tune with the NEP theatregoers, TEREVSAT could no longer survive, and on 26 June 1922, Olga Kameneva renamed it the Theatre of Revolution and offered it to Vsevolod Meyerhold.

WORKSHOPS OF COMMUNIST DRAMA

While the theatres of the RSFSR, the Proletkult and TEREVSAT provided the main storm troops for 'October in the Theatre', other groups, directors and playwrights were fully in sympathy with it, and worked to achieve the same ends. Most obviously, the Workshop of Communist Drama (MASTerskaya KOMmunisticheskoi DRAMaturgii – MastKom-Dram), established largely on the initiative of Meyerhold along lines suggested by Olga Kameneva,[65] was opened on 29 November 1920. It was created to explore ways of dramatising the new realities of post-revolutionary life, and thereby to create a new repertoire. It was to be Communist in ideology, and Communists were to run it, in order to avoid the 'culturalist tendencies'[66] which former members of 'People's Theatres' or cabaret companies often followed. So Dmitry Bassalygo, a Bolshevik Party member from 1904, was put in charge, and Pavel Ilin, another longstanding Party member, became chief administrator, and later directed some shows. The professional experience of these men was exceedingly slim, but their political credentials were unimpeachable, and they were 'balanced' by actors drawn mostly from the Komissarzhevsky theatre and a Board which included Meyerhold, Bebutov, Lev Prozorovsky, the company's chief director, other theatre directors, Pavel Ivanovsky and Alexander Razumny, and the playwright, Valery Yazvitsky.

Financed by central government, MastKomDram was regarded as important enough to assume the functions of TEO's Repertoire Section when it was closed on 8 February 1921. To create the new socialist drama it evolved a system, which began with plays written or created in its literary department. Both the ideology and the artistic quality of these plays were checked by a specially-formed 'foursome' – a writer, a director, an actor and either a designer or a critic or a musican. If they approved, the play was put into production, with the 'foursome' still available to advise on changes. It was then performed for worker audiences at MastKomDram's own small theatre, formerly Komissar-zhevsky's theatre, and then, if it was still acceptable, it was toured to clubs and then re-assessed. If at the end of this process the play continued to be approved, it was recommended to other groups – club theatres, factories, Red Army troupes and those based in rural reading rooms, and printed and distributed to them. This elaborate system may have produced little which has survived, but it highlighted some of the problems connected with creating a revolutionary theatre.

MastKomDram's work was centred on the actors, whose improvisations and other ideas moulded most of the plays. What they did was marked by 'sincerity of feeling' and 'ardent enthusiasm',[67] but the disappointing results demonstrated the falseness of Kerzhentsev's position, and that enthusiasm could never replace technical skill. Plays they helped into existence included Karpinsky's *Us and Them*, Antimonov's *The Tsars* and several by Yazvitsky and Neverov, who died before his promise fully flowered in 1923. *Red October*, *The Old Woman* and *The Civil War*, all by Alexander Neverov, showed some potential for symbolic action and staging, through the use of mass scenes rather than individual characterisation, as in the scenes of the requisitioning of food from the kulaks in *The Civil War*: when anonymous peasants, 'The Poor', drive out the kulaks in a highly choreographed and emblematic sequence, using individual voices, the singing of 'The Internationale', and a few stark props, like the haycart, the fixed bayonets of the soldiers and the red flag.[68]

In a similar mould was *The Festival of the Machine* by Vladimir Mass and Leonid Subbotin, performed at the first All-Union Agricultural Congress in Moscow in September 1923. The simple structure divides the play into three sections, the first consisting of a parade of old farm implements which are compared unfavourably with modern tractors, the second an argument between a young and an old peasant in front of their respective 'izbas', and the final section a speech by a Communist agronomist about agriculture's contribution to the strengthening of the economy. What is interesting about the play is that it is not written for a conventional stage, but is intended to take place all over the village square. Reality mixes with illusion almost inextricably – the agronomist's speech, for instance, which forms the third part of the play, is not written but is 'about topical matters connected with strengthening the economy'.[69]

MastKomDram also spawned a number of dramatic parodies. Dmitry Smolin's *Comrade Khlestakov* was fairly predictable, but Alexander Roslavlev's *Almost Gogol's 'Marriage'* was brought into the repertoire on Meyerhold's specific recommendation. Roslavlev was a journalist in Novorossiisk who had met Meyerhold there in 1919 and was so inspired by this and by the work of the local TEREVSAT that he gave up his profession to found his own little theatre. He opened with *Almost Gogol's 'Marriage'*, which uses devices such as having Pavel Milyukov, Foreign Minister in Prince Lvov's Provisional Government as Gogol's matchmaker. Unfortunately, Roslavlev contracted typhus and died in November 1920.

The parodies of which these are examples actually derive from the 'culturalist tendencies' embodied in the pre-revolutionary cabaret theatres. Mikhail Razumny's own cabaret theatre, for instance, had staged *'Woe From Wit' Through the Prism of Today* in the autumn of 1918. The Distorting Mirror and the Bat had closed in 1918 and 1920 respectively, but the cabaret of 'miniature dramas' had not died, despite persecution by the new regime. One cabaret which became particularly well-known, the Bi-Ba-Bo, had been opened in Petrograd shortly before the February revolution of 1917 by Konstantin Mardzhanov, Nikolai Agnivtsev and others. To the fashionable late-night audience who dined at little tables during the show, Agnivtsev proved an amusing writer, and Mardzhanov welded together a forceful ensemble. But conditions in Petrograd during the Civil War proved too much for the company, and they moved to Kiev in 1918, where several performers from Baliev's Bat Theatre joined them. In Januaray 1919, Mardzhanov's increasing politicisation led the group to change their name to Crooked Jimmy, and to adopt a more committed political stance.

In the spring of 1922 the Crooked Jimmy moved to Moscow, opening in the Summer Theatre on 13 May and moving to the Bat's old premises in October that year. They performed 'Jimmy-ades' on the lines of buffoonades, such as *Marriage*, described as 'almost in the style of Gogol',[70] this version being by Alexei Alexeev. They also revived several pre-revolutionary Distorting Mirror works, especially a season of Evreinov's miniature dramas, which were well-received. This may have encouraged Alexander Kugel in December 1922 to re-open the Distorting Mirror itself. Nevertheless, despite performing plays by Vasily Kamensky, Nikolai Erdman and Lev Nikulin in 1923, these cabarets became progressively milder in their 'satire', finally providing little more than relaxation for those who could pay under NEP.

Bi-Ba-Bo and Crooked Jimmy's director was the Georgian, Konstantin Mardzhanov, whose production of Lope da Vega's *Fuente Ovejuna* at the Solovtsov Theatre, Kiev, on 1 May 1919, would surely have won wider acclaim if it had first been seen in Moscow. How much Mardzhanov owed to Nikolai Evreinov's production of the same play at the Ancient Theatre eight years, but seemingly a whole historical epoch earlier, is debatable. It was, one critic has written, a 'popular-heroic' performance, displaying 'revolutionary incandescence which united auditorium and stage'.[71] The production's first impact came from the dazzling primary colours of Isaak Rabinovich's design, a green hill, an orange field, a blue sky. On it Mardzhanov, with his choreographer Mikhail Mordkin, staged crowd scenes of great dynamism and power, spilling off the stage into the auditorium in such a way as to maximise the emotional force of the work. The energy generated by the production is well-described by the leading actress, Vera Yureneva, who said Mardzhanov had encouraged the 'deep notes in my voice, a golden tan on my face and bare feet, health, energetic gestures and strong, honest, clear feelings'.[72] But when the action entered the castle, it was revealed as a gloomy interior behind drawn curtains – itself a kind of comment on the illusionist theatre Mardzhanov so deplored. In a final adaptation, Mardzhanov cut the ending to leave the people no longer dependent on the benevolence of the king, but victoriously shouting: 'There are no more tyrants!' The reception was electric: 'Kiev saw *Fuente Ovejuna*, and a wind swept through the hall of the old Solovtsy Theatre. We stood there for a long time, clapping and refusing to go home.'[73]

In February 1920, Mardzhanov moved to Petrograd, where he began work with a group of friends and supporters in two rooms of his own flat to create a Theatre of Musical Drama. The group worked on pantomime, dance and singing, acrobatics and rhythmic gymnastics, in an attempt to create a form which did not rely on an easy naturalism, but which through its performance rhythms would communicate a more stringent meaning than was usual in comic opera. 'Gesture, dialogue, movement, song and feeling – all must be saturated with the specific rhythm of the production,' he declared.[74] In May, Maria Andreeva inspected the work, acknowledged its importance, and handed the Palace Theatre to Mardzhanov, where he opened with a production of Donizetti's *Don Pasquale* in June 1920. He developed a repertoire which included Molière's *Le Bourgeois Gentilhomme*, Shakespeare's *The Merry Wives of Windsor* and a reworked version of Kamensky's *Stenka Razin*. In the basement of the theatre, he also opened a cabaret, the Limping Joe: 'Its stage area was tiny, uncomfortable and poorly furnished, with a low ceiling. The auditorium was sparsely furnished; instead of dining tables there were folding supports attached to the backs of the seats of the preceding row.'[75] The repertoire included parodies of *The Government Inspector* and *Woe from Wit*, satirical sketches such as *The Telephone Number of Your Beloved*, 'a powerful drama in one minute', Vasily Kamensky's *River Kamushka*, and material by satirical sketch writers like Argo and Agnivtsev. Mardzhanov himself also contributed, most notably the song of Limping Joe, 'lame, but eternally cheerful'.

Mardzhanov's work was undoubtedly significant for the development of revolutionary theatre, and his influence remained: it was because of his production that *Fuente Ovejuna*, for instance, remained in the progressive theatre's repertoire for decades. Unfortunately, with NEP, Mardzhanov's subsidy was ended, his theatres were forced to close and, after failing to find a base in Moscow, he moved to his native Georgia where for a further decade his work set a reputation for his Rustavelli Company which has remained.

The nationalised circuses did not lose their subsidies under NEP, and continued to play a part in the development of revolutionary theatre, as for instance in Vitaly Lazarenko's production of Mayakovsky's circus pantomime, *The Championship of the Universal Class Struggle* for the Second State Circus, Moscow, in November 1920. In 1919 Lazarenko had performed a turn based on Mayakovsky's political epigrams, *The Soviet Alphabet*, and in 1921 he was to appear as a devil in *Mystery Bouffe*. *The Championship of the Universal Class Struggle* was a clown show based on a wrestling match, with Uncle Vanya, played by Lazarenko, as the referee. He introduced the contestants in a style somewhere between that of the fairground barker and the circus ringmaster:

> Hear ye,
> Hear ye.
> Come in, people.
> Listen, people.
> Look, everyone who's eager:
> Lazarenko, in the role of Uncle Vanya,
> can pin any wrestler –
> of course, only if he's lying on a sofa.
> How many have been defeated by me!
> Almost unbelievable:
> Sidarenko, Karpenko, Enko.
> 4, 5,
> 16,
> 28,
> fortyteen.
> Who, who hasn't been beaten yet?
> But
> I'm not a wrestler
> today.
> I'm a referee.
> Now there'll be a championship:
> not an ordinary fight –
> but a class struggle.
> Now before your very eyes –
> the noblest nobles –
> athletes will strut by
> in well-matched pairs:
> they're here to eliminate each other.
> *Parade Allez!*[76]

The contestants who parade are: Lloyd George, champion of the Entente; Wilson, the American champ; Millerand of France; Pilsudsky of Poland; Siderov, a Russian speculator; Vrangel, the White General;

and Aprelev, the 'almost champion', a Menshevik, 'family unknown, living with fake credentials'. Uncle Vanya admits he did not wish to accept this last contestant, as he would only try to calm down the other combatants, and get them all to make concessions to each other. But Aprelev announces that:

> even though I'm a Menshevik
> I really want to fight now,

so Uncle Vanya permits him to enter the arena.

Once each champion has been introduced to the crowd, as professional fighters are – and presumably roundly hissed – the prizes are thrown into the ring: a crown, a huge gold coin and a bag with the inscription: 'Profit from an imperialist war'. Then an extraordinary and ridiculous free-for-all develops, which Uncle Vanya attempts vainly to control. Millerand appeals to him to stop Lloyd George biting, and Pilsudski complains similarly about Vrangel – 'he's biting my thighs'. At the same time, everybody complains about the Menshevik compromiser, who is contriving to get in everyone else's way. Finally, the referee blows the whistle. Everybody stops. A new fighter – Revolution – enters. Suddenly all the wrestlers on the stage look sheepish and begin to slink away, but Revolution challenges them. Eventually, Lloyd George faces him, but soon Lloyd George is in a 'head-circle tie-up', at which point the referee blows the whistle and announces a break. The Entente champion is wheeled out in a wheelbarrow as the referee turns to the audience and appeals to those who want the Revolution to defeat the Entente to join the Red Army. He adds that:

> I am
> ready
> to go there today.
> To get there faster
> I'll even take a carriage.

He then takes a carriage wheel – a circus hoop – and performs various tricks with it before he exits. Apart from the perhaps unintended hint of irony here, this is a much more satisfying ending to the one of similar import in, for example, *The Mexican*.

This is popular drama at its best, blowing raspberries at its so-called betters, fiercely partisan and shockingly disrespectful, and its success points to the heart of MastKomDram's failure as an institution. Having been established by a government department, and staffed by ideologically sound leaders, it was unable to acquire the irreverence necessary to popular drama. On 5 April 1921, Vladimir Blyum, the critic, asserted that not only had MastKomDram failed to produce an ugly duckling which might grow into a swan, it had failed even to hatch a chicken. A month later, on 6 May 1921, Alexander Serafimovich complained in *Pravda* that it had achieved nothing. For him, a writer, actors could never solve problems of play creation, and the work should be handed back to playwrights. To accomplish this, Serafimovich proposed the usual Communist remedy – reorganise the institution, in this case MastKomDram itself. At the board meeting that followed, there was an acrimonious debate, in which Lunacharsky sided with Serafimovich against Vsevolod Meyerhold, who put his trust in the actors, regarding playwrights in general, and especially the workshop playwrights, as 'purveyors of raw material'.[77] For the time being, no action was taken as a result of the meeting, but a perhaps unwarranted animosity between Meyerhold and MastKomDram grew and rumbled on through the summer.

'A SPECTACLE MOST EXTRAORDINARY'

Freed of the shackles of TEO from February 1921, Meyerhold was able to concentrate on his production of the second version of Mayakovsky's *Mystery Bouffe*, 'the revolution's trumpet of Jericho' as Bukharin called it. The rewritten Prologue presented virtually a manifesto for revolutionary theatre:

> For other theatrical companies
> the spectacle doesn't matter:
> for them
> the stage
> is a keyhole without a key.
> 'Just sit there quietly,' they say to you,
> 'either straight or sidewise,
> and look at a slice of other folks' lives.'
> You look – and what do you see?
> Uncle Vanya
> and Aunty Manya,
> parked on a sofa as they chatter.
> But we don't care
> about uncles or aunts:
> you can find them at home – or anywhere!
> We, too, will show you life that's real –
> very!
> But life transformed by the theatre into a spectacle most
> extraordinary![78]

This 'most extraordinary' spectacle was, according to Ilinsky, 'a major cultural event, and the whole of Moscow's attention was chained absolutely to it,'[79] when it opened at the Zon Theatre on May Day 1921.

It had been brought up to date by including references to the Civil War, it introduced a Red Army soldier, as well as the figures of Lloyd George and Clemenceau, and greatly expanded the part of the Menshevik-Compromiser, presumably after the success of this character in the circus pantomime, *The Championship of the Universal Class Struggle*. The part now provided Igor Ilinsky with his first great success. The whole of Act 5 in the Land of Chaos was also new, as was the climax of electrification.

Translated into German, the play was performed for delegates to the Third Congress of the Comintern in June 1921, and it was taken up by other groups throughout the country and given successful productions. It is important to establish the play's success, since some later historians have tried to minimize it. Alexander Fevralsky, who was in the audience on the first night, has recorded how at the end of the first act, the applause indicated unusual enthusiasm, and at the end of the play this enthusiasm was translated into stamping, cheering and clapping. Meyerhold and Mayakovsky, with linked arms, took repeated calls with the actors, and even the theatre technicians were called onto the stage. In 1966, Fevralsky wrote: 'After forty-five years it is difficult to recall another performance which was greeted with such enthusiasm from the audience.'[80] Moreover, Fevralsky records that he returned to the production several times during its run, and the response was always similarly ecstatic. Valentin Pluchek's revival at the Theatre of Satire in 1957 demonstrated that it was not simply 'a "hit" that for a time is all the rage'.[81] It made a remarkable impact, and other productions, in USSR and abroad, have demonstrated the play's tremendous drive and theatrical energy.

Mystery Bouffe is, according to Mayakovsky, 'the high road of the revolution', and as such it is an allegory in the medieval sense of the word and in a Bunyonesque manner: it tells a story of salvation through revolution. The Man of the Future shows the Unclean the way, as Evangelist shows Christian the way in *The Pilgrim's Progress*, and in *Mystery Bouffe* it takes them four acts to realize in action what his words have meant. That meaning, the central meaning of the play, concerns the abolition of social alienation, which is the real victory of the revolution: at the end of the play, the food belongs to those who need it, the tools and the machines to those who use them. All the characters recognise the Promised Land of the last scene as 'home', for every worker is 'at home' in the Promised Land of revolutionary socialism, and, conversely, the Promised Land is Manchester, Marseilles, Moscow, wherever is 'home', viewed in the new way; that is, without alienation. The masses thus take possession of their heritage.

Mystery Bouffe presents this popular expropriation through popular forms. Its journey is comparable with *The Pilgrim's Progress*, which has always attracted 'popular' rather than literary critical acceptance. Its spontaneity is akin to that of the *commedia dell'arte*, popular theatre much tried and admired by Meyerhold and his followers. Russian audiences would be likely to recognise some of the other echoes from popular culture with which the play is peppered. The Prologue, for instance, is delivered in the style of the Barker on the walk-up of a fairground booth, who tells of the delights he is offering, thus revealing the drama before it has begun. The Lady with the Hatboxes who embraces 'Beelzebubchik' at the end of the scene in hell recalls the old lady in the folk tale, *The Smith and the Demon*, who pays the devil to rejuvenate her: the devil 'took a pair of tongs, caught hold of the lady by the feet, flung her into the furnace, and burnt her up; nothing was left of her but her bare bones'. However, the Lady with the Hatboxes, unlike the old lady in the story, does not 'emerge . . . alive, and young, and beautiful!'[82]

The Prologue promises us 'life transformed by the theatre into a spectacle most extraordinary!' Spectacle is at the heart of popular theatre, and of Mayakovsky's dramaturgical practice. *Mystery Bouffe* has all the gaudy glitter of a popular carnival, and spectacular moments like the clown Lazarenko's startling slide down a rope onto the stage where he performed a series of acrobatic feats not only demonstrates this use of popular fairground or circus antics, it also 'introduces into the performance a feeling of *joie de vivre*'.[83] Meyerhold, in one of his *Theatrical Papers*, wrote at this time of 'the power of laughter in the theatre. It is the water on the wheel of an entertaining action.'[84]

At the base of Meyerhold's production, therefore, lay spectacle and laughter, which were presented with none of the trappings of traditional theatre. The stage at the Zon Theatre was not curtained, in contrast to the first version's production, and the backstage area was not masked. The audience could come and go as they pleased, and could interrupt the proceedings with shouted interjections. The auditorium was stripped of decoration, and banners like fairground gag cards were hung instead. The fronts of the boxes were removed so that a walkway ran round the auditorium, which was connected to the stage area by a wide ramp. In the centre of the acting area was a large half-sphere, representing the world, with a piece like a slice of cake taken from it. It was surrounded by platforms, like ships' decks, steep flights of steps and wires like rigging, but the play spilled out beyond the stage – the Things, Edibles and Machines, for instance, appeared in the frontless boxes at the sides of the auditorium. All this was in line with Mayakovsky's attempt to 'return the spectacular to the theatre', but he also provided Meyerhold with a gallery of grotesques to capitalise on – the pompous German businessman whose pleasure is in 'Scheidermann-izing' in pavement cafés (Scheidermann being the procrastinating

German Chancellor), the Menshevik-Compromiser who is thwacked over the head more often than a *Punch and Judy* puppet, the dithering Methuselah marking himself out by the length of his beard, the starving devils in hell, the monstrous Queen of Chaos, Lloyd George and Clemenceau like a vaudeville double act, and many more. The whole show – there is a point where 'play' becomes less than adequate as a descriptive term – is Aristophanic in its extravagance, its use of named contemporaries, and its gross caricature.

This is complemented by Mayakovsky's use of the mystery play framework. The flood as an image is taken directly from the biblical legend of Noah, a story which the makers of mystery plays found essentially dramatic. But *Mystery Bouffe* is a mystery play in reverse, and Mayakovsky's blasphemy is as all-pervading as the conventional mystery play's piety. One might compare it with Blok's inordinately blasphemous, but poetically stunning, climax to his poem, *The Twelve*, which depicts Christ at the head of the Red Guards. In *Mystery Bouffe*, in a dramatic moment calculated to demystify religion and metaphysics, Mayakovsky uses the common religious image of walking on water to show the post-revolutionary common man, the man of the future, performing the miracle. A few moments later, Mayakovsky turns the Sermon on the Mount upside down in a spirited glorification of the revolutionary fighter. Similarly, the proletariat is seen as the new Prometheus, stealing the fire of the gods, Jehovah's thunderbolts, which are, however, useless in the new materialist and socialist society. The Unclean's thunder is the roar of the railway engine and the giant steamship.

It is partly through the use of timeless images such as these that Mayakovsky is able to convey the spirit of the moment – the elation of victory, the contempt for and ridicule of the defeated Clean. *Mystery Bouffe* catches all the vivid vigour of what it felt like 'in that dawn'. This powerful contemporaneity derives at least in part from the timelessness of certain dramatic images, and is in turn largely responsible for the strong feeling of the movement of history in the play. We are made to feel the present in relation to the past and in relation to the future. This effect is partly cumulative, through the interaction of groups and types, rather than individuals; it is partly gained by the sharp, unmotivated breaks in the action, interruptions, as when the Unclean get drunk, or the new tsar, the Negus of Abyssinia, is thrown overboard. This is the basic method of construction in Mayakovsky's dramaturgical armoury: he picks the moment of maximum dynamic meaning and thrusts it forward with great intensity, relating it thematically to the preceding and succeeding moments, but tearing it out of the natural flow of time. Thus history is shown in the making, and a sense of how events affect, and are affected by, the common people is achieved. Mayakovsky thereby succeeds in suggesting that the people are no longer merely the passive victims of irrational, uncontrollable forces, but that they have the potential to 'move mountains' – the mountains of the Land of Chaos, which seem initially to make their route impassable, but which they do literally move out of their way.

Huntly Carter pointed out that *Mystery Bouffe* was entirely different in conception and substance from anything written for the conventional stage, and this is both its strength and its Achilles heel, for it was this strangeness which left it open to attack. As early as December 1920, Alexander Serafimovich, whom Meyerhold had imagined would support his 'October in the Theatre', used his position as head of the literary department of Lunacharsky's Commissariat to complain to the Central Committee of the Party that the play was 'anarchistic' and 'incomprehensible'. Mayakovsky responded by giving a number of well-received public readings of the play, and on 30 January a public meeting with the title 'Should *Mystery Bouffe* Be Staged?' was held, with representatives of the party, the government and other organisations invited. The atmosphere was 'incandescent', but Mayakovsky's champions passed a resolution which described the play as 'talented and truly proletarian',[85] and demanded it be staged throughout the country. Boris Malkin, one of the Party representatives, even undertook to persuade Lenin to support it, though without success, and his later efforts to get the Party leader to see the play were similarly fruitless. When the production went ahead, Zagorsky, Meyerhold's literary manager, distributed questionnaires to spectators and of 187 responses analysed, nearly seventy percent supported the play. One worker wrote: 'Now I understand what October in the Theatre means, and I see that such an October was possible, and I believe in its great future.' A young peasant added: 'The bourgeoisie didn't like it, they grumbled and even walked out, insulted, but the young girls and the lads were pleased.' A few objected to the play's attacks on Tolstoy or on religion, and one peasant wrote: 'This kind of propaganda gets on the nerves of us from the country.' But most of the responses were extremely positive.[86]

At this point, perhaps because of the success of *Mystery Bouffe*, perhaps with the connivance of the leaders of MastKomDram with whom Meyerhold had quarrelled, Glavpolitprosvet appointed a commission to enquire into the affairs of the former RSFSR Theatre No 1 (now MONO Theatre No 1). The commission concluded early in June that the theatre was extravagant and wasteful, and that it had no plans to tour workers' clubs. Vladimir Blyum in *The Theatre Herald* on 15 June insidiously reminded its readers of how Mayakovsky wore a decadent yellow shirt before the revolution! K. I. Lander of Glavpolitprosvet, noting the excessive spending, ordered the theatre to be closed, and a fellow bureaucrat, N. N. Ovsyannikov broadened the attack to include the levels of spending on theatre by both the Commissariat of Enlightenment itself and the Moscow City department (MONO), describing their budgets as 'astronomical' and homing in on the Zon Theatre for putting on such an extremely untalented and inflated play.[87] Finally, the head of the art department of Glavpolitprosvet, M. Bek, in *Communist Labour* on 5 July, called 'October in the Theatre' a 'Theatrical Sukharevka', a sarcastic reference to the cheap 'free' market, Sukharevka.

Meyerhold's theatre manager, Semyon Brailovsky, responded with a detailed, point-by-point rebuttal of the charges about overspending in *The Theatre Herald* on 11 July, and the prominent party activist, Lev Sosnovsky, who had been on board one of TEREVSAT's wagons on May Day the previous year, expressed surprise that because they were not making profits, 'theatres which are seeking a creative revolutionary path, like Meyerhold's and Terevsat, are being prepared for closure . . . I am not a great admirer of Meyerhold, but it sounds odd to me.' He added provocatively that perhaps the Zon should be handed over to a cabaret – that would make a profit.[88] After Sosnovsky's remarks, Lunacharsky felt able to defend Meyerhold and Mayakovsky again. He accused Lander of 'deliberate sabotage' by attempting to ban 'this most communistic work of communist art'. Lander continued to disagree, saying Mayakovsky's communism was distorted by Futurism, and what was more, doubts about his sincerity had been expressed! But with Lunacharsky resuming responsibility for RSFSR Theatre No 1, Meyerhold and his colleagues were able to continue through the summer at the Zon.

Two projects were in process at the time, though neither was able to come to proper fruition. The first of these was an adaptation of *Rienzi* by Valery Bebutov, in which he created a collage text from Wagner's opera and Bulwer Lytton's original novel, and staged it with a good deal of pantomime, aiming for dramatic, operatic and pantomimic elements to collide. The new text was put into verse by Vadim Shershenevich and an acting style developed from the monumentalism of *The Dawns*. The set too was in a similar abstract style ('the new baroque') by Shershenevich's friend, the artist Georgi Yakulov. But the piece was only seen in three public dress rehearsals, without Yakulov's set, in the Great Hall of the Moscow Conservatory after the season proper had ended.

The other project was a mass spectacle, *The Struggle and Victory of the Soviets*, planned by Meyerhold, with the writer Ivan Aksenov and the artist Lyubov Popova, for presentation at the Congress of the Comintern (where *Mystery Bouffe* was also presented). This drama consisted of twelve episodes, depicting the storming of the fortress, Capital, by the tanks and flame-throwers of Labour, an illuminated silhouette of a communist factory and a parade of troops, gymnasts, haymakers and workers. The finale was to reveal the 'city of the future' lit by search-lights and fireworks, and saluted by aeroplanes and a massed choir.[89]

Popova designed an extraordinary set with cranes, scaffolding and dirigibles on cords, while the production was to involve 200 riders from the cavalry school, 2300 foot soldiers, sixteen artillery pieces, five aeroplanes with Zeiss searchlights, ten searchlights mounted on vehicles on the ground, several armoured cars, tanks, motorcycles, ambulances, people doing their general military training, physical education students, military bands and choirs. The intended participation of those undergoing military training is particularly ironic, in view of Meyerhold's earlier attempts to involve them, and Lunacharsky's vision of their participation in 'our festive occasions'.[90] It is also ironic that Lunacharsky had asked Evreinov – but not Meyerhold – to stage a mass spectacle in Moscow on May Day 1921, which Evreinov had refused. Now the government decreed that money should not be spent on such extravagant pageants, and this work, which promised to be an important development for revolutionary theatre, was left uncompleted.

The RSFSR Theatre No 1, despite the backing of the Commissariat of Enlightenment, was also doomed. Meyerhold and Bebutov managed to cobble together a production of Ibsen's *The League of Youth*, which opened on 7 August, the day on which Alexander Blok, the great lyric poet who had worked with Meyerhold in their youth, and who had accepted the revolution, died. Two weeks later, Nikolai Gumilev, poet and playwright, was shot as a counterrevolutionary. That August, too, *The Theatre Herald*, the former mouthpiece of TEO, and Meyerhold's main organ at the height of his crusade for 'October in the Theatre', ceased publication. Subsidies to theatres were drastically cut, or stopped altogether, and only the academic theatres received adequate funding from the government. Other troupes were encouraged to become 'co-operatives'.

On 2 September 1921, while Meyerhold was on holiday, the order came from Valerian Pletnev at Glavpolitprosvet for his theatre to close, and for it to hand over its stage, its actors and all its property to MastKomDram. There may have been some intention for the two groups to negotiate, but Meyerhold knew that the order for closure resulted from the machinations of MastKomDram's leaders, who were still smarting from the ferocity of his condemnation of their work in May. Now his objections led only to a peremptory repetition of the order: there were to be no more performances, and Brailovsky was to hand over all the papers of the theatre forthwith. The last performance of *The League of Youth* took place on 6 September, and Meyerhold was left without a theatre and without a company. The dream of 'October in the Theatre' was over.

4

REVOLUTIONARY THEATRES
1921–1924

THE MASTER

After the defeat of 'October in the Theatre', Vsevolod Meyerhold never
thought of abandoning the struggle for a new revolutionary theatre, but
he changed the direction of his campaign. Instead of trying to organise
all the nation's theatres, he established his own exemplary model, with
three tiers – a public stage, an experimental workshop and a training
school – and able, through dialectical interaction, to develop contemporary significance in its dramaturgy, acting practice and stage
designs. The discoveries in the workshop would affect the teaching
in the school as well as what was exposed on the stage, and so on.
Through this would evolve the new democratic, collaborative and on-
going relationship with the audience, which was the explosive point
of revolutionary theatre.

After the dissolution of the RSFSR Theatre No 1, Meyerhold was
appointed head of the recently-established GVYRM (the State Higher
Directors' Workshop) situated in a former school on Novinsky Boulevard. From now he was known, not inappropriately, as The Master. He
was accommodated on the top floor, while the energetic young students
below, untainted by contact with the pre-revolutionary theatres, sought
new ways to deal adequately with the new revolutionary world. By the
time of GVYRM's official opening in October 1921, the students had
been joined in Novinsky Boulevard by the Meyerholdites of the RSFSR
Theatre No 1, who, jettisoning those members who were less than
wholehearted in their support for the Master's ideas, had formed the
Free Workshop of V. E. Meyerhold, which ran alongside the official
school throughout that autumn.

GVYRM's nominal head was Ivan Aksenov, Futurist poet, Shake-
spearean scholar and literary theoretician and apart from Meyerhold,
the teaching staff included his partner, Valery Bebutov. The course
'began with the student as listener, and soon inevitably a participant, in
the lectures, discussions and disputes, which were unusually interesting

because Meyerhold invited prominent public figures, literary people, artists and musicians to speak.' The ferment of ideas, experiments, arguments and practical research which characterised the new school was unique, and its results profound: 'everyone learned – students and teachers alike. It was a laboratory for working through the foundations of a new aesthetic.'[1]

Perhaps it was fortunate that the group had no theatre for the lack concentrated their minds on the working out of ideas without the need for public performance. The Zon Theatre was now in the hands of MastKomDram, which had expanded to create its own theatre company, the State Theatre of Communist Drama (GosTeKomDram), with fifty-eight active members, Bassalygo and Ilin still in charge, and Valerian Pletnev on the board. Their first production, which opened on 18 December 1920, was *Comrade Khlestakov*, adapted from Gogol's satirical masterpiece by Dmitri Smolin, and given Futuristic designs by Alexandra Ekster. But nothing could save the leaden script, and the play was a complete failure. So, despite the fact that Smolin's next adaptation, *The Communist In Spite of Himself* after Molière, was written, and even though Lunacharsky himself backed the group, GosTeKomDram collapsed, giving its last performance on 4 January 1922. A few days later Mast-KomDram itself also ceased to exist.

Thus, the Zon Theatre was again empty, and a number of groups tried to lay claim to it. The most serious contenders were Konstantin Mardzhanov, looking to establish himself in Moscow after he had lost his subsidy in Petrograd, Konstantin Nezlobin, whose theatre beside the Bolshoi had been awarded to the new State Children's Theatre, and Meyerhold. The Nezlobin company, who had spent two months in the former Bat cabaret, now concluded a tactical alliance to share the theatre with Meyerhold, thereby putting paid to Mardzhanov's hopes, and the Actors Theatre was formed, with Meyerhold at its head. He promised to merge the two groups, but performances were at first given exclusively by the Nezlobin actors, who remounted their old, rather dull productions – Tolstoy's *The Fruits of Enlightenment*, *The Two Little Orphans* by Adolphe D'Ennery and Eugène Cormon, Eugène Brieux's *The Red Robe*, and others. Meyerhold appeared unconcerned. Not only was he beginning married life with one of his young students, Zinaida Raikh, at this time, he was also seeing the emergence of an appropriate structure for his work: the school (which changed now from GVYRM to GVYTM – the State Higher *Theatre* Workshop), the experimental Free Workshop and the public Actors Theatre.

The revolution's original concept of 'collective creativity' resonated here. Consciously or not, Meyerhold's practice followed Bogdanov's line of 'comradely organisation' to make theatre a weapon in the struggle to transform society.[2] The lectures on philosophy, politics and aesthetics in GVYTM were strictly relevant: Garin remembered that 'the personal question of one's professional technique became in Meyerhold's school a question of one's world outlook, one's vision.'[3] Meyerhold wanted the spectator:

> in our theatre, to acquire that dynamic which he does not acquire in other theatres, that strong-willed effort towards construction which he needs. Our task comes down to bringing onto the stage good, healthy laughter, and if something touches the spectator, he should not pull out his handkerchief, but shake his fist. We live in a militant epoch when we don't have to tolerate our powder getting wet from tears.[4]

Meyerhold turned to Pushkin for justification of his stance, and for a way forward. 'Drama originated in a public square and constituted a popular entertainment,' Pushkin had asserted. But it 'had betaken itself to stately halls at the behest of a cultured, elite society' and there it had 'lowered its voice [and] doffed the mask of exaggeration ... shed its universally comprehensible language and assumed a fashionable, select and refined idiom'. Meyerhold's work was concerned to return the drama to 'the common people' in the 'public squares'.[5]

The search for intellectually acceptable popular forms resulted most noticably in non-psychological character creation ('the mask of exaggeration'), which provoked 'good, healthy laughter' even if it was hardly 'fashionable' or 'refined'. In an attempt to help the actor towards such character realization, Aksenov, Bebutov and Meyerhold published *The Set Roles of the Actor's Art*,[6] which included a list of 'types' such as Hero, Lover, Mischief maker, Clown, Villain, Outsider and Braggart. It should be emphasised that this concept of 'type' was the opposite of *stereotype*; it might be seen in musical terms as the theme upon which the actor is invited to play variations.

To achieve this, the actor must place greater than usual emphasis in his playing on what Stanislavsky called 'the super-objective',[7] and allow that rather than the more detailed intentions or the inner stimuli of the emotion memory to dominate his work. Other non-naturalistic acting styles, Expressionist acting, for example, require a similar approach, but the Expressionist actor's super-objective is related to the proximity of chaos, or the terrifying closeness of the disintegration of his 'soul', as in Professor Raat's humiliating but compulsive pursuit of Lola in *The Blue Angel* or Karl Thomas's increasingly desperate search for understanding in Toller's *Hoppla! Such is Life!* In Meyerhold's system, by contrast, the super-objective is geared towards integration, it is celebratory and looks to life, the future, the building of a new revolutionary society. Consequently, where Expressionist drama is sombre or alarming, revolutionary drama, even when it treats the destructive power of sexual jealousy (as in *The Magnanimous Cuckold*), has a buoyant and energising drive.

This method of acting derives ultimately from Diderot's thesis that good acting is rooted in reason, not in feeling:

> Look you, before he cries *'Zaire vous pleurez,'* or *'Vous y ferez ma fille'*, the actor has listened over and over again to his own voice. At the very moment when he touches your heart he is listening to his own voice; his talent depends not, as you think, upon feeling, but upon rendering so exactly the outward signs of feeling, that you fall into the trap. He has rehearsed to himself every note of his passion. He has learned before his mirror every particle of his despair. He knows exactly when he must produce his handkerchief and shed tears; and you will see him weep at the word, at the syllable, he has chosen, and not a second sooner or later.[8]

Though movement, not speech, formed the foundation on which his system was erected, the self-awareness and the calculation highlighted by Diderot are both crucial to Meyerhold's approach. Constant-Benois Coquelin also noticed the apparent duplicity of the actor, and it was from his description that Meyerhold devised his algebraic formulation:

$$N = A_1 + A_2$$

where N is the actor, A_1 is the controlling brain, and A_2 is that which executes A_1's idea. The intellectual training in GVYTM was dedicated to training A_1, while the practical work was to train A_2. The practical training constituted Meyerhold's famous 'biomechanics', which still resonates through the best acting schools across the world. Through it, the actor learns physical expressiveness and control, and also to be able to sense easily his body moving in space and through time. Its exercises and practices are gathered from any source which seems appropriate, especially from dance, acrobatics and sport, and the emphases are first on self-consciousness (in the best sense):

> Co-ordination, attention and persistence are the elements of our system. Concentrated attention to the physical plan is required above all. The free condition of the spontaneous human being (as in Duncanism) is not tolerable. With us everything is organised, each step and each small movement is calculated. The eye is judging things all the time in the work.

and second, on efficiency of movement, so that action is quickly and clearly communicative. 'The first principle of biomechanics is: the body is a machine, and the person working it is a machine-operator'.[9] These emphases, Meyerhold believed, would help to reveal the super-objective.

The first step towards mastery of this movement-based system is the 'silhouette', the still picture. Meyerhold was able to demonstrate how if an actor takes up a sad posture, he begins to feel sad, and the emotion is shared by an audience. Thus, the pause, or the pose, are of especial importance in the movement-based biomechanics. From the stillness of the silhouette, a gesture of the hand, a movement of the head, even a flicker of the eyes becomes more potent, especially if there is a slight 'recoil' before the movement to accent or underscore it. There is a natural progression from this to the more gymnastic movement work associated with biomechanics, as there is in the development into self-contained dramatic 'études'. 'The Stab with the Dagger', for instance, is one of several recorded on film.[10] It may be described in sections, which run smoothly into one another in performance:

1 Two actors, A and B, face one another in the stance of a boxer and execute a Dactyl – slowly they raise their hands from their sides to head height, then clap rapidly twice while jumping on the spot at each clap, then relax back to the original position. The Dactyl focuses concentration and creates a receptive frame of mind.

2 Slight pause.

3 Actor A watches intently while Actor B, looking into A's eyes, feels for the imaginary sheathed dagger in his belt on his left hip with his left hand. B backs slowly away with bent knees and bent back for about three paces, left hand still on the sheath. He stops, flourishes his right hand, brings it to the 'dagger' handle, draws the dagger rapidly. A straightens quickly, then again follows B intently. B slowly backs off another three paces, crouching.

4 B and A straighten quickly, face one another.

5 B and A move slowly together, knees bent, arms bent, looking at one another.

6 When close, they slowly bend their knees and backs till they are crouching, looking down, heads side by side, arms bent, left feet forward, B's left knee between A's knees, A's left knee between B's knees, but not touching.

7 They jerk up to standing. B's weight is on forward left foot, chin thrust forward, right arm with imaginary dagger raised high. A's weight is on both feet, she arches backwards, hands clasped over stomach or falling vertically downwards (see illustration 11).

8 B holds A with his left hand behind A's back, A leaning backwards over it. B stabs A in the chest with a short, quick jab. Short pause.

9 B withdraws the dagger, turns away, and with bent legs, moves 3 or 4 paces quite rapidly away. A remains arched.

10 B turns sharply back to look at A. A straightens quickly, then slowly sinks forward to the floor, putting her hands down, dropping slowly to all fours, faces the ground, arms bent. B standing, watches.

11 Biomechanics. 'The Stab with the Dagger'.

11 After a short pause, A slowly rises, stands, arches her back as she moves almost to the crab position, arms dangling, then sinks to the floor on her back.

12 With a wide flourish, B replaces the 'dagger' in the 'sheath', and walks purposefully to behind A's head.

13 B indicates to A. A straightens to lie rigid at attention on her back, her head at B's feet.

14 B puts his hands under A's neck. A remains completely rigid while B lifts her smartly up.

15 B turns his back to A's back, A relaxes backwards carefully onto B's back. B walks a few paces, bent nearly double with A lying on her back on his back. Then B runs smoothly away with loping strides.

The whole procedure outlined above lasts about one minute ten seconds. Such an *étude* can be developed into a complete scene, and it can also be used for teaching techniques of 'pointing', as when A straightens quickly in (3) above.[11]

Through that intense, cold winter of 1921–22, Meyerhold's group of actors and students worked on these and similar techniques, locating much of their work in an unlikely text by a minor Belgium playwright, Fernand Crommelynck, *The Magnanimous Cuckold*, translated by Aksenov. In April 1922, Meyerhold seems to have judged it time to show this work to the world, or perhaps he was simply worried that the Nezlobin actors were becoming totally identified with his Actors Theatre. At any rate, he organised his young followers into brigades early one morning, and seized the Zon – a typical piece of theatrical-military bravado, like the founding of the RSFSR Theatre No 2 in a night raid. Stage flats were carted out, backdrops rolled up and dragged into the courtyard, the dust stood in columns, but by the end of the adventure, the trappings of bourgeois theatre were gone, and the building's grimy, whitewashed brick walls were starkly visible.

First Meyerhold flung together a production of *Nora*, adapted from Ibsen's *A Doll's House*, with the Nezlobin actors. 'Nothing will ever erase from my memory the impression left on me by those three days of rehearsals,' recalled Sergei Eisenstein, who with Vladimir Lyutse, Alexei Kelberer, Vasily Fedorov and Zinaida Raikh, was responsible for the defiantly impertinent 'design': the discarded flats propped back to front against the bare walls – a rejection of the box set, but also a three-dimensional space for actors. 'I remember shivering continuously. It was not cold, it was excitement, it was nerves stretched to their limit.'[12] And five days later, on 25 April 1922, came the première of one of the twentieth century's most significant productions, Meyerhold's version of Crommelynck's *The Magnanimous Cuckold*.

There is no need here to add to the numerous detailed accounts of this momentous work.[13] It is worth noting, however, that an acting style was established through the triumphant playing of Meyerhold's ensemble which may be regarded as almost definitive for revolutionary theatre. It was rooted in biomechanics, of course, and the three leading players, Igor Ilinsky, Maria Babanova and Vasily Zaichikov were so in harmony they became known collectively as 'Il-Ba-Zai'. But the point to stress is that the effect they created was joyful and dynamic. They were clowns, not unlike the circus-style clowns created immediately after the revolution by Annenkov and Radlov. The ancient *skomorokhi* could also be seen in them; the buffoons of the fairground booths and the comedians of the *commedia dell'arte*. But though they were fast, acrobatic and quick-witted, they had a newly modern sensibility. Their ability to combine echoes of popular tradition with something distinctly and consciously contemporary was at the heart of their achievement.

The designer for the production was Lyubov Popova, who had been associated with Meyerhold's abortive mass spectacle *The Struggle and Victory of the Soviets* the previous year. She was now a professor at GVYTM, and her contribution perfectly complemented the director's. A modern critic has asserted that 'Popova's productions in Meierkhold's theater are a benchmark in the history of theatrical Constructivism: all that went before them is its prehistory; all that went after, its development and continuation.'[14] It is difficult now to understand the startling originality contained within Popova's arrangement of platforms, stairways, slides and doors for *The Magnanimous Cuckold*, for we have become used to stage sets which offer volumetric playing-space to the actor, but all previous abstract or non-objective stage designs had been conceived in painterly terms. Popova's set was neither the popular theatre's trestle stage nor a 'generalised' windmill, though it had elements of both. Instead of walls, levels or surfaces, it was simply space, shaped to show off the skill of the actor and it responded to the emotional intensity of the action when the propeller-like mill wheels whirred round faster or slower, or came to a stop. It reminded Sergei Tretyakov of 'the scaffolding of a house under construction. These are the ladders and gangways which our muscles must conquer'.[15]

For Meyerhold:

> the fact that the stylistic extremes displayed by this production . . . were greeted *with delight* by the widest possible audience, proved that an urgent desire for just such a theatrical style was felt by [the] new audience, which regarded the theatre as one of the many *cultural* conquests of the Revolution.[16]

But not everyone shared the 'delight'. The ever-vacillating Lunacharsky labelled the play 'obscene' and wondered about a 'Communist' director working on it at all. At the end of April, Nezlobin and his company, suddenly almost wholly marginalised, walked out of the Actors Theatre,

12 Model of the set for *The Magnanimous Cuckold*, designed by Lyubov Popova.

which in June was officially liquidated, though some performances of *The Magnanimous Cuckold* were still given. Meyerhold wrote furiously to the press, threatening to emigrate,[17] and a new deal was struck: Meyerhold would become head of the new State Institute of Theatrical Art (GITIS), based in the former Institute of Music Drama, and the Zon would be at the disposal of the new organisation.

GITIS drew into itself immediately five Workshops – those of Meyerhold, Boris Ferdinandov, Nikolai Foregger, and the Armenian and Jewish Theatres – and these were soon supplemented by the Music Drama Workshop of Nikolai Malko, the Synthetic Theatre of Nikolai Aksagarsky, and Andrei Petrovsky's Workshop. For one reporter present at the opening ceremony on 17 September 1922, GITIS was 'a place unique on the planet, where the science of theatre is studied and theatre itself is being constructed. Exactly – "science" and not "art" – "constructed" and not "created".'[18]

It was during Meyerhold's short period at GITIS that he and Eisenstein worked together most closely, and one phase of the particular synthesis of revolutionary theatre was clearest. The work they were able to do together combined Futurism, circus and *commedia dell'arte* in a unique way. Futurism typically dislocates conventional sense to release new kinds of meaning; circus stimulates the adrenalin with its boldness and spectacle; and *commedia dell'arte* creates narrative through action. United in Meyerhold and Eisenstein's work, they generated a uniquely theatrical energy, first in the projected *Heartbreak House*, which Eisenstein wanted to stage with lions and tigers in cages on stage throughout, then with the production of Alexander Sukhovo-Kobylin's nineteenth-century black farce, *The Death of Tarelkin*. Though sometimes considered unsuccessful, this production nevertheless appealed to some important spectators, including Moscow Party boss, Lev Kamenev[19], and it was important for its director and his assistant in cementing the revolutionary style, which Eisenstein described as 'a strong and colourful grotesque, moving in places into pure clowning'.[20] Rudnitsky hints at how this worked:

A carnival atmosphere invaded the auditorium. Coloured balls flew through the hall. During the intermissions enormous prop apples were lowered from the balcony and the spectators eagerly tried to grab them. Posters were tossed out: 'Death to the Tarelkins – Make way for the Meyerholds.'[21]

Meyerhold had travelled far since his clowns were the dreamy Pierrots and decadent Harlequins of the pre-revolutionary years. The show was staged around strictly functional white-slatted furniture which cracked, tilted or otherwise tricked the actors, like the fireworks under the audience's seats. It was nerve-wracking and exhilarating.

But the cracks between the various members of GITIS were also making themselves felt. After a series of bitter confrontations, Boris Ferdinandov, whose Experimental-Heroic Theatre had been the main user of the Zon Theatre with Meyerhold's troupe, quarrelled irrevocably with the Master and left GITIS, followed shortly after by Meyerhold himself. He had been invited by Olga Kameneva to take over the Theatre of Revolution, the descendant of TEREVSAT whose board she chaired. Meyerhold accepted, for it enabled him to complete his exemplary model: he had his school, his Free Workshop became the experimental Theatre of Meyerhold at the Zon, and the Theatre of Revolution provided him with a conventional stage. He entered 1923 ready once again to turn the theatre world upside down.

THEATRE EXPERIMENTAL AND HEROIC

After the formation of GITIS, Meyerhold shared the Zon Theatre with the Experimental-Heroic Theatre, an inherently unsatisfactory arrangement, for the Experimental-Heroic Theatre had several productions in their repertoire, whereas Meyerhold had only *The Magnanimous Cuckold*. Soon Boris Ferdinandov, leader of the Experimental-Heroic Theatre, and a hot-tempered and somewhat self-righteous man, suspected Meyerhold of trying to oust him. He gathered his troupe together in his studio on the fourth floor of the Zon, and led them like a brigade of shock troops down the echoing stairs to the floor below, where Meyerhold was working. The door flew open. Ferdinandov, in his short sheepskin coat, his bald head shining, his face red, flicking his knee-high riding boots smartly with his cane, faced his imagined persecutor. 'Meyerhold!' he screamed, and spat out a high-pitched shriek of demands and insults too frenzied to be comprehensible. There was a pause, filled with writhing tension and heavy breathing. Then Meyerhold, who had been forewarned of the interruption, walked forward and proffered his hand. 'Sit down. Let's talk,' he said. There was another fraught pause. But Ferdinandov's bristling pride was too strong. He turned on his heel and marched out, leaving GITIS shortly afterwards.

He was a man of quarrels. He had come into GITIS after having quarrelled with his theatre's former landlord, the Rogozhsky-Simonovsky district theatre on Taganka Square, which he had tried to commandeer to the exclusion of the local groups who were entitled to use it. And in February 1923, shortly after the group had moved out of the Zon Theatre, he quarrelled with Vadim Shershenevich, his partner, and they went their separate ways. Ferdinandov's fiery temperament partially concealed his real talent. Born in 1889, he had studied at the school of Sophia Khalyutina, and worked briefly at the Moscow Art

Theatre and the Theatre of Music-Drama before joining the Kamerny Theatre as actor and designer. He designed *King Harlequin* and Tairov's adaptation of Debussy's *The Toy Box* in 1917, and, in 1919, *Adrienne Lecouvreur* by Eugene Scribe. He gave 'a sort of Cubist Rococo'[22] to the production which remained in the repertoire till the 1940s. As an actor, he appeared as Harlequin in Schnitzler's *The Veil of Pierrette*, the Young Syrian in Wilde's *Salomé*, Boris in *The Storm* by Ostrovsky, and Tybalt in *Romeo and Juliet*, when one critic commented that he captured 'something of Verona's sunniness, of the brightness of the Italian Renaissance'.[23]

Alexander Tairov claimed that Ferdinandov's line of development was parallel to his own but for Ferdinandov they met at a crossroads, Tairov's work becoming ever more esoteric and his own ever more 'scientific'. His complaint that Tairov employed him only when he had no money for more famous artists added a typically personal edge to their differences. Meyerhold mischievously suggested that Ferdinandov deserted Tairov because he could no longer stand the latter's 'resounding banality, the advertised "nudity on stage", the pseudo-acrobatic posing, the declarations about "neo-realism"',[24] while Ferdinandov derided Tairov's 'grandmother's tales [about] the inscrutability of the foundations of theatrical creativity'.[25] He and another Kamerny actor, Konstantin Eggert, were determined to find fundamental laws and a scientific basis for theatrical creativity, and they moved to the theatre on Taganka Square. Eggert soon left, but Ferdinandov was joined by Vadim Shershenevich, who had created the new text of *Rienzi* for Bebutov earlier in 1921. Futurist, founder of the Mezzanine group and translator of Marinetti, Shershenevich's poetry was described as 'baroque urbanism' by one critic, and his first play, *Swifthood* was seen as 'a poor imitation of Mayakovsky'.[26] After the revolution he became a leader among the Bohemian Imaginist poets, with Sergei Esenin, Anatoly Mariengof and Nikolai Erdman. He had appeared in the notorious film, *Drama in Futurist Cabaret No 13*, and also produced the brief manifesto, *A Declaration About Futurist Theatre*, in 1914, which argued for a grotesque theatre of mixed genres and tone, in which words would be less important than movement, and stage sets less important than lighting effects. Probably following Marinetti, he argued against psychology on stage, and for 'modern' themes. These concerns were developed in a poetic context by the Imaginists, who declared that 'the only law of art, the only and incomparable method, is the representation of life through the image and the rhythm of images.'[27] Images (or 'signs' in Formalist terminology) were 'independent' in Shershenevich's system, but 'linked', and none was more important than another.

Ferdinandov and Shershenevich's approach to dramatic performance paralleled this. For them, the key to spoken text was to be found not so much in the words as in the pauses, the caesuras, the beat of the sentences and the rhythms of the language, which together made up a series of theatrical 'signs'. It led to a speaking mode which was part singing, part recitative, and part heavily- and regularly-accented speech. This was to conform with the 'fixed laws' of theatrical presentation, which Ferdinandov and Shershenevich connected with rhythm – the rhythm of life, growing up, growing old, dying – but mapped out in diagrams, sketches and figures. Like many revolutionary artists, the attraction of science and industry proved almost irresistible, and where Meyerhold 'invented' biomechanics, this theatre 'discovered' metro-rhythmics, a 'science' rooted (like biomechanics) in Taylorism, time-and-motion, the *efficiency* of movement, and Pavlov's laws of reflex stimulation, as opposed to the kind of free emotional flow of Jacques-Dalcroze or Isadora Duncan.

In the summer of 1922, Vladimir Mass had discussed the potential of 'the mechanics of art',[28] and Meyerhold and Ferdinandov were by no means the only theatre practitioners to explore it. Nikolai Lvov's Laboratory Theatre of Expressionism used 'rhythmised action, Taylor-ised theatre, anthropo-cinematics, and reflexology,'[29] in an attempt to abolish theatre as art and introduce a new form of socially-rational action. The relationship of this programme to Expressionism is not clear, but in any case his leading collaborators, including Vitaly Zhemchuzhny and Valentin Parnakh, could not agree on methods, and the theatre failed. It merged with Evgeny Prosvetov's Workshop of Organisational Theatre, which had grown out of the Proletkult Ton-Plas Studio, and which took its name from Bogdanov's 'organisational' theory. Prosvetov had developed his own style of rhythmised action and rhythmo-dynamics, and now took *agitki* into factories, and was gener-ally engaged in educational and training work. The new grouping, called the Projection Theatre, specialised in self-created revue-style programmes, like those pioneered by TEREVSAT (lectures, mimes, sketches, and other 'attractions' to create revolutionary propaganda), but they also performed the 'non-representational' dramas, *AOU Tragedy* and *The Conspiracy of Fools* by Anatoly Mariengof, with designs by Solomon Nikritin.

The methods of Lev Kuleshov in his Film Workshop were also couched in pseudo-scientific language. Originally a unit within the State Film School on Neglinny Drive, the Experimental Film Workshop was led by Kuleshov and Vasily Ilyin, an architect and artist, who based his work on the Delsarte system of movement. Kuleshov was closer to the Formalists, being anxious that the actor's movement should be under-stood as a system of signs. His main concern therefore was that the actor should not attempt to 'relive' what he was doing, but that he should find the appropriate 'sign' for it. Holding up as an example the docker 'because many years at the job have made his movements sparing, deft and well-calculated,'[30] his exercises broke movement down into the smallest possible units:

A person enters the room – the first part of the assignment.

A room may be entered in different ways (we begin the analysis with the door being opened).

Which hand should be put on the door handle? How best to hold the hand itself? Which leg enters the room first? In which attitude will the body be held? What will the other hand be doing; in what position will it be? How will the head be held?[31]

Once the actor has confronted the problems of movement in space, its tempo and rhythm must be considered:

The metronome sets the tempo . . . as in music: either two-quarter or three-quarter time or else their combination. Just as in music the three-quarter metrical time division (the waltz) agrees best with lyrical themes, while the two-quarter division (the march) suits bold, energetic themes . . . the accented dominant beats set off one measure of movement from another.

Finally, Kuleshov introduced 'axis work' to give range and sensitivity to movement in a way which almost prefigures the work of Rudolph Laban:

A movement can be stressed or unstressed (strong or weak), long or short, i.e. its behaviour in time must comply with all the laws of a harmonious process. Each gesture has its duration, which can be recorded in special (musical) notation, studied and reproduced. The alternation of stressed and unstressed units will create a metre and a temporal pattern (as with montage). A strong movement is the result of a special plastic combination with the preceding and the following elements and a particular distribution of the axes in the metric space grid.[32]

Despite the pseudo-scientific language, Kuleshov's actors, including Alexandra Khoklova, Boris Barnet, Vsevolod Pudovkin, Porfiri Podobed and Vladimir Fogel, mastered an agile, unfussy, stylised acting system, the dynamism of which can still be appreciated in films like *The Extraordinary Adventures of Mr West in the Land of the Bolsheviks*. The shortage of film stock in the early Soviet years meant that the group had to present their scenarios, 'films without film', as theatrical performances. In *The Venetian Stocking*, Khoklova as the jealous wife performed a fit of hysterics 'in the most complex, semi-acrobatic series of movements'. Later 'she gives him a slap, and he performs a "back flip".'[33] Kuleshov's scenarios usually contained clowning, farce and dance, as well as self-contained 'études' such as two characters unaware of one another on either side of a street kiosk, mirroring one another in the style of Harpo Marx. The intention was to create a rhythm of theatrical images in shows which toured street cafés and restaurants:

> The fat thriving tradesmen sitting at the tables dully watched our 'rhythmic shows', their ugly champing mugs alternately reflecting horror and lust. Khoklova's gauntness horrified them. During the interval she was surrounded by gypsy women from the band who fingered the glass beads around her neck and kept asking, 'Diamonds? The real thing? Where didya get 'em?'

Not all the experiences were as bad as this:

> We also performed at workers' clubs, schools, even in the Hall of Columns. We loved taking our shows to children's homes, where we got a very special payment: we were allowed to eat as much white bread as we could, provided we didn't take any away.[34]

In the summer of 1922, Ilyin left the company, and that autumn, at the invitation of Boris Ferdinandov, they moved into the Zon Theatre.

Ferdinandov's practice had much in common with Kuleshov's. In October 1922, at the time of the founding of GITIS, Shershenevich outlined the programme of the Experimental-Heroic Theatre.[35] Starting from Diderot's premise that art was not 'inspired' but subject to 'fixed scientific laws', he argued that theatrical performance should conform to the laws of motion, which were centripetal and centrifugal, based on metre and rhythm, strict and free. Therefore a 'metro-rhythmical' system was required, for only that kind of system could accept and utilise an arbitrary individualistic work of creativity, harnessing it through metre and letting it express itself through rhythm. Shershenevich and Ferdinandov worked on methods of creating a 'score' for a production which would not omit 'architectural-pictorial set building' (Shershenevich claimed the Experimental-Heroic Theatre's use of Constructivism preceded the production of *The Magnanimous Cuckold*). Nor would it forget music, which was used in the Experimental-Heroic Theatre 'as part of the harmony and tempo of the metro-rhythmical structure of the performance' in contradistinction to the Kamerny Theatre's 'lyricism'. The company's training programme required students to keep journals of work, to make models and masks, and to learn the 'Synthetic-theatrical gymnastics of the Experimental-Heroic Theatre'.[36] Parallel with this was an 'Experimental Line', comprising five sections:

1 The Alphabet of theatre – recording word, gesture, emotion, the individual 'part' (a musical term, as distinct from the theatrical

'role'), the 'complete score' and 'theatrical harmony, counterpoint and orchestration'.

2 Elementary Physical Analysis – including plasticity and stage lighting.
3 The Organisation of Work for a Production – directorial plan, 'orchestration' and so on.
4 Recording and Study of a Production.
5 Theatrical Composition – ideological premises, the technique of composition, examples of theatrical-technical forms, and building an original production.

The programme attempted to train actors in the 'mechanical' calling forth of emotion, frequently with the use of the metronome, and laid stress on breaking down text and movement into rhythmic compartments, which sometimes made Ferdinandov's actors seem like marionettes.

Despite the theatre's name, the repertoire was eclectic, including classical tragedy, farce, Shershenevich's 'harlequinade', *All Utter Nonsense*, and a spoof detective drama. The young company made its debut on 3 October 1921 in Shershenevich's adaptation of *Oedipus the King*, directed by Ferdinandov (who also played the hero). In a rudimentary Constructivist set, the masked actors tried to put into practice the director's theories about the rhythm and metre of words, and their relationship to movement. A year later, Shershenevich found it 'crude, shallow and primitive',[37] but it was in fact a not unimpressive start, and perhaps more accessible than the next production, Ostrovsky's *The Storm*, where an attempt was made to relate the rhythm to the construction of life. The text was adapted to compartmentalise rhythmical sections, and the playing was strongly regulated by the monotonous beat. The effect created may have been interesting but it certainly diluted any tragic intentions.

After Gogol's *Marriage* and Shershenevich's *All Utter Nonsense*, the company produced Labiche's *The Money Box* as a rhythmical construction of the word. Boris Erdman, the designer, created a raked stage with several levels on it, tapering to the back, with original music by Yuri Milyutin structuring the action. It went from:

the sliding ballet *glissando* to the circus tumbling and jumping, executed with the precision and the courage of an aerial gymnast. Such 'circusized' vaudeville, on the one hand, became bravura, with the actors outstanding as masters of dare-devil precision, and on the other hand, raised the methods of variety, music hall and cinema to a keen expressiveness.[38]

The last production of the Experimental-Heroic Theatre at the Zon Theatre was Shershenevich's *The Lady in the Black Glove*, a satire on the filmed detective thriller. Staged on a gigantic cube, with ladders, triangles, horizontal bars and more, the play was largely a series of chases, tightly controlled by the music. The breathless actors had time for little other than snatched and panted dialogues, but the effect of a crazy parody was achieved. Shershenevich had once proclaimed that 'every epoch differs from the others not by its episodes, anecdotes or facts, but by its general rhythm.'[39] This production may have come nearer to embodying the rhythm of the twentieth century than any of his poetry, and it suggests that the company might have been well-advised to present more contemporary plays – Shershenevich's 1919 tragedy, *The Eternal Jew*, for instance, remained unperformed, and plans to stage Nikolai Erdman's play, *The Mysteries*, came to nothing. In fact, when the Experimental-Heroic Theatre left the Zon shortly after this play's première, it was the beginning of its end.

Shershenevich left in dudgeon in February 1923, and Ferdinandov had to return to the Kamerny for two seasons: his Experimental-Heroic Theatre becoming part time, though not finally disbanding until 1926. Afterwards, he left Moscow to direct plays in other parts of Russia and later worked in the literary section of the State cinema organisation. Shershenevich, too, after ten or more years at the heart of Moscow's literary and artistic bohemia, faded from the scene, though he appeared in the film *The Kiss of Mary Pickford* in 1927. The Experimental-Heroic Theatre may have been short-lived, but its metro-rhythmics added a unique dimension to the revolutionary theatre, which can still be identified in early Soviet films.

THE DANCE OF LIFE

In May 1921, with Lenin's blessing, Isadora Duncan arrived in Moscow to found a school of dance. Her aim was 'to find those primary movements for the human body from which shall evolve the movements of the future dance in ever-varying, natural, unending sequences.'[40] For those attempting to forge a revolutionary theatre, this notion of the flow of 'natural' dance, and indeed everything which Duncan (and Jacques-Dalcroze) stood for, was anathema. Revolutionary dance work was done by practitioners like Inna Chernetskaya, who had left Duncan to open her own Studio of Synthetic Dance which concentrated on developing acrobatics, mime and gesture, in a consciously dramatic context; Vera Maya, who also discarded her original Duncanism to investigate the potency of acrobatics and pantomime in her studio; and Lev Lukin, whose Free Ballet became notorious for the dancers' near nudity and sensuality, for instance, in *A Danced Caress*. These *avant garde* choreographers were interested in expressive movement, which responded to Radlov's 'express trains and aeroplanes' and Mayakovsky's electrification. Lukin demanded that 'the epoch of the materialist Renaissance must reverberate through our work,'[41] and made a number of 'eccentric' dances, as well as a ballet from Shershenevich's spoof thriller, *The Lady in the Black Glove*.

The conventionally-trained Alexander Gorsky, who had worked in the Imperial ballets till the revolution, formed his own company in the summer of 1918 and presented a season at the Aquarium Theatre, including *Lyric Poem*, on the old avant-garde theme of Columbine and Pierrot. His *Stenka Razin* at the Bolshoi later that year was noteworthy for its heroic tone, its dynamic sets and its wild Russian dances. These works suggested a move towards a more 'Sovietised' choreography, and this was confirmed in his last full-length production, the children's ballet, *Ever-Fresh Flowers*; he suffered a mental breakdown and died on 20 October 1924. Though still structured largely traditionally as a series of divertissements, he introduced 'revolutionary motifs' – hammers and sickles, bare-chested blacksmiths, revolutionary banners – and made serious attempts to bridge the gap between stage and auditorium. Thus, during the performance, characters spoke directly to the audience, and in the intervals, games were played in the auditorium, sweets shared, and garlands and ribbons given out. At the climax:

> the smith suggested that they form a procession. The children-actors and children-spectators formed a line headed by a military band and went out into the lobby to the sounds of a march. Having gone through the building singing revolutionary songs, they came back into the auditorium.[42]

But such work, according to Nikolai Foregger was 'plastitution' ('plastic prostitution'). He asserted that 'the future is in dance and film. But while the film fantastically gallops ahead and becomes firmly established . . . the dance peacefully dreams along in the shadow of the Good Fairy's *tutu*, using a plastic bust-bodice as a pillow.'[43] He upheld the example of Chaplin, who 'turned upside down the usual way of playing a scenario, with its psychological diarrhoea, which, having messed up the drama, has begun to shit on the film.' Chaplin's playing was:

> always precise, never using decorative gesture for the sake of gesture, and in his work his intentions and his actions are always clear. His playing is concrete, he reacts precisely to things. The whole experience is inconceivably stark, and one doesn't remember 'his eyes' or 'his profile' because his whole body is at work as a complete mechanism.[44]

In 1919, Foregger had crossed swords with Meyerhold concerning the relevance of circus to theatre. For Meyerhold, the difference was both crucial and clear: the theatre actor had to master rhythm whereas the circus artist had to master metre. But Foregger argued that while the two forms were certainly different, the theatre actor needed the technical mastery over his whole body which the circus artist possessed, and he complained that it was still generally true that whereas the theatre actor *pretends*, the circus performer *does*. (It is worth noting that when, in the summer of 1920, Meyerhold was in danger of losing his tenure of the Zon Theatre, Foregger protested extremely vigorously and publicly.[45] And in April 1923, his workshop, MastFor (MASTerskaya FOReggera) was invited to perform alongside Meyerhold's own at the Bolshoi Theatre for the celebration of the Master's Jubilee.) Referring to Zola's praise for the Hanlon-Lee Brothers acrobatic clowns, Foregger called for a performance art which would be spectacular, energetic, bright, dynamic, made from the images of modern life, but clear, precise and understandable. Acrobatic tricks were the artistic equivalent of technological wizardry, but they had to be as smoothly functional. For Huntly Carter, 'Foregger was an inventor of genius, who took the mechanical age into the theatre and sought to interpret some of its wonders.'[46]

MastFor had opened in 1921 after Foregger had met Vladimir Mass at the TEREVSAT Studio, where both were working after the Civil War. They agreed on the need to form a contemporary version of the old Theatre of Four Masks, and they obtained a barely adequate base in the House of the Press, helping the members of their small company to survive by registering them as students of GVYTM. In August 1921, *Labour* noted the company's 'very interesting and promising' parodies, which it described as 'very witty'.[47] After an increasingly successful autumn, during which a Deburau-style pantomime, *The Mannequin*, and a thriller, *The Pearly Necklace*, among others, were added to the repertoire, Vladimir Mass's adaptation of Mayakovsky's poem, *Kindness to Horses*, was presented on New Year's Eve, 1921. It caused a furore, and on 2 January 1922 Mayakovsky spoke enthusiastically in Foregger's defence at a 'dispute' on the new production.

Over the next eighteen months, MastFor's repertoire continued to grow, as it presented cabaret-style programmes of short, sharp, self-contained numbers. He wrote:

> 'When the dominant waves of art reflect an already defined reality, then the "little forms", like foam on the crests of the waves, carry in their spray the smell and tang of new waters which will come to wash the world. In the domain of theatre, it is the music hall (cabaret) which must play this role.'[48]

MastFor became No 2 theatre in GITIS (Ferdinandov's was No 3) with a permanent theatre holding fewer than 200 spectators on the Arbat. For a year or more, under Foregger's artistic direction, MastFor held a place in the foremost ranks of the revolutionary theatre. It had an extremely talented core of artists, including Mass as writer in residence, Sergei Yutkevich and Sergei Eisenstein as designers, Matvei Blanter in charge of music, and Andrei Senerov, Vladimir Fogel, Boris Barnet, Regina Baburina and others as performers. But it was partially trapped in the political and social net of NEP. To pursue its most original line, it offended its bourgeois patrons; if it pleased them, as with the frankly erotic *Dance of the Hooligans*, it outraged its fellow 'Leftists'. In late 1922, Eisenstein left, having failed to present his *risqué* parody, *Columbine's Garter*, 'a contemporary tragic *balagan*',[49] dreamed up with Yutkevich after Meyerhold's pre-revolutionary *Columbine's Scarf*. Yutkevich and then Mass followed him out of MastFor, and Foregger was forced to try to make his repertoire more acceptable to the authorities. He adapted Toller's *Hinkemann* and created a patriotic performance, *Budyonny's March*, about the Bolshevik Civil War hero. But in January 1924, the little theatre burned down, and MastFor was 'reorganised' out of existence.

MastFor's programmes were of three kinds. It first made a name with theatrical parodies, especially after the widely-noticed evening at the House of the Press on 28 March 1921. The performance included *One Operetta Is Enough for Every Wise Man*, culled from Ostrovsky's *Enough Stupidity for Every Wise Man*, but mocking Nemirovich-Danchenko's current pretensions to be a grand opera director; *The Tsar's Mother-in-law*, parodying Rimsky-Korsakov's *The Tsar's Bride*; and *The Phenomenal Tragedy of Phetra*, mocking Tairov's Kamerny Theatre production of Racine's tragedy. Later parodies were *Don't Drink Unboiled Water!* satirising TEREVSAT's 'Living Newspapers'; *The Proposal*, after Chekhov's vaudeville (it was somehow turned into a mass spectacle and a parody of *The Dawns* with biomechanics, crowds cheering and booing, and a parade to celebrate the revolution); *Are You Deaf, Moscow?* after Eisenstein's successful production of Tretyakov's 'agit-guignol', *Are You Listening, Moscow?!*; and Nikolai Erdman's parody of *The Magnanimous Cuckold*, *The Rhinoceros*, punning on the Russian titles: 'Nosorogie' – 'Rogonosets'. Each parody lasted perhaps twenty minutes, and if they were primarily laughter-makers, they had a serious underlying purpose reflecting the struggle of 'Left' artists to find a revolutionary theatre.

Probably of more significance were MastFor's 'parades' – the original cabaret-style dramas, organised musically at 'an American tempo' and with characters deriving from Foregger's updated *commedia* 'masks', which were linked by jazz numbers, acrobatics, chorus lines, or Cossack dances. The 'masks' which appeared most frequently in MastFor's shows were: the female Communist with briefcase and leather jacket, reminiscent of Alexandra Kollontai and prefiguring Milda in Tretyakov's *I Want a Baby*; the Mystical Intellectual, a Symbolist like Bely or even the revered Blok, who had reconciled himself to the Revolution;

the Imaginist poet, a mixture of the peasant Esenin and the urbane Shershenevich; a Militiaman, a kind of Russian Keystone cop; the NEP man, ostentatiously 'nouveau riche'; and an Auguste, butt of everyone's violence, always in the way when least wanted. Each was crudely characterised by two or three features, exaggerated make-up and typical costume, and in each playlet the 'type' was modified by the action, the actor's inventiveness and the particular play. MastFor's dramas deliberately eschewed conventional dramatic structure, in favour of interruption and syncopation. This provided the audience with plenty of shocks, and many of them responded with unruly laughter. The dramas often resembled partial surveys of the contemporary world, sardonic, without illusions, but dynamic, awry, topical and very fast.

One of MastFor's strengths was that Foregger did not work from unwritten scenarios, as for instance Radlov had at the Petrograd Popular Comedy; his collaboration with the writer, Vladimir Mass, in the creation of his shows was vital to both artists. Foregger seemed to spur Mass on to create much sharper, spicier dramas than his more obvious agit-prop work; his plays for MastFor were usually one act buffoonades in the style of Mayakovsky, an important supporter of the Workshop. *How They Organised* was one of Mass's earliest plays for Foregger, and concerned the defeat of the interventionist foreign powers in the Civil War, with a comic sideswipe at Isadora Duncan. The 'masks' in this show included the returning emigrant, the sceptical professor, the cigarette-selling spiv, and others, whose appearances and disappearances were orchestrated by the compère. There was plenty of topical comedy, some acrobatics, and a brazen feeling of contemporary Moscow in the performance.

Perhaps the most brilliant example of this new genre was *Kindness to Horses*. Mayakovsky's original poem tells of a cab-horse which falls in the street; everyone is amazed and amused, except the poet who sees a tear in the animal's eye. Heartened by the poet's solidarity, the horse gets up and trots happily away. The play opened with an actor in a mask of a horse's head entering, then falling, and a crowd gathering round as in the poem. But this was the cue to explore various social types and discuss issues of the day in comic and satirical fashion. In a later reworking of the drama, this section came to be called *Tverboul*, after TVERskoi BOULevard, and featured a former self-proclaimed hero of the Civil War (akin to the traditional Braggart Soldier) and a 'Soviet miss' in short skirt and high laced boots. On the boulevard the NEP entrepreneurs establish a 'Poet's Café', complete with Imaginist Poet, whom Eisenstein dressed in two halves of completely different costumes – one half a peasant's cap and smock to represent Esenin, the other half a smoking jacket and top hat like the dandy Shershenevich.

The horse's recovery is the signal for a satirical cabaret, featuring comic dances and songs, parodying Mistinguett, Isadora Duncan, western variety shows, and so on. For this, Yutkevich designed a 'mobile' set, with moving stairs, rotating scenery, trampolines and energetic lighting effects, and Eisenstein invented a costume for the female dancers which was little more than two hoops: one at the neck, the other at the knee and joined by different coloured ribbons, between which most of the dancers' bodies were visible. Isadora Duncan was played by a man in see-through red veils, who danced to the Chopin Nocturne which Duncan had used to dance before Lenin on the fourth anniversary of the Revolution. When 'she' raised her arms, the compère informed the audience that this was the proletariat triumphant; when she lowered them, the proletariat was enslaved; when she raised and lowered them alternately, it indicated the uncertainty of the proletariat before the Bolshevik revolution. *Kindness to Horses* was extremely popular, constantly revised, and was kept in the repertoire till MastFor closed.

Other 'parades' which should be mentioned included *The Promenade, the Passion, the Death*, in which a young typist with a white face was courted by a Chaplin-like 'little man'. Their relationship was interrupted by a Strong Man and they danced an acrobatic trio. When the Strong Man died, his arched back made a bench for the lovers to sit on. *The Locomotive* was even more striking: after a scene on the station platform in which a hooligan robbed a breadseller of her loaves, the night train was seen departing. This was created by lighting effects, rhythmic clapping accompanied by a sheet of thunder, and then as the noise diminished to represent the engine pulling away, actors made sparks from lighted cigarettes. Later productions of already-existing plays tried to recreate some of these effects, but not very succesfully. Thus, in *Jocrisse the Juggler* by Adolphe D'Ennery and Jules Brésil,[50] revolving metal discs crossing beams of light attempted to give the impression of cinefication, and in Charles Lecoq's *The Mysteries of the Canary Islands*, Yutkevich tried to create a Constructivist setting, though it seemed in many ways more like the cubistic Futurism of earlier years. This production was marked by slapstick buffoonery, actors like badly-painted dolls who moved like marionettes, and western smoochy music.[51]

In these shows Foregger's company danced all the most modern dances – the cakewalk, the shimmy, the foxtrot, the tango and many more. Their most original dance, however, was the 'machine dance', first shown in *Machine Dances* on 13 February 1923. The idea may have derived from Valentin Parnakh's solo 'mechanical' dances, accompanied by a 'noise orchestra', but Foregger's inspiration soared beyond that. Dressing his actors in tight black-and-white costumes somewhere between sports outfits and circus acrobats' leotards, he created a kaleidoscope of mechanical patterns which were dazzling and soon internationally famous.[52] There was a whistle. The performers ran on

13 A 'machine dance' by Nikolai Foregger.

stage, formed up, and swung agilely into a pyramid, several people high. A pause. Slowly the machine began to get going, the pistons pumping, the gears engaging. The movement was accompanied by a 'noise orchestra' – drums, Jew's harps, the shaking of bags of broken glass, the clanging of metal objects, the whispers and shrieks of the players themselves. Then came the 'transmission belt', in which two men stood about two and a half metres apart with their arms out. As they turned, their arms formed sprockets for a chain of actresses, the drive belt, to go round. The programme included *The Blacksmith's Forge*, with hammers made from human fists or whole people, and *The Saw*, wherein two men held an actress, 'the saw', rigid between them by her shoulders and feet. Two other actresses formed a log of wood, splitting gradually apart as the 'sawing' proceeded. Everything was performed in strict tempo, with maximum precision, and with no expression on the performers' faces. The aim was clearly Constructivist, in the sense that it inherently commented on human efficiency and on taking possession of man's mechanical heritage. The laughter it provoked was an integrating laughter, implying the forward drive to a better society:

> A German visitor to MastFor suggested the dancers were like Priests, celebrating in dance the new God of the Machine. Their bodies became correctly constructed appliances, they no longer moved, they 'functioned' . . . The new dancing tries to express the most general movements of the human organism, rhythm no longer individual but universal. All the gestures are, therefore, as far as possible transformed into partial functions of a total movement, and strictly geometrised. The spectator is intended to recognize in the activity of each single group of muscles a motor reflex within the frame of the whole great stage machine. Dancing is intended to be nothing but a vivid demonstration of the adequate organisation of the human machine.[53]

This is a far cry from Isadora Duncan's search for 'the perfect expression of the individual body and the individual soul'.[54]

To achieve these performances, Foregger designed his own system of theatrical and physical training, 'TePhyTrenage', to develop:

1 Control of one's movements. Work on coordinating exercises for the separate parts of the body.
2 Speed of the plastic memory; attention to oneself and to one's partner (coupling). The trainer demonstrates the exercise several times and outlines it once. Exercises in pairs or larger groups.
3 Emotional colouring of the exercises.
4 Precision and speed of reaction. Boldness. Interrupted movement. Arbitrary alternation of the chain of exercises.

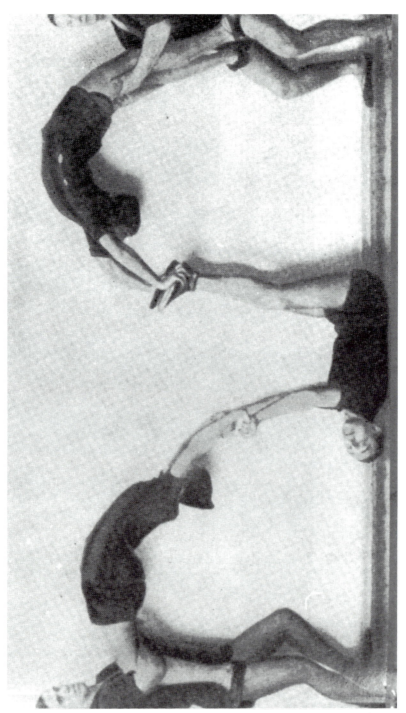

14 TyPhyTrenage. Constructivist movement at MastFor.

5 Inventiveness and ingenuity. Development of plastic thought . . . The shaping of the musical phrase, etc.[55]

For Foregger, the body should be regarded as a machine, controlled by an operator, the muscles, which are subject to the performer's will. His exercise 'The Wandering Leg', exemplifies this:

1 Stand at ease, feet apart, hands loose at the sides.
2 Tremble the right leg violently, while bringing it very slowly forward, foot just off the ground.
3 With the right leg still trembling, lift both hands straight out in front of the chest, arms straight; then lower both hands onto right thigh.
4 Stop trembling, shoot the right leg backwards, taking the left leg with it.
5 The body falls forward, the hands break the fall, the performer lies on his stomach, face down.
6 Jerk the face up, look forward, angry and puzzled.

TePhyTrenage included over 300 such exercises, for the body and for psycho-physical development, including exercises for concentration and for the physical, and plastic, memory. Foregger tried to distinguish between constructivist movement, such as 'The Wandering Leg', and grotesque movement, such as his exercise, 'The Beggar':

1 Stand at ease.
2 Bend both knees as far as possible to crouch; simultaneously, hook the right hand behind the left knee, bend the back, look piteously upwards, raise the left arm straight up.

The actor needed command of both kinds of movement, and Foregger also advocated instruction in specific techniques, such as wire-walking, particular dances, boxing, acrobatics, somersaults, vaulting, and so on. His programme was comprehensive, not to say diffuse, but whether it was ever actually implemented in its entirety remains uncertain.

After the fire in his theatre, and after some vicious criticism from 'workers' who called *Machine Dances* 'pornographic' and 'anti-Soviet',[56] MastFor was not permitted to reopen in its previous form, and the dance section was moved to Petrograd, where Foregger staged the acclaimed *An American on Ligorsky Boulevard*. He also worked freelance for the Aquarium Theatre, the Theatre of Satire and the Blue Blouse, and acted in Kozintsev and Trauberg's film, *The Devil's Wheel*, but in 1929 he moved out of Moscow to become artistic director of the Kharkov Theatre of Opera and Ballet. In 1934 he moved to Kiev, presenting circus as well as opera and ballet, and in 1938 he became artistic director of the Kubyshevsky Theatre. He died in 1939, having almost single-handedly created a style of machine dancing which influenced many of his contemporaries and followers. It informed the work of the Blue Blouse[57] and mainstream ballet as much as it did the mass choreography glorifying Stalin, which could be seen in Red Square on revolutionary holidays in any year in the 1930s.

The 'miniature forms' of MastFor were like the elements of the medieval Carnival or the theatres of the fairground, or even the best of cabaret. They subverted the claims to attention of the legitimate theatre housed in the Bolshoi, the Art Theatre and such venues. Parody, the 'parades' and machine dances embody the best of the revolutionary theatre, but they were little appreciated by the political revolutionaries who turned out to be cultural conservatives, unable to think through the logic of their own philosophy. What Foregger presented was not their formulaic *socialist* realism, but *theatrical* realism in which the body of the actor, and the actions he or she performs, are the centre of attention. As Foregger himself proclaimed: 'The people of the Middle Ages, suffocating under the yoke of the Church, created the "Dance of Death". In the joyous construction of a new world, the "Dance of Life" must resound.'[58]

THE FACTORY OF THE ECCENTRIC ACTOR

In Moscow GITIS provided, at least for a few months, an umbrella for all those seeking a revolutionary new theatre, but in Petrograd matters were not so simple. The former TEREVSAT group at the Free Comedy Theatre, with Nikolai Petrov, Konstantin Mardzhanov, Nikolai Evreinov and Yuri Annenkov, promised much, and mounted a few interesting productions, most notably, in February 1921, Evreinov's *The Main Thing*, which ran for over a hundred performances. The group also established its own late-night cabaret, *Balaganchik*, in the autumn of 1921. But its contribution to the creation of a new kind of theatre was disappointing, as was that of Ligovsky Dramatic Theatre, also known as the Theatre of New Drama, whose leaders were all former students of Meyerhold: Vladimir Soloviev, Alexei Gripich, Vladimir Dmitriev, Konstantin Tverskoi and Konstantin Derzhavin. This backwardness was less true of dance, where the earliest experiments of Georgi Balanchivadze (later known as George Balanchine), took place. In 1920, his *La Nuit* featured Olga Mungalova in an acrobatic and 'erotic' performance which aroused some controversy, and his Young Ballet, founded in 1922, provoked similar reactions, including responses to the 'utterly preposterous' sets designed by Vladimir Dmitriev. Equally controversial was Fedor Lopukhov's *Jim from Cincinnati*, about which the young Leonid Trauberg enthused in a typical comparison with a new car: 'Benz 1923 : Ford 1913 = *Jim from Cincinnati* : the one-step from Maxime's'.[59]

Trauberg was a contributor to the 'Dispute on the Eccentric Theatre' at the Free Comedy on 5 December 1921, with Grigori Kozintsev and Georgi Kryzhitsky. When their declarations were published the following year, a similar statement from Sergei Yutkevich was added to the manifesto. At the time, Yutkevich and Kozintsev were mere boys, aged 18 and 17. They had known each other in Kiev, where they had wanted to stage *Vladimir Mayakovsky, a Tragedy*, and had worked with Konstantin Mardzhanov, whose acquaintance proved extremely useful when they came to Petrograd. In Kiev, Mardzhanov had handed them a small empty theatre and suggested they study clowning:

> We all adored the circus. At that time there were some gifted clowns, Fernandez and Frico, at the Kisso Circus. They performed some classical clowning which ended in a funeral: the 'corpse' fell out of the coffin and ran after the procession with anguished cries and torrents of tears. Frico hobbled in boots three feet long and peeled off innumerable waistcoats. Fernandez sparkled with flowers and butterflies spangled on his white clown get-up. They played tunes on bottles and motor-horns, swapped blows and fled from the ring, slipping, tumbling, and producing hidden crackers from their pantaloons. It was the old popular comedy in all its poetry.[60]

Some of these techniques they tried to transfer to the Petrushka puppet show which they traipsed round the streets, before Yutkevich left Kiev, and Kozintsev, still only fourteen, decided to stage the old comedy, *Tsar Maximilian and His Son Adolf*, which many years later Trauberg, perhaps disingenuously, named as a 'principal source' of their eccentrism.[61]

The extreme youth of three of the four authors of the Eccentrist Manifesto – Kryzhitsky was the odd one out at thirty – was perhaps its most extraordinary feature. They had had no contact with the old *avant-garde* theatre, as had Meyerhold, Radlov, Mayakovsky, Mardzhanov, even Ferdinandov and Foregger. They simply knew they liked American films and jazz bands, the energy of which seemed to match the revolutionary mood. Their Eccentrist philosophy therefore began from the iconoclasm of youth: 'Better to be a young June-bug than an old bird of paradise', crowed Kozintsev, echoing Mark Twain.[62] More than a clown with an outsize trombone, and not quite the same as the beautiful Beast,[63] this Eccentrism deliberately violated normal expectations, causality, sequentiality and logic; while their awareness of the concrete world prevented them from sliding into Surrealism, Kozintsev, Trauberg and Yutkevich were, as Nikolai Lvov noted, committed to 'the extraordinary, the unexpected . . . whatever contradicts the normal direction of everyday activity'.[64] 'Today's tempo,' announced Kozintsev, 'is the machine's rhythm, concentrated in America, pumped into life from the street,'[65] and those three elements were the basis of the group's theatre work. The machine's rhythm related dynamism and speed of performance to the industrial drive; Americanism embodied the new life to Kozintsev: 'either Americanization or the funeral hall,'[66] and the 'life of the street' centred on crowds, posters, cheap novels, especially the detective thrillers about Nat Pinkerton, and also the music halls and cinema, especially the popular American cinema of Charlie Chaplin and Pearl White.

On 9 July 1922 the Factory of the Eccentric Actor (FEKS) opened. It had already brashly announced courses by Evreinov, Annenkov, Miklashevsky and Tatlin; now it boasted the support of Nina Tamara, a star of music hall and operetta, clown Serge, Takoshimo the Japanese juggler, and various 'street characters'. Its first production was to be Gogol's *Marriage*, though 'not according to Gogol'. One poster read:

AMERIKA VORWÄRTS! AMERICA FORWARD!
AMÉRIQUE EN AVANT!
IN THE PRODUCTION – OPERETTA, MELODRAMA,
FARCE, FILM, CIRCUS,
VARIETY, CHARLIE CHAPLIN AND THE LOVELY BETTY
DEMONSTRATION OF THE THEORY OF RELATIVITY OF
PROFESSOR EINSTEIN
ELECTRIFICATION OF N. V. GOGOL ??? [67]

On the evening of 25 September 1922, as the audience waited with increasing impatience outside, the actors (who had only gained access to the Proletkult Hall, where they were to perform, two hours before the announced time of curtain-up), were still dress rehearsing, with Sergei Eisenstein in the auditorium urging them, 'Too slow! Too slow!' Eventually, seventy-five minutes late, and only after the militia had been called, the spectators were admitted.

The play opened with the bringing on of a chamber pot. Gogol himself solemnly sat down upon it, whereupon it was wired up and electric shocks were set through him via his backside! Next moment, echoing Pudovkin's technique in *The Iron Heel*, but using it more dynamically, a sequence from a Charlie Chaplin film was shown, and in front of it the action continued. Podkolyosin, the hero, was renamed Musichall Cinematographovich Pinketonov, and Miss Agatha's other suitors were the Steam Bridegroom, the Electric Bridegroom and the Radio Bridegroom, each on roller skates. Taurek the Clown appeared as Albert, and Serge was Einstein. The audience booed, cheered and whistled, as a fantastic kaleidoscope of theatrical trickery was shaken out before it – melodrama, clowning, dance, acrobatics, film. Multicoloured lights flashed, the pianist played a two-step, hooters hooted, bells rang, rattles rattled, and the performers cracked topical jokes and recited rude rhymes. There was even a can-can, and in the end – perhaps unsurprisingly – Gogol expired pitifully and in despair.

The whole was a phantasmagoria, brilliant and bewildering, yet Kozintsev's comments, written many years later, explain why the show was not just a meaningless mish-mash:

> It was a case of trying to find [theatrical forms] which could convey the intense sentiment of the new life. Unless this last point is recognised, our creations of that period would become incomprehensible. All these experiments, all these quests for new forms came because we had an intense feeling of an extraordinary renewal of life ... Thus, in our production of *Marriage*, a preponderant place was accorded to rhythm, because the novelty of things was initially felt not in themes nor in characters, but in rhythm. *Art had changed rhythm.* The new epoch had found its first expression in rhythm ... The young artists felt life in all its richness and colour, and artistic forms seemed naturally to take on the artistic forms of a great popular carnival. In the middle of every kind of privation a sort of fair was going on. The young artists bore the common fate gaily, so fine did the time in which they lived appear to them.[68]

Kozintsev's comment about rhythm is the key to understanding his art, and indeed revolutionary theatre itself. 'The performance is a rhythmical beating on the nerves,' he said in his manifesto, and this was achieved through 'a synthesis of movement: acrobatic, athletic, dance, constructivist-mechanical'. 'The actor is mechanized movement.'[69] His colleague, Kryzhitsky, having saluted 'Boklaro the Clown (N. N. Evreinov)' in his manifesto, added tellingly: 'Theatre is a sense of the tightrope, of exhilaration, it is the healthy, joyful springiness of our total being, of our total life energy. We catch our breath, we feel air spinning in our mouths.'[70]

The members of the Factory realised that if they were to solve the problems which this fizzing show had thrown up, they, like Meyerhold, Ferdinandov and Foregger in Moscow, must learn more about the actor's business. In 1921, Kozintsev had urged the actor: 'Forget about emotions and celebrate the machine, forget passion and turn to jest',[71] and though the pun seems not to be in the Russian, what he sought was a way to conflate 'jest' and 'gesture'. In the Factory, it seems Trauberg taught most of the theory, and Kozintsev took most of the practical work. This included mime, acrobatics, gymnastics, clowning, boxing, fencing and film acting, especially that of Chaplin. When the eighteen-year-old Sergei Gerassimov applied to join FEKS, the eighteen-year-old

'Master', Grigori Kozintsev, auditioned him by getting him to play Hamlet in mime and modern dress. The technical secret of the style, he believed, lay in circus, as Anatoly Golovnya, a film cameraman, put it a few years later:

> I believe that the highest form of art is the circus. When a man can walk on a tightrope – he can walk. When he can not, he breaks his head. And all that is very *visible*. In the circus you *have* to work.[72]

The new version of *Hamlet* was called *Foreign Trade on the Eiffel Tower*, and was presented on 4 June 1923 at the Musical Comedy Theatre. This play centred on a chase through the sewers of Paris and up and down the Eiffel Tower, as a mad American tried to sell a special kind of coal made out of air, and the World Fuel Corporation determined he should not do so. He was saved from the Corporation's hired desperadoes by a little girl, played by clown Serge. The drama again used film, this time made for the play: it caught the attention of officials at Sevzapkino, who invited the Factory of the Eccentric Actor to make a similar fantasy comedy as a film. This was *The Adventures of Oktyabrina*, which opened on 9 December that year, and Kozintsev and Trauberg never returned to the theatre.

But their short career had taken theatrical Eccentrism to its furthest point, and their distortions had disturbed and disoriented the spectator. 'The centre cannot hold', wrote Yeats at just this time,[73] and FEKS's excentricity argued the need for artistic re-evaluation and social rearrangement. The revolutionary theatre practitioners had subverted Tolstoy, Sukhovo-Kobylin, Sophocles, Ostrovsky, Gogol and other icons of accepted culture, and had turned them tendentiously to topical usage – *The First Distiller* aligned with the Bolsheviks' anti-alcohol campaign, *The Death of Tarelkin* proving the importance of Taylorism, now *Marriage* arguing for electrification. But these productions were neither moralistic nor portentous, and FEKS particularly filled them with zany laughter, and the joy, energy and hope of youth:

> We read poetry and looked at paintings, and the inner gaiety of which I speak shone in our eyes, not only in the eyes of fourteen-year-old Grisha Kozintsev but also in those of Konstantin Mardzhanov, who was then nearly fifty. It was not a matter of age – it was, if you like, a matter of the age of the Revolution.[74]

THE WORLD TURNED UPSIDE DOWN

When the theatrical revolutionaries turned their attention to acting, they found non-psychological, 'inconsistent' forms related to the intensity and grotesquerie of circus, and the gestic sequentiality of silent

15 Sketch by Sergei Yutkevich of Zinaida Tarkhovskaya in *Foreign Trade on the Eiffel Tower* by the Factory of the Eccentric Actor, June 1923.

cinema. But this was applied almost exclusively to established classics, and the new plays they attempted, *The Lady in the Black Glove*, *Kindness to Horses*, *Foreign Trade on the Eiffel Tower* and others, were all extremely slight pieces, so that it became common currency that there was a 'crisis in the repertoire'.

It was Meyerhold who first tried to meet the crisis. Ever since the founding of the Theatre of Revolution at Olga Kameneva's behest on 26 June 1922, Meyerhold had kept a supervisory eye on its work. Its first performance was of *Night* by the French pacifist, Marcel Martinet, directed by Alexander Velizhev on 29 October 1922. Though Meyerhold attended some rehearsals, he was organising the new GITIS and directing his own production of *The Death of Tarelkin*, and the opening production of the new theatre was a disappointment. Its next presentation, Toller's *The Machine-Wreckers*, was better received, and at the end of the year, as the GITIS experiment faltered, Meyerhold became more involved with the Theatre of Revolution, while at the Zon the Theatre of Meyerhold demonstrated the products of its 'workshop'. On 22 January 1923, they presented Aksenov's adaptation of Claudel's *Stale Bread* and *The Hostage*, directed by Fedorov, Act Three of Meyerhold's adaptation of *A Doll's House*, directed by Valery Inkizhinov, with Anna Bogdanova as Nora and Constructivist settings by Alexei Kelberer, scenes from *Mr Troplong's Wooden Leg* by Sergei Bobrov, directed by Vladimir Lyutse, and students read poems by Aseev, Mayakovsky and Tretyakov, and performed biomechanical études. On 18 March they showed a self-created piece, *The Paris Commune*, celebrating that uprising's fiftieth anniversary, directed by Naum Loiter, scenes from Mirbeau's *The Epidemic*, given as an 'agitka' in circus Eccentric style, directed by Nikolai Ekk, and *Immac-Concep*, from 'Immaculate Conception', an anti-religious clown show about the establishment of the Komsomol by Sergei Tretyakov, directed by Ksenia Goltseva. Many of these pieces also toured clubs and factories, as Meyerhold and his followers sought new audiences among non-traditional theatregoers.

Meanwhile, a committee, chaired by Olga Kameneva and including Lunacharsky, Yuzhin, the poet Bryussov and others, was charged with preparing Meyerhold's Jubilee celebrations at the Bolshoi Theatre on 2 April 1923 (Tretyakov called it 'the daring boarding of an old barge by a detachment of revolutionary guerrillas of art'),[75] and Meyerhold was created People's Artist of the RSFSR. But behind this facade, he was begging Kameneva to help him obtain some form of subsidy,[76] for that week the electricity to the Zon Theatre was cut off. Meyerhold, though at work on *A Profitable Post*, which was to be his debut at the Theatre of Revolution, threw together with typically rapid brilliance a new production of *Night* for the Workshop, and this proved enough of a commercial success to save the Zon.

Martinet's *Night* tells of an old widow woman, Mariette, whose son is fighting in the war. When the soldiers decide to rebel, and stop fighting, the generals on either side agree to unite against them. Ledrux, the soldiers' leader, is assassinated, the war is restarted, and Mariette's son's corpse is brought home. At the end of the play, she and her daughter-in-law prepare to face another dreary day. When Sergei Gorodetsky's translation of *Night* was published in 1922, no less a person than Trotsky hailed it as a 'landmark play'. It was, he said, a 'noble work of art' with 'social, political and revolutionary significance . . . It generates a mood which will seek a way out in thought and in deed,' he wrote. 'The insurrection is put down,' but the spectator goes out 'with a clenched fist,' vowing, 'this grief shall not be repeated!'[77] These comments and Lunacharsky's recommendation probably steered Meyerhold towards *Night*, which he hated. He disliked:

> the slackness in the play's action, the predominance of monologue rendered in the spirit of French pathos, the monotonous dramatic rhythm, the abundance in the Russian translation of particles and empty words, necessary only for the preservation of the rhythm.[78]

When his production opened on 4 March 1923 it had a new title, *The World Turned Upside Down*,[79] and a completely remade text. It was the work of the Futurist poet, Sergei Tretyakov, a member of Meyerhold's literary department and also joint editor with Vladimir Mayakovsky of *LEF* magazine.

In his own word, Tretyakov created a 'montage' of the text of *Night*.[80] He reduced the five long acts into eight self-contained episodes or 'links', he cut thirty-five per cent of the text, and substituted a more vernacular style, with concrete phrases replacing rhetorical flourishes. Thus, when the Soldier brings news of the ending of the war, and the Man from the Hills responds, the original has:

> Is it true?
> You see how wretched we all are.
> Some of us are old folk, women, and children,
> We have suffered so much,
> We have suffered enough
> To last us the rest of our days.
> Do not deceive us, do not make fun of us.[81]

Tretyakov's Man from the Hills simply says:

> You're not lying?

In the scene of the political meeting, Goutaudier is the first to speak to the crowd. In Martinet's play, he begins:

Comrades!
It is not any one of us in particular, as you know,
Whose thought it was that we should meet here.
No need for that! The idea, as you know,
Had been, so to say, alive in us for a long, long time.
For a long time, if we had dared to look within,
Long, long ago, we should have said to ourselves:
'Here we are, countless in numbers; the masses, armed;
'None can stand against us if we have but the will.
'Why should we endure this dreadful trade, this daily
    martyrdom? . . .

and so on for no fewer than fifty-eight long lines, ending with:

And if anyone has ever known what it is to have brothers,
I think that we have seen and done enough together
To say that what we have to do now is to join hands and to love
    one another like brothers.
That is what I wanted to say to you, comrades, and you must all
    have understood me.

In Tretyakov's version, Goutaudier simply says:

Comrades,
We've got our guns,
Now we want our share of power.
Murder and torture have gone on day after day.
But united, we can stop all that.
We need to decide
What we're doing, why we've come together.
Isn't it true for us,
Comrades,
That we've seen so much and lived through so much,
That it's time for us to stand together, to live like brothers.
That's all, comrades.

Structurally, while keeping Martinet's parallel between Mariette the old woman, and Generalissimo Bourbouze, who are both aged seventy, Tretyakov makes Ledrux, the revolutionary leader, Mariette's soldier son, thereby tightening the focus considerably. The three generations of the family now become the centre of the revolutionary action. This also helps to clarify the struggle as one between the peasantry and the 'Black International' – 'the proletariat are absent from the play,' as Tretyakov notes.[82] Nevertheless, the implications of the action are pointed up by Tretyakov's use of slogans projected onto screens. These operate like punctuation marks. Thus, in the scene when the Soldier brings news of peace, the peasants are defiant at first, and then determined to make a fresh start. The action is marked by captions: 'The author of war – industrial capitalism.' 'Down with the gold insignia of rank.' 'Peace to the cottage, War to the palace.', 'Knock off the crown of the last of the tsars.', 'The floor is yours, Comrade Tractor.' They perhaps more than anything else destroy Martinet's windy poetic rhythms, emphasising the moments of maximum impact rather than the play's flow. 'The reformed action complied with the principles of montage,' Tretyakov declared, 'making psychological scenes into posters.'[83]

The slogans also provide opportunities for Tretyakov's pervasive irony. As Favrolles, the turncoat, disputes the general will, the slogan, 'Workers of the World, Unite' appears; as the Emperor lowers himself, trouserless, onto his chamber pot, there is a caption, 'Rule by terrifying your enemies'; and when the contentious Favrolles accuses Ledrux bitterly of 'dictatorship', there appears the sign, 'Long Live the Dictatorship of the Proletariat.' All these have the effect of stirring the spectator, making her or him clench his fist and determine that 'this grief shall not be repeated.' Tretyakov himself argued: 'The problem for the playwright is to lift the playgoer out of his equilibrium so that he will not leave serene, but ready for action.'[84]

To achieve this end, play construction must be united with play production, and Meyerhold directed the play to maximise each moment's impact. Thus, Erast Garin:

> played the clownish cook with the live rooster . . . The Emperor had already fallen asleep in a sack and been wheeled off in a barrow. White Guards officers hauled him out of the sack, recognised him, and paid their homage. Next was my entrance. In a white jacket and hat, armed with a huge knife, I chase a live rooster in order to turn him into soup. I stumble and the rooster flies out of my hands . . . Then the chase begins; it was a comic improvisation. The audience loved the chase. The rooster stopped, blinded by the lights, and looked around him. I gave a jerk in order to catch hold of him, but he pulled out of my hands, flapped his wings madly and flew right into the audience![85]

There was the low farce of the Emperor ('a crafty Punchinello' in Trotsky's memorable phrase) defecating on his chamber pot, while the band played *God Save the Tsar*, and a few episodes later the heart-rending tragedy of the hero, Ledrux, brought home in death:

> Slowly, to the steady sound of a motor, a lorry drives onto the stage. A pause. The close friends bid farewell to the body of the deceased; the coffin is loaded onto the lorry. The motor runs softly during the pause, as if to replace the funeral march with its

humble sound. The final farewell. The lorry slowly begins to move, the motor's rhythm changes, and the lorry disappears from the stage with a roar of the motor that continues to be heard in the distance off-stage. Those attending the coffin freeze in place . . . The hypnotic sound of the motor lingers in the ears of the spectators gripped by the scene's dramatic effect.[86]

The pictorial dimension was just as critical as the aural one. Designed, like *The Magnanimous Cuckold*, by Lyubov Popova, the setting for *The World Turned Upside Down* had a stark reality which the earlier work never aspired to. Instead of making space through the construction of a windmill-cum-trestle stage, the space was itself. Anything which entered it did so not as a stylisation of something else but as a real object. Typewriters, field telephones, lorries, projection screens were what they were. This:

> fusion of art and life, and the imperative to transform life itself, led to the idea of the 'artistic' being a direct product of the real world of objects. In other words, life was transforming art and the concept of what was 'beautiful'.[87]

Moreover, the projected signs and slogans (one of which, a text by foreign minister Georgi Chicherin, remained throughout while others changed unpredictably), echoed those of the real revolution of a very few years earlier, and made a direct impact on the spectators' apprehension. And in Popova's graphic designs, they became an element of the montage themselves.

Meyerhold's staging and Popova's setting were again at one, but this time the play text itself was an equal partner in the creation. Even though it was an adaptation, not an original work, the play had a tragic dimension not seen in any earlier revolutionary drama. *The Communist* said that with this production 'the left front has achieved in the theatre . . . exactly what we workers and peasants did five and a half years ago.'[88] *The Workers Gazette* recorded that the performance was greeted with 'delirious applause'[89] and Alexander Fevralsky said that Tretyakov's script 'sounded crisp and hard-hitting', characterised by 'in some places a poster-like brilliance and in others a tragic strength'.[90] Fedorov wrote that it was 'the greatest achievement of the current season and the first major achievement in the sphere of revolutionary theatre. The immensity and simplicity, verging on grandeur, prevented the production from becoming a nine day wonder.'[91] In July, a worker named Evgeny Babin, who had seen the play on tour, wrote that:

> In *The World Turned Upside Down*, I lived through what I lived through in 1917. And this coincidence of living through it tells me

of the absolute truth of *The World Turned Upside Down* . . . As I was leaving the theatre I said to my comrade, also a Bolshevik, 'Did you recognise yourself on the stage?' and he replied, 'Yes.' We were both proud that they had produced this for us . . . From me, a Bolshevik and a soldier of the revolution, thanks to Meyerhold and his theatre: they have raised my spirits with *The World Turned Upside Down* back to the heights of the great years of 1917–21.[92]

There could be no better proof of revolutionary theatre's ability to make ordinary people take possession of their heritage than this spectator's reaction. As the Formalists pointed out, everyday life dulls us to experience. By presenting revolutionary experience in an unfamiliar context, by using clown tricks, projected slogans, deeply felt pathos, a startling, empty stage upon which real things unexpectedly intruded, Tretyakov, Meyerhold and Popova made the experience of revolution 'strange' again. Those slogans were associated with political action, not with theatre. Clowns belonged in the circus. Wrenched out of context, they had to be re-evaluated, each moment of the play had to be looked at, focused on, understood. And only then was the spectator able to reassemble the pieces of the experience offered, 'remake it' for him or herself, and thus 'take possession' of it. 'Art is a way of experiencing the making of a thing,' wrote Viktor Shklovsky, the Formalist critic who was a close friend of the authors of this production. By his criteria, the production demonstrated transparently the 'vital dynamism of the work of art'.[93]

The production was not a panacea for all revolutionary theatre's problems, but it pointed a way forward, and by 23 December 1923, *The World Turned Upside Down* had been performed a hundred times. On that day Tretyakov made a statement before the performance. He spoke of the significance of *The World Turned Upside Down* in the struggle for a new art, and of the role of the revolutionary theatre in the 'restructuring of society'.[94] The theatre's ability to penetrate reality seemed particularly clear the night the production's dedicatee, Leon Trotsky, came to the performance:

During one of the acts, turning by chance to Trotsky's place, I saw that he was not there any more. I thought that the performance was not perhaps to his taste, and that he had left the theatre unobtrusively. But after two or three minutes, Trotsky unexpectedly appeared *on stage* and, in the very midst of the play, the actors gave way to him. He made a short speech about the fifth anniversary of the Red Army which was very appropriate to the occasion. After a stormy ovation, the action on stage continued in the most natural way and Trotsky went back to his seat.[95]

141

BACK TO OSTROVSKY

12 April 1923 marked the centenary of the birth of the nineteenth-century Russian playwright, Alexander Ostrovsky, and Anatoly Lunacharsky called on the contemporary theatre to celebrate the date with new productions, suggesting in an article in *Pravda* that they were 'going back to Ostrovsky not only in order to appraise the correctness of the fundamental basis of his theatre, but also to learn from him some of the features of his craftsmanship'.[96] Lunacharsky went on to discuss a 'Theatre of the Red Way of Life', which would deal with the heroism of the Red Army, 'the Civil War which often divided loving hearts . . . the creation of a new state apparatus, the advancement of the economy, the elaboration of the new ethos in the convulsions of tormented hearts'.[97] One modern critic has noted 'the closeness of Lunacharsky's formulation to the Socialist realism formula eventually canonised.'[98] For Lunacharsky, Ostrovsky's craftsmanship, his realism and his ability to touch the heart were all models for modern dramatists.

Meyerhold might have been expected to propound an alternative, but his production of Ostrovsky's *A Profitable Post* on 15 May 1923, his first presentation at the Theatre of Revolution, was strangely uncontroversial, and his next at the Theatre of Revolution, *Lake Lyul*, by the contemporary writer Alexei Faiko, which opened on 7 November that year, also did little to stimulate its audiences in Meyerhold's usual way. But brewing up behind this respectable façade at his major theatre was one of Meyerhold's most extraordinary productions, Ostrovsky's *The Forest*, presented by his experimental workshop at the Zon Theatre on 19 January 1924.

Following Tretyakov's method, the text was reduced from its conventional five act structure into a montage of thirty-three episodes, each marked off by a blackout and a projected title. Contrasting episodes were juxtaposed to create a dynamic rhythm, within which images and ideas collided and reverberated. 'This is not a show,' wrote one reviewer, 'but some kind of volcanic eruption of emotions – loud, frothing, thundering, piled one on top of the next, like a snowball.'[99] An example of such a scene was that between the clown Schastlivtsev, played by Igor Ilyinsky, and the maid Ulita, which was staged on a seesaw. The sexual rhythm of the seesaw's motion, the girl's squeals as she rose and fell with skirts fluttering, and the finale when she sat aloft astride the plank while Schastlivtsev sat at the bottom and blew cigarette smoke out in a delicious gratified sigh, shocked and delighted the often-prurient Moscow theatregoers. The characters were painted as social types, the estate owner as an exploiter in red wig and riding breeches, the Priest in golden wig and beard. Aksyusha, the poor relation, became a modern, progressive girl, but healthy and full of energy, not the kind of leather-bound Communist *apparatchik* of Foregger's satire. Neschast-livtsev was played as a romantic actor in flowing cloak, while his companion Schastlivtsev was a circus clown. Similarly incongruous juxtapositioning was evident in the set, which had a Constructivist ramp, a 'real' thing hung from the ceiling by steel cables, facing the 'theatricalised' reality of the rural estate, and between them a rotating swing, or 'giant stride'. The whole set, as provocative as any of the sets Popova had designed, made a distinct contribution to the production's urging of the transforming power of the theatre.

Yet Meyerhold's *The Forest* might have been impossible without the Proletkult's earlier version of Ostrovsky's *Enough Stupidity for Every Wise Man*, which was presented on 26 April 1923. The production partially revived the theatre of the Proletkult, which since *The Mexican* had been sunk in wrangles and overambition. After the scandal over the pamphlet, *We Are Collectivists* [100] in November 1921, Nikolai Demidov led a group of his actors from the Sidelnikov Studio (formerly the First Central Studio) out of Proletkult to become part of the newly-established Fourth Studio of the Moscow Art Theatre, leaving Evgeny Prosvetov to run both the remnants of this Studio as well as his own Ton-Plas Studio. This was clearly unsatisfactory, and the residual Sidelnikov Studio soon asked Nikolai Foregger to take charge of their work. This he did, but his commitment was obviously to his own MastFor, and in March 1922 they asked Valentin Smyshlyaev to take over. He had been working with the First Workers Theatre group since its foundation in May 1921, but his pseudo-Stanislavskian approach was not popular with them, and in March 1922 they had parted company with him. Finally, in May 1922, the Hermitage Theatre was removed from Proletkult, leaving them without a base. It was then that Boris Arvatov proposed a drastic reorganisation of the Proletkult's theatre work to the Central Praesidium. Arvatov's premise was that Proletkult, still a basically amateur organisation, though with professional leadership, should not try to compete with professional theatres, but should concentrate on two specific areas: experimental work which aimed to develop new forms of theatre to express the new Soviet reality and agit-prop work, arguing the case for Communism through the use of 'miniature forms' pioneered by TEREVSAT and presented in workers' clubs, street corners and similar venues. This was accepted, and the Ton-Plas and Sidelnikov Studios were disbanded to make way for a mobile agit-prop group, called Peretru (PEREdvizhnaya TRUppa Moskovskogo Proletkul'ta), and a new Director's Workshop, Rezhmas, (REZHiccerskaya MASterskaya). Many members joined both groups, which were put under the direction of Sergei Eisenstein.

Proletkult's troubles were not yet entirely over. The First Workers Theatre group asked the testy Valentin Tikhonovich to lead them, and he began working on Ernst Toller's *Masses and Men*. But they found themselves at odds with him, and asked Nikolai Beresnev to take over. Work began on a different production, Upton Sinclair's *Prince Hagen*. When problems arose with this in November 1922, Boris Arvatov proposed that the First Workers Theatre should also be amalgamated with Peretru and Rezhmas. Heated opposition to this came from Valerian Pletnev, who saw in the proposal a further contraction of Proletkult which might have been fatal, coming after Lenin's latest attack and the removal of all state subsidy. However, on 8 December 1922, a compromise was reached whereby Eisenstein's groups would be taken into the First Workers Theatre and Beresnev's group would continue to work independently on *Prince Hagen*. Unfortunately, when this work was shown to the public in a dress rehearsal on 23 February 1923, it was so poor that it was stopped forthwith, leaving Peretru as the only performing group within the First Workers Theatre of the Proletkult.

Since October 1922 when Proletkult's subsidy had been removed, Peretru had been working on their version of *Enough Stupidity for Every Wise Man*.[101] Now, less than two weeks after Ostrovsky's centenary, in the erstwhile Proletkult Central Arena, formerly the Hermitage Theatre, before that Morozov's banqueting hall, they presented *A Wise Man*, in 'a magnificently keen and trenchant' adaptation by Sergei Tretyakov.[102] The setting was a green carpeted arena, almost wholly surrounded by audience. It was a circus ring, or a riding school, a contructivist space, focused but decentred, and it set up a spectator-performer relationship beyond anything Meyerhold had ever dared. At the back was a small construction with a curtained-off interior and a platform above reached by ladders. Strewn about or hanging from the ceiling were ropes, rings, trapezes, ladders; all the paraphernalia of a big-top show.

Within the magic circle, the performance 'was very witty and gay, and went at a great speed, almost too quick for some spectators . . . Perhaps the most amazing thing was the vitality of the players.'[103] The action was transferred from nineteenth-century Russia to contemporary *emigré* Paris, but the show mocked more than political spying and the *emigré* opposition: it also hit at conventional religion, sexual morality and more. Every character was conceived on three levels – the person in the story, his or her equivalent from circus or popular entertainment, and a political enemy. Thus, Glumov, played by Ivan Yazykanov, was the White Clown, and a subversive NEPman; Gorodulin was a juggler, but also the recently-empowered Mussolini, apt to exclaim 'Mama mia!' when surprised; Mamaeva was a circus equilibrist and a vamp; Mashenka an *ingénue*, as well as Mac-Lac the dealer in stocks and shares; Kurchaev, a lion tamer in fleshings and leopard skins, but also simultaneously three 'extra-polished hussars'; Mamaev, an acrobat and Milyukov (at least in Tretyakov's script, though Eisenstein seems to have made him a

16 Rezhmas, Proletkult's Director's Workshop, August 1922. Valerian Pletnev is seated in the centre of the front row, with Sergei Eisenstein next to him, right

Lord Curzon equivalent); and Golutvin, the 'mysterious' person, was Harry Piel, the film detective, and also a double-dealing NEPman; with Krutitsky becoming General Joffre and Manefa the matchmaker as Rasputin, an unremitting kaleidoscope of popular entertainment and popular perceptions of politics bubbled and sparkled, climaxing when Mamaev dragged another character onto the stage by his coat tails shouting: 'Back, back to Ostrovsky!'

As if this were not exhausting enough, the play was accompanied throughout by music, mostly fragments or themes which Zinovy Kitaev worked out with Eisenstein to intensify the emotion, or to contrast with it or to parody the action. 'Music was an indispensable, active element of *A Wise Man*,' wrote Alexander Levshin, who played General Joffre; 'the actors would not have been able to play without it.'[104] It gave them boldness to use the techniques of circus, *commedia dell'arte*, silent cinema and music hall freely. Glumov, the chameleon, even changed costume on stage, and in one breathless scene moved between Mamaev, the complaisant husband, who advised him how to amuse his wife, and Cleopatra Lvovna, the wife, who panted ardour and passion in another part of the ring:

MAMAEV.　What sort of relationship do you have with your aunt?
　　　　　　　　[*Mamaeva becomes visible above on the platform.*]
GLUMOV.　I can dance the One-Step, I don't need to be taught manners.
MAMAEVA.　[*holding out her hand*]. Kiss my hand, your problem is solved.
GLUMOV.　[*runs to her*]. But I haven't asked you anything.
MAMAEVA.　I guessed it.
GLUMOV.　Then thank you.　　　　　[*He turns back to Mamaev.*]
MAMAEVA.　Where are you going?
GLUMOV.　Home. I'm so happy.　　　　[*He returns to Mamaev.*]
MAMAEV.　Well, what I've got to say is stupid, perhaps. [*Mamaeva mimes appropriately behind.*] She's still young and beautiful . . .

A little further in the scene:

MAMAEV.　Maybe you could make eyes at her – I dare say you know how to.
GLUMOV.　No, I don't.
MAMAEV.　You don't, old fellow. Look, like this. [*He demonstrates. Glumov goes to Mamaeva and copies him.*] Like Sashenka Kerensky . . .

Two scenes from Ostrovsky's original are intercut here, one interrupting the other. Meyerhold used the device with the first two long scenes of

The Forest, which he cut together, but Tretyakov employs it relentlessly in *A Wise Man*:

> JOFFRE.   What kind do you need? [*to Mashenka*] Forty per cent comes to me for brokerage. Bank on bread rising . . . [*to Turusina*] The kind you need . . . There are plenty of them . . . [*to Mashenka*] I'm taking a million poods of American wheat. [*to Turusina*] I know exactly who you need.

The play crackles with stunts, surprises, and tricks, each 'sold' to the audience, as Eisenstein put it. The Red Clown, who becomes Glumov's mother, first appears wrapped in a huge parcel which is mistaken for American Relief Aid. When they decide to smuggle Glumov, the White Clown, out of Russia, they first try to put him in one of several sacks, each labelled with the name of a well-known prison, then they try to grind him in a pestle and mortar labelled respectively *Pravda* and *Izvestiya*, and they finally put him in a coffin, which is pierced with a sword at the German border by the border guards in a well-known circus trick: 'If there was anything alive in there, it's dead now.' When the Red Clown reappears in France, he zooms in on roller-skates. When Kurchaev sketches his cartoon of Mamaev, it is on paper stretched over a hoop, and when Mamaev sees it, he somersaults through it in fury. Turusina wears a flimsy skirt and a top (little more than two inverted lampshades), to cover her breasts; these light up or flash at moments of excitement in a refinement of Popova's revolving wheels in *The Magnanimous Cuckold*. And in what Eisenstein later called an 'Aristotelian-Rabelaisian' moment, Mamaeva escapes from the lecherous Joffre by climbing the greasy pole, or 'perch'. 'Now I'm right up the pole!' she shrieks. 'Now you're like Moscow,' replies Joffre, 'impossible to get to.' 'Yes,' she agrees, 'I'm as unattainable, and as dauntless, as Soviet Russia.' Amid such a *tour de force*, no wonder that that 'even the parts given in the manner of naturalistic theatre seemed to have eccentric attractions.'[105]

The ending piled absurdity on *coups de théâtre* in a manner Lewis Carroll might have envied. Glumov has run away, so Kurchaev will marry Mashenka. But since Kurchaev is played by three actors, a mullah will have to conduct the ceremony as his religion allows polygamy. He is brought in seated on a plank, singing a mock-holy song, then leaps off the plank to perform a Cossack dance. He holds up a sign: 'Religion is the opium of the people.' Then there is a chorus song and dance. Finally, the bride and her three grooms are packed into a large box and pots are smashed against it in a parody of ancient marriage rites, while three guests sing a comic song. Glumov returns, discovers his bride has wed another and makes to hang himself. As he ascends,

17 *A Wise Man.* Glumov in the box at the back approaches the German border, left, with France to the right, May 1923.

however, he fixes wings to his shoulders, takes a candle, and parodies the Ascension itself. Eventually, his enemy, Golutvin, appears, Glumov descends and they duel. Golutvin falls, and reveals a label – 'NEP.' 'So!' cries Glumov, 'you're a NEPman!' The two decide to return as speculators to Russia – Golutvin on the high wire above the heads of the audience, Glumov, with his servant, 'by the back way'. The Red Clown is left alone. 'Everybody's gone. But they've forgotten somebody,' he says, parroting Firs at the end of Anton Chekhov's *The Cherry Orchard*. Glumov's servant returns down the tightrope, holding onto a pulley by his teeth. The two Clowns have a water fight, the Red Clown turns to the audience: 'The end!' Fireworks explode under the seats of the spectators.

Part of the effect is gained from the danger of *real* tightrope-walking and greasy-pole climbing, complicated here by being inextricably mingled with the fantasy and grotesquerie of the drama. And all are a kind of playing. Eisenstein remembered when he was a boy playing with a friend:

> He is interested in the locomotives and the way they work. I prefer an awkward toy character whom I make late for the train and who runs between the rails like a red clown in the circus and who gets confused by the signals. Nearby real locomotives whistle and now and then you even hear the station bell. The sounds of real trains synchronise with the toy railway and the illusion of the game becomes more powerful.[106]

The relationship between theatricalisation, playing and reality is further illuminated by Eisenstein's account of the climax of the play:

> Up this wire, balancing an orange parasol, dressed in a top hat and tails and to the accompaniment of music, Grisha Alexandrov walks . . . without a safety net. There was one occasion when the upper part of the wire had been smeared with machine oil . . . Grisha sweats, puffs and pants. Although he is gripping the wire with his outstretched big toe, his feet, wearing deerskin soles, slip mercilessly backwards. Zyama Kitaev starts to repeat the music. His feet slip. Grisha will not make it. Eventually someone realises what is happening and holds out a walking stick to him from the balcony.[107]

The conflation of art with reality is deliberate, and is closely related to the Formalists' idea of 'baring the device'. At the end of the first act, Glumov says to his mother: 'That's the first step finished.' 'And the first act, too,' she replies. When Joffre asks Glumov what medal he would like, he asks for 'The Order of the System of St Stanislav'. 'I'm not playing by Stanislavsky's System,' Joffre answers. Later Mashenka asserts

'I'm no heroine out of Ostrovsky or Turgenev', and near the end when Glumov realises he has lost his precious diary, and Mamaev and his wife hurry away, bumping into Turusina, the actress squawks, 'Excuse me, my name is . . .', giving her own name.

The Epilogue includes two short sequences of film, one showing Golutvin's escape from Glumov by aeroplane, the other a visual representation of Glumov's diary, in which by trick photography he is seen to be all things to all men. By heightening (or perhaps undercutting) the overt theatricality of the piece, and transposing the action to another – apparently more realistic – medium (film), Eisenstein and Tretyakov lead the spectator to reassess not so much the subject of the play as his or her relationship with the world beyond the theatre. This is the sense of Tretyakov's assertion that 'ideology is not in the material art uses, ideology is in the processes of the development of that material, ideology is in the form.'[108]

The form was described by Eisenstein in what is probably the most important theoretical justification of revolutionary theatre, *The Montage of Attractions*.[109] In this he rejects the 'figurative-narrative theatre' of the First Workers Theatre at the Central Arena, in favour of the 'agitational theatre of attractions' developed in Peretru by Arvatov and himself. He defines an 'attraction' as 'any aggressive moment in theatre', such as those from *A Wise Man* described above, which each provoke some sort of 'emotional shock' in the spectator. These are then put together to create an 'effective structure', that is, one which 'moulds the audience in a desired direction'. This is the '*montage* of attractions'. It is in effect a sophisticated and dynamic rhythmic configuration, and a method of play construction quite different from that of naturalism. It seems highly dubious today (now that time has put Pavlov's theories into better perspective) whether a montage of attractions can evoke a specified response or reaction, or whether the audience can be 'moulded' as Eisenstein asserts (indeed, he says that the 'emotional or psychological influence' exerted by particular attractions can be 'verified by experience and mathematically calculated'). Nevertheless, as an antidote to Lunacharsky's plea to dramatise the anguish of 'loving' or 'tormented hearts', this is refreshing, and as provocative as Tretyakov's formulation: 'The theatre show is to be replaced by the theatre blow.'[110]

The montage of attractions, which sprang from the non-psychological acting styles developed by Meyerhold, Eisenstein and others, thus points the way to an appropriate method of playmaking. 'What do the masses and the Revolution want from the theatre? Only (answered Eisenstein) what goes back to the sources of traditional forms of popular spectacle: circus, fairground, attractions.'[111] There is a sense in which revolutionary theatre found its true self in this production.

TWO SERGEI MIKHAILOVICHES

'Let the theatre be an arena of action,' cried Romain Rolland. '*Joy, energy* and *intelligence*: these are the three fundamental requisites of our people's theatre . . . great emotions shared, and shared often.'[112] If any theatre this century has come close to meeting these aspirations, it was surely that run by Sergei Mikhailovich Eisenstein and Sergei Mikhailovich Tretyakov for the Moscow Proletkult in 1923–1924. Living, loving and working together in cramped rooms down an alley at the side of the Morozov mansion, in something like Bogdanov's 'comradely co-operation', they were genuinely attempting to fulfil his precept to make a working-class intelligentsia. Eisenstein and Tretyakov, indeed, were middle-class, but almost all the others were from genuinely working-class backgrounds: Judith Glizer, for instance, later an Honoured Artist of the USSR, had been a seamstress. But still the group came under unrelenting attack from Bolshevik critics and less adventurous artists alike, and they even had their access to the performance space in the mansion removed or at least restricted. But their next two productions were still as formidable and brilliant as *A Wise Man* had been.

Like many of the Russian revolutionary theatre groups, the First Workers Theatre of the Proletkult aimed not only to mount productions, but also to study, think and experiment together. It was probably the most successful of all the laboratories for new theatrical ideas: the publication of Eisenstein's *The Montage of Attractions* in May 1923 inspired energetic exploration, development and refinement of its ideas. This entailed both theoretical and practical work, and the group employed specialists like Valentin Parnakh to teach them modern dance, the popular variety artist, Viktor Khenkin, for 'comic story-telling', and artists like Armand, Tserep, and Petr Rudenko of the Three Georges for circus skills. They also studied eurhythmics, which Eisenstein later decribed as 'that useless activity, propagated by those who follow the fallacious system of Dalcroze'.[113] This was perhaps a sideswipe at the Proletkult's old Ton-Plas work, which he believed had led nowhere. But Eisenstein needed to find out why this system was, in his word, 'fallacious'. Emile Jacques-Dalcroze saw the body as 'a marvellous instrument of beauty and harmony when it vibrates with artistic imagination and collaborates with creative thought', and objected, for instance, to Nijinsky's *L'Aprés-Midi d'un Faune* because the movement was taken from sculpture, and:

> the series of pictures, most artistic in effect, [were] intentionally deprived of all the advantages given by time duration – I mean continuity – all the details of slow development, the easy preparation and almost inevitable climax of plastic movement in space.

151

Isadora Duncan, Dalcroze noted approvingly, 'surrenders her body to *continued* movement and these interpretations are the most filled with life and meaning.'[114] Aside from the comparison between Nijinsky's 'attitudes' (to use Jacques-Dalcroze's phrase) and Meyerhold's 'silhouettes', the jagged rhythm to which Jacques-Dalcroze objected was surprisingly close to montage as Tretyakov and Eisenstein defined it. But these two Proletkult leaders were also dissatisfied with Meyerhold's eclecticism which took études and exercises magpie-like from wherever he found them, and they worked out their own programme from a study of the German practitioner, Rudolf Bode, and his predecessor, François Delsarte.

Delsarte's system is based on triads, sets of three, which is how he understands what controls and directs all movement, namely:

1 The sensitive or vital states of man which find 'eccentric' modes of expression.
2 The moral or affective states which have 'normal' modes of expression.
3 The mental or reflective states which are expressed in 'concentric' forms.

Practically, this may be seen in exercises such as this one for the head: 'In the normal attitude, the head is neither high nor low. In the concentric attitude the head is lowered; this is the reflective state. In the eccentric attitude the head is elevated; this is the vital state.' Every aspect of the body must express in this way:

> If the chest is greatly dilated, this is the eccentric state – the military attitude, the sign of energy. The normal, when the chest is in a state more homogeneous, less contentious, more sympathetic. The concentric, when the chest is hollow, with the shoulders elevated and inclining forward.[115]

Interestingly, in the light of Jacques-Dalcroze's comments, Delsarte worked out his fundamental idea of 'harmonic poise' by examining classical statues, but he advised against being content with 'the brain's knowledge . . . what we are aiming for is unconscious cerebration'. The expressive quality of movement is consequently embedded in his practical exercises, as for instance, the 'spiral movement':

(a) Bring arm directly in front of body, muscular force acting only in upper arm. A rotary movement of the arm has turned the eye of the elbow (commonly called crazy bone) to the front. Now follows the evolution of motion.
(b) Putting force in upper arm, raise it to level of shoulder in front. The forearm and hand must be decomposed.

(c) At level of shoulder, force flows into forearm and unbends it; upper arm still rising. When arm is straight,

(d) a rotary movement of wrist turns hand;

(e) force flows into hand, raising it on line with arm, palm in. The arm is now directly over head, fingers pointing up.[116]

Delsarte is behind Rudolf Bode's work, which begins, for instance, with the triad, Relaxation, Contraction and Progression. Preliminary exercises aim to give the participant:

1 'Totality', that is, a sense of how the whole body participates in every movement.
2 An understanding on a physical level of his or her centre of gravity.
3 'Emancipation', that is, the body's ability to deal with the forces of gravity and inertia.

Once these principles are mastered, the participant progresses to Expression-Gymnastics proper, which aims to 'bring the organism into a psycho-physical condition which will make possible a free development and a complete control of its motor powers'.[117] Bode's exercises are much more gymnastic than Delsarte's: Deep Swings and Deep Bounds, for instance, and presses and pulls with partners which faintly recall some of Meyerhold's biomechanical études, especially those related to work movements.

Bode's Expression-Gymnastics provided the direct physical base upon which Tretyakov and Eisenstein built their system of Expressive Movement, with its concern for the centre of gravity, relaxation and organic unity. It was founded on the gymnast's mastery of movement, but Tretyakov and Eisenstein were careful to note the distinction between reality created by Expression-Gymnastics or Expressive Movement and real life itself.

> It is pointless to think that the sawing of wood expressively on the stage will earn for that actor a high rate on the sawer's labour exchange, just as the best qualified sawer will make a minimal impression on the stage.

But Tretyakov and Eisenstein also distinguished between Expressive Movement and Expression-Gymnastics. Movement becomes expressive, Eisenstein argued, when it varies from the perfect norm: a certain grotesqueness, a person limping down the street, say, expresses more than someone walking merely athletically. But perfect movement, which demonstrates complete control of the body's motor powers, can be expressive when it is theatricalised, if it:

> carries a certain accent. It is not enough to do a somersault correctly, to sit on a chair, to walk a wire, to make a threatening

gesture. The movement must also be 'sold', in the expression of circus performers: the movement must be *underscored*.[118]

This is reminiscent of Meyerhold's technique of 'pointing'.

In the 'selling' of the action lies the distinction between this system and more naturalistic styles: Eisenstein and Tretyakov's actors had to learn not 'sincerity', but properly 'infectious' movement, like the high-wire circus artist who 'infects' the watcher by his contradictory attitudes towards the act and the audience. He needs full concentration on what he is doing, yet he must also be fully aware of his audience. This duality was behind the thirsty Tarelkin's action in Meyerhold and Eisenstein's *The Death of Tarelkin*. Unable to reach the cup of water, he winked at the audience, then jauntily but surreptitiously took a swig from a bottle he (the actor) had in his pocket. Eisenstein explained the process with reference to *A Wise Man*: 'Theatre-style depiction of emotion was expanded into the abstract style of circus movement.'

The final distinction Eisenstein and Tretyakov made was between their system and circus itself, a distinction located in their approach to characterisation which Eisenstein called 'typage', and which was somewhat reminiscent of Meyerhold's 'set roles' and Foregger's 'four masks':

> Ostrovsky's drama of everyday characters suggested its own expansion into the interplay of the stylised, masked characters of the Italian *commedia dell'arte* and its great-great-grandchildren to be found in the modern circus ring. This was successful because Ostrovsky himself . . . had carried out the reverse process: he had personified the range of conventionalised, masked characters in the actual, everyday characteristics of a gallery of typical Muscovites of his own time.[119]

For Eisenstein, the conventional masked characters were *personae* distinguished by their expressive movement, thereby tying in with the original Expression-Gymnastics. The actor must learn basic movement and also train in an eccentric (and concentric) circus style:

> You know that in primitive or early language the word 'go', the concept 'go', does not exist, but forty designations exist for different goings. You go rollingly – that's one designation; you go quickly, you go stumblingly. Thirty to forty designations for shades of meaning, but not one generalised concept of going. And there we have it: a general concept of going and a series of divisions, quick, limping, jumping, etc.[120]

The product of all these ideas can still be seen in some of Eisenstein's films: in *The Strike*, for instance, in the scene when the two *agents provocateurs* meet the boss, and in *October,* when the soldier with the flag is confronted by the angry bourgeois. Both these scenes are marked by a grotesque style, actions 'sold' to the camera, and a focus on action rather than character by the performers' manifest attitudes. This last feature is achieved largely by rhythm – Eisenstein lingers fractionally on a face or a pose, interrupts the expected flow momentarily with a sculpted 'silhouette', and fractures expected responses in doing so.

The discoveries which led to this style of film-making, as well as those developing Tretyakov's skills as a playwright, were first exposed on 7 November 1923, when the First Workers Theatre of the Proletkult presented the 'agit-guignol', *Are You Listening, Moscow?!*, at the Dmitrovsky Theatre. The play tells the story of a German Count who, to keep his people in order, plans a festival for them, where a pantomime glorifying his family will be presented and a bas-relief of one of his ancestors will be unveiled. But his plans are subverted, the festival turns into a rebellion, and the bas-relief when it is uncovered turns out to be of Lenin. Expressive movement governed the presentation of the aristocrats and their hangers-on, as in the scene when Marga, the Count's mistress, haughtily cries: 'Tie my boot-laces!'

> [*Everybody throws themselves at her feet; the Count, wheezing, at last gets down on his knees with difficulty.*]
> VOICES.　What legs! Like marble! She's a goddess!
> POUND.　In a New York music hall she could make a fortune.
> MARGA.　[*squealing and laughing*]. Don't tickle! Whose are those whiskers? Count, stand up![121]

Eisenstein directed the episode so that while the Count was doing up the laces on Marga's high boot, she placed her other boot on his neck in the pose of a big game hunter with a 'trophy'. Such silhouetted 'attitudes' were deliberately contrasted with the expressive efficiency of the workers.

This gives some clue to the characterisation, or 'typage'. The workers wore their own clothes, and Kurt, the type of the hero, was seen refusing the lascivious blandishments of Marga, and he even encouraged his brother to shoot him so that the weapons for the uprising could be smuggled in. This is Grand Guignol in Eisenstein's 'sense of direct reality . . . where eyes are gouged out or arms and legs amputated on stage'.[122] But so is the type Marga represents. When the Count displays his biceps and boasts of his prowess at sword-fighting and hunting, Marga adds: 'And embracing!' Her red handkerchief symbolises 'passion', not revolution, and she is entirely contemptuous of the lower classes. Then there is the informer, Stumm, whose hand 'twitches', who speaks 'secretively', 'turns away, scared', 'listens carefully' and counsels the would-be rebels to be cautious. He stutters when challenged, his teeth chatter and his shiftiness is responsible for his

18 *Are You Listening, Moscow?!* The end of the play when Lenin's portrait is revealed. November 1923.

untimely end. And the two artists, Grubbe and Grabbe, are the Count's 'Michelangelo' and 'Shakespeare', grossly self-satisfied, and as silly as Tweedledum and Tweedledee.

Characterisation of this kind shades into 'attraction-ness'. Is Marga's entry on a camel characterisation or a typical Eisensteinian attraction? What about:

> the official court poet . . . in armour and on stilts – just like his stilted poetry. The knightly costume envelops his figure and stilt legs, forming an iron giant. At the critical moment the straps break, and, with a clatter like that of empty pails, the empty armour falls from the poet.[123]

The ending, too, seems to fuse elements of both. As the play within the play begins, with a 'plastic ballet' (presumably à la Dalcroze) and the reading of the ridiculous doggerel, the performers, portraying primitive people, 'apparently accidentally' cross a hammer and a sickle, and the rebellion begins. The Count tries to rescue the situation by insisting on the unveiling of the monument, Marga gives the signal with her red handkerchief, and in a thrilling *coup de théâtre* the huge portrait of Lenin is revealed. The workers, symbolically echoing Thaelmann's Hamburg revolutionaries, call out to the audience, 'Are you listening, Moscow?' and the audience replies, 'Yes, we're listening!'

The montage here was considerably tightened and disciplined compared to *A Wise Man*, so that the audience were never as confused as they were in that play. This was partly because here Tretyakov found a central image – the building of the festival stage and setting, which provided a dynamic central focus for the action. Within this, he managed to find scenes which echoed and illuminated each other – the Fascist conspiracy, for instance, vulgar, complacent, expressed to the accompaniment of heartless laughter, was implicitly compared with the Communist conspiracy, with its urgency, seriousness and hope. The function, to arouse the audience, make them clench their fists, was certainly fulfilled. One spectator wanted to shoot Glizer, as Marga, and when she was thrown down the ladder at the end, a student called out 'Serve her right!' so vehemently that a lady in furs near him was constrained to run out of the theatre for fear of the same treatment. A group of young workers did rush the stage one night; and the questionnaires which Tretyakov circulated in order to measure audience reaction came back with strong expressions of approval.[124]

The need to arouse is, of course, a key reason for building a performance as montage, but Tretyakov and Eisenstein also incorporated a distinct ambivalence into the play world's relationship with reality. The play-within-the-play which ends the show inevitably draws attention to the theatre's theatricality at the moment of maximum emotional agitation, especially with the final direct address to the audience, and the subsequent joining of actors and spectators in the singing of 'The Internationale'. Furthermore, this climax is supposedly set on the date of the performance, 7 November 1923: in other words, stage time becomes real time, and the play becomes part of real life.

Three years later, assessing Eisenstein's film, *Battleship Potemkin*, the critic Alexei Gvozdev wrote:

> Anyone who wants to appreciate the significance of *Potemkin* and to understand the sources it derived from, should not forget that Eisenstein was a pupil of Meyerhold . . . His work in Proletkult in Moscow is the next link in the development of 'Theatrical October'. A remarkable show Eisenstein staged in the Proletkult Theatre, *Can You Hear Me, Moscow?!* . . . was, and in the history of revolutionary theatre will always remain, a magnificent model of the maximum possible saturation of theatre with agitation. In this production Eisenstein sharply and decisively dissociated himself from the old theatre and its methods [and] borrowed the methods of the circus and the music-hall, driving them to a convincing artistic and agitational limit, beyond which beckoned the destruction of the old theatre and the formation of the new. This frightened people and in the atmosphere of theatrical reaction of recent years, in conditions of the 'persecution of leftism', Eisenstein was forced to leave and abandon work in theatre. He went into film and made *Strike* and *Potemkin*, two great triumphs that are now acknowledged by the very same people who 'rejected' left theatre. But we must not forget that his method of work has remained the same.[125]

The play *Gas Masks*, which followed *Are You Listening, Moscow?!*, is often dismissed as a failure,[126] but a performance in Birmingham, England, in August 1989, succeeded 'in bringing this long-neglected play to life . . . [and] breathed a remarkable immediacy' into it,[127] and Mayakovsky called it 'an extremely interesting work'.[128] It is in fact a more subtle piece than Tretyakov's previous plays, taking as its theme the effect of the revolution on everyday life, by dramatising an account of an industrial near-disaster from *Pravda*. Perhaps because the group now had no permanent performing space of their own, the play was first presented on 29 February 1924 at the Kursky Voksal gasworks, 'in the body of the water-powered factory [in front of] a huge machine, with a wooden platform with stairs and floorspace in front of it.'[129] This was an attempt to make the play's central image – the repairing of a fractured gas main – more immediate. But though interesting on one level, Eisenstein's decision to play here was clearly a mistake: the reality of the play related to its theatricality, not its gasworks setting.

In the play, a pipe in a gasworks is cracked but there are no gas masks for those who would repair it, because the director has spent the money stocking his personal drinks cabinet. Nevertheless, working three minutes each before they are overcome by toxic fumes and carried to the sick bay, the gasworkers heroically save the plant. Their dilemma is clear: if they duck the hideous challenge and fail to save the factory, their jobs (in the NEP period) will disappear. They are supposedly the new masters: have they the nerve and the strength of will to accept their responsibility? One worker, Foma, supported by his wife, wants to turn his back on his mates. The rest do what has to be done and in their determination become a 'mass' hero. But they are no longer the symbolic 'masses' of Mayakovsky's *Mystery Bouffe*: they are specific gasworkers with individual names in a particular plant.

The dilemma of the director and his son is woven around this story. As a good Komsomol the son wants to help the workers, but he is stopped by his father because he has a weak heart which will not stand the strain. In the end the son takes his turn in the mending work, and is killed – effectively murdered by his father who failed to buy the gas masks. The particularisation is perhaps over-schematised but the clash is real enough: the son runs away from the danger momentarily, then faces up to it. When he is carried away, the director demands special treatment for him from the medical staff, then when he thinks he is saved, has a drink and mouths revolutionary slogans. When he hears the truth, he orders his own arrest. The characterisation seems typical – the director is scornful, selfish, arrogant – but we suddenly see him as a father and his need to persuade his son is desperate and real. Typage has unexpectedly developed into something 'exemplary'.

Other characters are more nearly types – Yegorich, the boss's stooge on the works committee, is a pot-bellied hypocrite, happy to voice 'Red' slogans when they might be useful, but otherwise cynically sycophantic. He is implicitly contrasted to Dudin, the 'rabkor' newspaper 'worker-correspondent' – a good example of Tretyakov's genius as a topicaliser, for the network of 'rabkors' was only established by *Pravda* in the autumn of 1923. His transparent integrity wins the workers to the fight, but he is left pondering the truth in a remarkably modern-seeming, downbeat ending. Again, a type becomes an exemplar, and the theme is generalised. 'Who was right? Tretyakov gives no direct answer. The play exemplifies his distinctive ability to present a general social problem in concrete terms.'[130]

Despite this new thoughtfulness, Tretyakov still employs the montage of attractions to give his work immediacy and urgency. There is, for instance, the 'turn' overseen by the director, precariously perched on top of a ladder, when Vaska enters, intent on destroying the icons. He is pursued by Valkyrie-like icon-wielding women, who set about him with their holy placards. In a few moments, the icons are smashed to firewood, and Vaska holds his head but wonders, looking at the fragmented images: 'Who did the thunderbolt actually strike, me or God?'[131] Other attractions include the Komsomols vaulting athletically over the benches, the attack on the director by one choking worker (which 'balances' the near-defection of Foma), the bodies on the stretchers, the sound effects – hissing gas, factory hooters, Komsomol singing, and of course, the anonymous voices calling out. Tretyakov's new confidence in his stychomythic dialogue adds its own momentum to the show.

The montage is again dependent on the use of a known popular theatre form – in this case melodrama – and the audience's response is again governed by this 'displacement'. After *emigré* Paris had been presented as a circus, and the German revolution portrayed as *grand guignol*, the building of socialism was here conveyed by melodrama. Eisenstein hoped to create a specific distancing effect by contrasting this highly theatrical dramatic form with the harsh reality of the gas works with its real, not Constructivist, machines and walkways, its unnatural light and its smell of gas. At the beginning a worker came and sprayed the area to cleanse the air, and at the end the real night shift arrived to switch on the gas, to demonstrate that the fractured pipe was working again. The director of Kursky Vokzal gasworks, initially flattered to be host to such a show, soon found it thoroughly disruptive, and after a very few performances, he withdrew his permission for the use of the space. Nevertheless, a valid experiment had been tried, and one worker-correspondent wrote in *Pravda*:

> I see this as the first play of its kind. The play gives one a great shot of energy. It is not a rest, and it's a good thing that it's not. The play raises class consciousness, and class pride, through its hero. When you left, you stood stronger on your feet.[132]

The achievement of Eisenstein and Tretyakov was perhaps the pinnacle of revolutionary theatre. The heady buffooneries of Mayakovsky and Kamensky, the mad chases in Radlov's pseudo-circus, the engulfing monumentalism of the mass spectacles, the pinpricks of the living newspapers, the biomechanics and constructivism of Meyerhold's theatre, the modern masks and machine dances of Foregger's, all reached their tightest focus and their brightest manifestation in Eisenstein and Tretyakov's theatre. This consummation began to evaporate immediately. That winter, 1923–1924, Foregger's little theatre burned down; Lyubov Popova died; Boris Arvatov fell ill and became confined to a psychiatric hospital; Boris Ferdinandov's theatre became part-time; Sergei Tretyakov took up an appointment in China; Meyerhold withdrew from the Theatre of Revolution; FEKS switched from theatre to film-making; Sergei Eisenstein did the same; even the *avant-garde's* most enduring love affair, that of Mayakovsky and Lily Brik, cooled decisively. When the German Communist uprising in Hamburg failed in October 1923, (it had been directly encouraged by Trotsky and Zinoviev), the dream of world revolution began to fade too. And on 21 January 1924, Lenin died. The revolutionary period was symbolically at an end.

5

'WHAT HAS HAPPENED TO US ALL?'

A TANGLED WEB

The revolutionary theatre began to fade from 1924 onwards, but it did not simply disappear. On the contrary, the two 'lines' which fused in the work of Eisenstein and Tretyakov, agit-prop and epic theatre, continued and some new heights were scaled. Meyerhold's productions of both new and classic works, for instance, expanded the achievement of revolutionary theatre considerably. Perhaps inevitably, he was unable to sustain his work at both the Theatre of Revolution and the Zon while maintaining his training school, and he brought in first Valery Bebutov as assistant at the Theatre of Revolution, and then handed it over entirely to his former pupil, Alexei Gripich.

Bebutov had organised his own Romantic Theatre in Moscow in the summer of 1922, but without much success. Meyerhold tried to 'rescue' him by inviting him to the Theatre of Revolution, where he staged *Spartacus* by Vladimir Volkenstein on 6 September 1923 and a new production of Kamensky's *Stenka Razin* on 6 February 1924. But Bebutov seemed to have been left behind by developments, and these apparently revolutionary works were accorded a treatment reminiscent of RSFSR Theatre No 1's *The Dawns*, monumental and static. Gripich's production of Vladimir Bill-Belotserkovsky's *Echo* was certainly more dynamic, having a moving set, flashing lights, revolving floors, and plenty of steel girders, catwalks and other constructivist trappings. And his next production, in February 1925, *The Meringue Pie*, had an extraordinary success. Meyerhold, however, found both play and production alien to all he had striven for, and painfully, he severed his connection with the theatre, and its chairman, his long-time champion, Olga Kameneva.

At the Proletkult, Valerian Pletnev's *Over the Precipice* was presented in November 1925, and Alexander Afinogenov's first play, *They Came Across*, adapted from a Jack London story, received its premiere in February 1926. Film of this latter production has survived, and shows a lively and energetic non-naturalistic treatment of its story, which is set in New York and concerns an out-of-touch professor of political economy who 'comes across' to the proletarians. The actors' physicality, their sense of irony and the way they play to the audience are surprising considering the author's later adherence to socialist realism, but the fact that the production was designed by Meyerhold's sometime designer, Viktor Shestakov, directed by his former student, Naum Loiter, and included several of Eisenstein's group in the cast – Judith Glizer, Fokin, Kalinina, and L.A. Alexeev – may help to explain its vigour and style. Once Afinogenov became Proletkult's literary manager in 1927, the directness and athleticism were toned down.

More significant contributions to revolutionary theatre were made by another ex-Meyerhold pupil, Sergei Yutkevich who made his debut as a director with a political review, *Komsomol Christmas*, which 'created an atmosphere of great intensity on the stage',[1] and by Vitaly Zhemchuzhny in whose *An Evening of Books*, designed by Varvara Stepanova, characters stepped out of a huge book. This wild fantasy pitted Nat Pinkerton, Tarzan, God and others against heroes like John Reed and Upton Sinclair, in the battle for working-class literacy, and ended with the triumph of the Party's anti-illiteracy campaign. God, acknowledging his mistakes, agreed to make amends by appearing as an extra for Meyerhold!

Equally sensational, though less successful theatrically, was Vladimir Tatlin's production in May 1923 of *Zangezi* by Velimir Khlebnikov at the Petrograd Museum of Painting. *Zangezi* is built on a principle not unlike Eisenstein's montage, but its component parts do not yield easily to the understanding:

> Quiet! Quiet! He will speak!
>
> ZANGEZI. Ring the glad tidings of the mind! Sound the tocsin of reason, the big bell of the mind! All the different shades of the brain will pass before you in a review of all the kinds of reason. Now! Everyone sing after me!
>
> I
> Goum.
> Oum.
> Uum.
> Paum.
> Soum of me
> And of those I don't know.
> Moum.
> Boum.
> Laum.
> Cheum.
> Bom!
> Bim
> Bam![2]

19 Design by Vladimir Tatlin for *Zangezi* at the Petrograd Museum of Painting, May 1923.

More substantial than this was the work of Igor Terentiev, who had been a member of the Futurist group, 41° in Tiflis after the revolution. Terentiev first made his mark as a theatre director with *John Reed* at the Leningrad Red Theatre in 1924 – as a production, 'it stood somewhere mid-way between the experiments of Radlov and Foregger and Meyerhold's larger-scale political revues.'[3] In 1926 at the Leningrad House of the Press, he staged *Foxtrot* by Vasily Andreev, a sensational and unsentimental delving into the underworld of gangsters, prostitutes and rapists, and followed this with his own play, *A Tangled Web*, which was not only a fearless indictment of the widespread swindling in Soviet society, but also included directorial surprises such as a 'shadow show' and a 'sound montage' – dialogue counterpointed by a pre-recorded urban cacophony.

The next year Terentiev presented at the House of Press Gogol's *The Government Inspector*, which was designed, as was the whole House especially for the occasion, by students of the eccentric Pavel Filonov, who had designed *Vladimir Mayakovsky, a Tragedy* in 1913. The show was a deliberate response to Meyerhold's controversial production of the same play, but in place of Meyerhold's controlled terror, Terentiev presented a slapstick farce, and in place of Meyerhold's dozen polished doors, Terentiev used five tall, dark, distorted cubicles, which were unexpectedly mobile. The potential of these standing cupboards was enormous. For instance, 'the comedy began with all officials sitting on toilets and the mayor punctuating his soliloquy with pauses for groans of defecation.'[4] Later, Khlestakov took the mayor's wife, then his daughter, into a cubicle, each lady having divested herself of almost all her clothes before she went in, and each 'absence' from the stage was marked by lurid gurgles and telling sighs. Other attractions included two white mice running along a tightrope when the mayor blurts out: 'All night I dreamed of two mysterious rats', and there was a stunning finale when Khlestakov returned to the frozen group of bureaucrats to read Gogol's character notes about each of the petrified figures.

Terentiev's directorial work was a significant contribution to revolutionary theatre, and by this time a number of writers were contributing plays built more or less by a montage of attractions. Mayakovsky's last plays, *The Bedbug* and *The Bathhouse*, for instance, are dramatic spectacles which expose contemporary society with a ribald sense of humour and a seething fury, and then confront the audience with possible futures which could spring out of the present. His very last 'play' was the circus show, *Moscow Is Burning*, produced at the First State Circus, Moscow, by Sergei Radlov, with designs by Valentina Khodasevich, on 21 April 1930 – just one week after the author's death. It was, noted one participant:

an entirely new phenomenon in the field of circus pantomime. It was a sharp political satire developed in motion-picture style in separate sequences. Mayakovsky would not use a plot nor the plot structure traditionally used in circus pantomime. Instead he presented a montage of effective, independent *tableaux vivants* done in poster style and in the spirit of a circus performance.[5]

Radlov's experience made him an ideal director. Unfortunately he fell ill a few days before the opening and the production was taken over by Andrei Petrovsky. Nevertheless, it was full of spectacular and extravagant attractions, some of which, such as the Cossack riders, could only occur in the circus. One particularly breathtaking moment occurred when a Cossack was shot by a sniper hidden in a factory. The rider fell from his horse and rolled down a ramp, while the whole factory appeared to collapse. Another was the obligatory comic chase sequence, when the policemen (clowns) rushed at a group of workers:

> The workers scatter. A policeman runs after one of them. Meanwhile the 1st Worker sticks a pamphlet on another policeman's back. Laughter. The policemen run after this worker. He adroitly and nimbly climbs up a rope to a trapeze. The policemen pursue him and clumsily get their sabres and holsters entangled in the ropes. The worker swings from one trapeze to another, hurling down pamphlets, until he reaches a sanctuary in the cupola.[6]

Most astounding of all was the descent of the 'class pyramid' from the cupola into the ring. This was a vast, circular, tiered stand, rather like a gigantic wedding cake, upon which was an emblematic representation of the class system:

> The lights come on. A huge pyramid about 33 feet high appears in the arena. On the lowest level, shackled workers are at work; on the second level greedy representatives of the state bureaucracy (grafters, usurers, government officials); on the third, police and military officers; on the fourth, priests, mullahs, rabbis; on the fifth, the bourgeois, capitalists, high-ranking Czarist dignitaries and landowners; and at the very top, the little Czar Nicholas II, wearing a huge crown.[7]

The show was something of a throwback to *The Storming of the Winter Palace*, but it made a lasting impression on those who saw it.

Other significant contributions to the revolutionary repertoire were Nikolai Erdman's *The Mandate* and *The Suicide*, which exposed the ludicrous *non sequiturs* of early Soviet society, and the still underestimated plays of Isaak Babel and Evgeny Zamyatin. Mikhail Bulgakov's epic *Flight*, the somewhat later operas of Dmitri Shostakovich (*The Nose* and *Lady Macbeth of Mtsensk*) and the dramas of Evgeny Schwartz, all employed a montage technique more or less rigorously, but it may be that the plays of Sergei Tretyakov exemplified the new form best.

Roar, China!, produced at the Meyerhold Theatre on 23 January 1926, was a tendentious but penetrating critique of imperialism as it was operating in China, and was presented without any exotic 'chinoiserie' – so much so, indeed, that Meyerhold's old device from *The Dawns* was revived and in some performances despatches from the Chinese revolutionary struggle were read at appropriate moments during the performance. There is some justification for claiming that *Roar, China!* was the most successful of all revolutionary plays, after it was included in the Meyerhold Theatre's repertoire for its international tour in 1929. In Germany it made a powerful impact, and was described by the disapproving British Consulate General in a despatch to the Foreign Office:

> The theatre was packed, and the impression created in the audience was one of mingled pity, disgust and rage. Whilst some left the building before the performance was over, others shouted 'pfui England', 'pfui Europe', 'Nieder mit England', and other choice things.[8]

There were several other productions of *Roar, China!* in the Soviet Union, and it was also performed in Germany, Poland, Estonia, England, USA and Canada. It was produced in Japan, in India, and in China (first in Canton in 1930, then in Shanghai in 1933). After Tretyakov's death, it received some of its most memorable productions – by Jewish inmates of Czestochowa concentration camp, Poland, in 1944, where it 'was an example of passive resistance'[9] – and:

> in the fall of 1949, during the successful take-over of China by the communists, *Roar, China!* was again staged, this time in the Canidrome of Shanghai in a large open-air set with rapid scene changes made possible by lighting techniques.

Noting another production in Zurich in 1975, Walter and Ruth Meserve, who researched this play's stage history, ask: 'one wonders why *Roar, China!*, of the thousands of propaganda plays, has lasted so long, heedless of time and space, nationality and race,' and they give at least part of the answer:

> What began as a simple documentary drama became an expression of human feeling and abused human dignity throughout the world, strong enough to demand the attention of people who at various times and in many places felt themselves bound by sympathetic emotions.[10]

Such was the aim of all revolutionary drama.

BLUE BLOUSES

However interesting the development of a revolutionary epic theatre was in the second half of the 1920s, it was eclipsed for a time by the vigour of the agit-prop movement.

A good example was the work of the Meyerhold Workshop, which since its successful spring programme,[11] had acquired a subsidy and a new name, GEKTEMAS (State Experimental Theatre Workshop – Gosudarstvennaya EKsperimental'naya TEatral'naya MASterskaya) in the summer of 1923. Through the winter of 1923–1924, the members of GEKTEMAS visited factories, housing estates, and military and student quarters, discussing Marxism and the arts, demonstrating Meyerhold's techniques, lecturing, leading practical sessions, analysing and creating plays. The most spectacular results were a series of outdoor performances and mass spectacles performed the following summer, Vladimir Lyutse's *The Firm of God the Father, Son and Company*, V. Izaakson's *Two Kinds of Wife*, and Pavel Urbanovich's *An Unjust Trial*. These shows were each watched by up to 15,000 spectators, and led on to *The Crushing Defeat of the Trade Delegation from the USSR in Berlin*, created by Isaakson, Lyutse and Alexander Nesterov and presented on 15 June 1924 before 65,000 spectators, including delegates to the Fifth Congress of the Comintern. The audience was directly involved in the show, becoming German workers or Soviet demonstrators, and marching about the arena 'with such enthusiasm that when the comrades who played the German police had to disperse the demonstrators, they almost came to blows with bayonets'.[12] Nesterov, Lyutse and Mikhail Koronev then reworked Tretyakov's *The World Turned Upside Down* for outdoor performance, incorporating military personnel, mobile detachments on lorries, cars, motorcycles and so on, and a total cast of 1,500. Unfortunately the day of the performance was marred by drenching rain, but still 25,000 spectators braved the elements and received the show with great enthusiasm. On the same wet day, in the Ryansky district of east Moscow, a group under Nikolai Bogolyubov presented *Proletarians of All Countries, Unite!* with up to a thousand participants. And finally, on 20 July more than 1,500 people, including members of drama clubs, choirs, brass bands, Pioneers and members of the Red Army, took part in *The July Days, Lenin and the Party*. This was organised, prepared and shown within the space of seven days, and marked the climax of a remarkable summer's work.

The best known agit-prop group, because of its international tours, was the Blue Blouse, not, as Alexander Macheret was at pains to point out, the name of a group, nor a type of play, but a method for creating a specifically Soviet kind of play, with actuality as its subject and accessibility the key to its treatment.[13] The first Blue Blouse troupe was a living newspaper group based in the Moscow Institute of Journalism, led by Boris Yuzhanin, which first performed in October 1923. By early 1924 the group was being funded by the Moscow Trades Council and had turned professional. The success of their work led to the foundation or affiliation of a myriad of similar groups, a few managing to become professional, such as Leningrad's Left Flank theatre company, led by A.Vvedensky and Daniil Kharms, but all united through the publication of Yuzhanin's magazine, *The Blue Blouse*, which, like the earlier *Red Shirt*, printed scripts, details of staging, photographs and theoretical discussions. In 1927 they toured Germany, giving nearly a hundred performances before perhaps 500,000 people, and their success was so immediate, that they spawned innumerable Blue Blouse groups abroad, in England, France, Czechoslovakia, Latvia, China and USA as well as in Germany itself.

The magazine, *The Blue Blouse*, pinpointed the salient features of the form in an article 'What Is The Blue Blouse?': it was a living newspaper, a presentation in 'agit-form' of reality, a 'montage of political facts'; it was adaptable to widely different conditions of performance; it was created by the working class; it used all the means of theatrical expression, especially those derived from the work of Vsevolod Meyerhold and Nikolai Foregger; and its texts aimed for the qualities exemplified in the work of Vladimir Mayakovsky, Nikolai Aseev and Sergei Tretyakov – brief, precise, and compelling; it was derived from 'popular forms'; and it sought out its working-class audiences in their own locations.[14]

Few Blue Blouse shows lasted more than an hour. As with TEREVSAT, the opening was usually a strong, assertive march and song by the whole company, often the Blue Blouse 'signature tune':

> We are the Blue Blouses,
> We are trade unionists,
> We are not musical nightingales,
> We are only cogs
> In the great soldering together
> Of one working family![15]

The whole show always included plenty of music, jazz where possible, or folk songs often with new words, as in one sketch when Herriot and Macdonald enter arm-in-arm singing 'I Love You'. Dance featured frequently: 'The military exercises of the infantry, cavalry, and artillery were represented with dance,' says one report; 'the fleet too was represented . . . with the expressive means of the body.' Contemporary film also records highly polished folk dance being performed, and in Germany the Blue Blouse group presented 'a propaganda scene for physical proletarian culture which is simultaneously a critique of bourgeois sports competition. First a dancing couple is shown, then a grotesque boxing match, and finally gymnastic exercises.'[16] Given that Sergei Yutkevich, Alexander Macheret, Vladimir Mass and others graduated from Foregger's workshop to the Blue Blouse, we need not be surprised to learn that:

> One of their most effective skits is entitled 'Industrialization'. One after another the actors come out in fantastic costumes, adorned with symbols indicating factory buildings, installation of electrical stations or other items in the program of industrialization. Finally, chanting in chorus lively verses, they scramble on each other's backs and shoulders, forming a structure which is supposed to represent the finished industrial system.[17]

Other dramatic attractions included tantomoresques, mass declamations, monologues by latter-day *raek* men, farcical sketches and clowning.

Though the Blue Blouse used effects and methods consciously drawn from the fairground shows and music halls of popular culture, like TEREVSAT it treated them in such a way as to create an entirely new form of theatre, one which expressed, rather than merely reflected, the reality of revolutionary social life. When the first Blue Blouse troupe made its debut in 1923, there were no resources available for fantastic costumes, even if they had wanted them. The typical costume for the decade when the Blue Blouse was in existence consisted of blue shirt or blouse, black trousers or longish skirt, and red headscarf, though 'ingeniously made costumes are slipped over them and used both back and front'.[18] This suited characterisation which was deliberately representative and traditional, like the 'grandad' with beard of flax or the anarchistic mischief-maker like Laidakov in Dmitri Kurdin's sketch, *An Agitator at the Barracks*, who spits on the ceiling – because he has been told not to spit on the floor. Contemporary types included Red Army men, Red sailors, Chinese coolies and youthful Komsomols, villains like priests, landlords, and speculators, Mensheviks, and foreign imperialists. But such apparent simplifications did not make the Blue Blouse actor's task simpler: like the old Italian comedian, the Blue Blouse performer required extraordinary versatility. He or she had to be able to sing a song, take up a pose, tell a story, hold up a placard, somersault, dance, walk on his or her hands, manipulate a puppet and more. A play like *The International Circus*, presented in 1926, required the banker J. Pierpoint Morgan to introduce 'Europe' as a trained horse, the Italian fascist as an equestrian acrobat, rich English and Turkish petrol salesmen as a pair of clowns, and a Chinese juggler whose poles symbolised the political situation in that country. The actor was both helped and hindered by staging, which was minimal both in terms of stage space and decor – any sketch had to be adaptable to clubrooms,

20 The Blue Blouse. A worker snared in the web of capitalism.

street corners, factory canteens, village greens and the back of a lorry. Consequently it is no surprise to learn that 'the eccentric and grotesque styles pioneered by Meyerhold and Eisenstein were injected with earthy popular humour and wit which made them less abstract and immediately understandable and accessible to spectators without formal education.'[19]

Another description of the Blue Blouse audiences – 'in the first place they were young – and then lively, bubbling, thinking'[20] – suggests the success of their work, but also implies that they posed a threat to the developing dictatorship. Stalin had defeated the 'Left Opposition' and Trotsky by the time the Blue Blouse was celebrating its quinquennial, and the party's Central Committee now instigated an enquiry, to discover how it could be used in the new intensified 'class struggle' for collectivisation and the Five Year Plan. Pavel Kerzhentsev, now Deputy Director of the Party's Agit-Prop section, decided to give the Trade Unions a much greater say in Blue Blouse policy-making. Then, in the summer of 1928 the magazine, *The Blue Blouse*, was closed, and in the autumn the leading personnel, including Yuzhanin himself, were replaced. The Blue Blouse was ordered to concentrate on rural performances, and to devise little plays to propagate the Party line (and after 1930 to praise Stalin specifically), thereby shifting the emphasis from satire to exhortation. Not surprisingly, the groups, no longer self-motivated, faded away in the early 1930s, and with them went their contribution to the political debate, tendentious and challenging as it had been.

Rivalling the Blue Blouse in the mid-1920s was the Leningrad State Theatre of Agitation which grew out of the Petrograd railwaymen's Central Dramatic Studio of the immediate post-revolutionary years.[21] In 1921 this group presented an extremely tendentious drama about the suppression of the Kronstadt Rising which alienated not only most of their audiences but the company as well. The leader, Viktor Shimanovsky, gathered a new troupe, including several who had not left after the Kronstadt fiasco, and restarted the company. They mounted a number of mass spectacles in Petrograd, they advised and helped amateur groups, and began to stage their own form of agit-prop drama. This was not strictly the same as a living newspaper, being more self-consciously thematic, like *Three Days*, a literary collage about the Decembrist Rising first presented on 22 January 1922. Over a period of months the group staged more and more conventional kinds of drama, culminating in a production of Ernst Toller's *Masses and Men* in June 1923. Forced to choose between conventional drama and agitation and propaganda, Shimanovsky opted for the latter, and changed the group's name to the State Theatre of Agitation. He staged another mass spectacle, *The Constitution of the U.S.S.R.* on 6 July 1924, while now

21 The Blue Blouse. 'We stand for the proletariat.'

touring agit-prop sketches more in the Blue Blouse idiom. For example, Vladimir Voznesensky's *The Affair of the Second International* showed Labour leaders of the Second International like the Swiss Otto Lang, and the Germans, Gustav Bauer and Philipp Scheidermann, jokingly accusing one another of taking capitalist bribes. Since they had all accepted such bribes, no-one could judge them. But an ordinary worker arrives. He can – and does – pass judgement. Mikhail Rokhman's *The Waltz-Polka of the Co-operative* is perhaps more typical in that it shows young women, Masha, Olya, Nadya, whirled into the co-operative, with a good deal of clowning from the accordionist and his sidekick.

As with the Blue Blouse, the struggle against Trotsky and the 'Left Opposition' seems to have led directly to this theatre being 're-organised'. On 30 September 1927 it lost its chief dramatist, Zadykhin, its head of music, Vasily Velikanov, and others. On 10 December, Shimanovsky himself was relieved of his duties. The company was redirected towards the struggle in the countryside, where their agitation was needed by the Party. But the enthusiasm was gone, and the group faded away. Their progress from a railway workers' amateur drama group, through mass spectacles and urban agit-prop, to state-sponsored touring in rural areas, is entirely exemplary.

Finally, Leningrad also gave birth to TRAM, the Theatre of Young Workers, which scored some spectacular successes in the late 1920s, often through the use of techniques pioneered by the practitioners of revolutionary theatre. They were a group of enthusiasts when they gave their first public performance, on 21 November 1925, of Mikhail Sokolovsky's production of *Sashka the Tearaway* by Arkady Gorbenko. The idea of dynamic youth theatres supporting the Party became something of a craze, and by 1928, when Sokolovsky's original troupe turned professional, there were eleven TRAM collectives. Two years later, this had grown to seventy, and by 1932 to 300. But the Communist Party, unable to keep its fingers out of any pie, decided that TRAM would have to be reorganised. In 1932 the leadership was removed, the movement's tasks were redefined, and inevitably it sank rapidly into oblivion.[22]

I WANT A BABY

In many ways, the representative figure of the revolutionary theatre was Sergei Tretyakov, an artistic polymath whose contributions to the development of broadcast radio, journalism, documentary, film and poetry are only beginning to be appreciated. His last play's title, *I Want a Baby*, poignantly symbolises the fate of the revolutionary theatre, which yearned for progeny but which was brutally suppressed.

I Want a Baby itself was only given its Russian première in Moscow in

February 1990. The play is constructed as a montage of attractions, and has all the energy and intensity which characterise revolutionary theatre. It tells the story of Milda, a Latvian Party worker, who wishes to contribute to the revolution by bearing a child, but has no wish for a husband. The first scenes show her in the overcrowded flat block where she lives and where drug addiction is rife, and squalor, lubricity, petty illiberality, corruption and even gang rape rub shoulders with attempts to remain respectable or to adapt to a new kind of idealism. Milda chooses a good proletarian building worker, Yakov, to be the father of the child, though he is hardly a morally irreproachable Communist, and he has a *fiancée* as well. However, once he gets her with child, he becomes sentimentally paternal, until Milda despatches him back to Lipa, his girlfriend, with a hit over the head. The last scene is set three years into the future, as Milda dreams of what may be. At the 'Exhibition of Children', she receives the first prize, but it is shared with Lipa, and the next prize is won by the child of a drug addict, whom Milda had urged to have an abortion. As all the children are raised aloft, Yakov cries, in an uncanny premonition of Stalin (who was to become 'Uncle Joe', provider of 'happy childhoods'), 'Hurrah for the heroes of our age!' The non-conformist Saxoulsky is arrested, and the mothers and fathers march past jauntily – or insensitively – to music played by their children.[23]

The ending is deeply ambiguous. As Tretyakov said himself:

> The play is constructed deliberately problematically. The task of the author is not so much to give a kind of single final prescription as to demonstrate possible variants, which might provoke the healthy discussion which society needs on the serious and important questions which are touched on in the play.[24]

Later, he put it more trenchantly:

> I will not bow any more to plays which end with some kind of approved maxim, which emasculates any struggle towards understanding. The intrigue has been worked out, the conclusion has been presented, and the spectators can go and put on their galoshes in peace. I think plays which stimulate in the spectator something that lasts beyond the theatre are more valuable.[25]

This explains why he presents a montage of vivid glimpses of the diverse doings in the large flat block which is home for all the characters. Its demolition and rebuilding during the course of the action provides the central dynamic image which focuses the play's meaning. Are the Volunteer Organisers Brigade, who officiously over-arrange the 'new way of life', or the hooligans, who lurk in the shadows with hyperdermics and clenched fists, building or demolishing? What of the vast panorama in between, the undertakers, supervisors, prostitutes and flower sellers, working women and housebound housewives, circus-trained fathers, patriotic Russians in traditional blouses – a spectrum as broad as a cherry-stone counting rhyme? Out of this jostling, seething, squalid multitude, can a worthwhile and possible future be plucked?

The question leads to the nub of the play – the getting of children, the representatives of the future. The question of the selective breeding and rearing of children was much argued over in the young Soviet society as it was in the West by H. G. Wells, George Bernard Shaw and others. As the twentieth century has worn on, the problem has grown more devastatingly urgent, and today there are 'test-tube babies' growing into adults, while sperm banks store the genetic inheritance of 'men of genius' for use with suitable mothers. Such sperms can even be purchased at a price. Milda (the name, ironically, is that of a Lithuanian love goddess)[26] in some measure represents this trend. She directs her sensuality away from sex, which disgusts her, towards the act of child-bearing. Her body, she declares, is her own, and her emotions are not available for possession by someone else, least of all a man. The play thus links the question of genetic heritage with the nature of female sexuality and a woman's control over her own body, subjects whose importance has also come to be seen as increasingly important in the decades since Tretyakov wrote.

I Want a Baby is therefore in no sense a 'period piece'. Nor is it a 'love story', though like the very first revolutionary play, *Vladimir Mayakovsky, a Tragedy*, it is about love as it manifests itself both socially and personally. But Tretyakov remarked that 'in constructing this play, I have set myself a task – to discredit the so-called love intrigue, that commonplace of our theatrical art and our literature.' 'Love' is simply the means by which the real subject can be broached:

> Up to now on stage, love has been a spicy stimulant. The tension of it gripped the spectator, turning him into an 'illusory lover'. In *I Want a Baby*, love is put on the operating table and what is socially significant about it is exposed.[27]

This is achieved by laying bare all the goings-on in the block of flats, among all sorts and conditions of relationships, each one potentially fruitful in that a child could result from any of them.

There is, for instance, Saxoulsky's insouciant seduction of the vain and naive Kitty; the flat-block supervisor's blustering and banal attempts to do the same to Milda; there is Varvara's infatuation with the failed poet and drug addict, Filirinov; Andryusha's self-deluding and cowardly desire to enjoy Ksenichka; and Dr Vopitkis's narcissistic attempts to impress. Then there is Lipa, the 'girl next door', who simply wants to settle down and have a family; Laskova, who will cock her eye at anything in trousers; and the frighteningly large number of men who take advantage of Ksenichka's defencelessness and join the gang rape. Milda herself imagines that love can be planned and organised formulaically, like a Party campaign, with terms of endearment manufactured like industrial products. She asks Varvara what she should say to Yakov:

> VARVARA. Well, I'd say something like: 'Sweetie-weetie,' 'umpsy-wumpsy,' 'itsy-bitsy'.
>
> MILDA. So you can just take an adjective and add '-umpsy' or '-itsy'?

But all her careful planning for the seduction of Yakov is at the mercy of chance: when Laskova unexpectedly turns up at her flat and starts to make eyes at him, the whole edifice almost crashes to the ground. As Tretyakov himself pointed out, Milda, despite her leather briefcase and Party-inspired efficiency, is truly naïve.

Tretyakov's device of interposing one or more onlookers between the audience and the action ('selling' the action, to use Eisenstein's word), encourages us to 'struggle towards understanding'. In the first scene the fallen dummy and the drugged poet Filirinov are overlooked by all the frightened residents; Saxoulsky's ballet, the 'plastic symphony of the emancipation of women', is watched by the Factory Club Secretary ('Charming! Every gesture! Every movement of Katerina Sergeevna is fit to be cast in bronze!'); the NEPpeople's shimmy is overlooked by Yakov and Grinko; Milda's seduction of Yakov is spied on by a variety of grotesque eavesdroppers – a man in his braces, a 'horrible woman' and her little girl, a party of drunks, and an old woman who swears she 'won't peg it till I've seen how these Bolsheviks fornicate'. Even when there are no stage spectators, characters tend to 'act', as when Saxoulsky flamboyantly seduces Kitty, though even their lovemaking is interrupted and commented on by Milda. The whole play ends with the 'Exhibition of Children', and Lissitsky designed a setting for Meyerhold which used space as if for an exhibition: the audience was to be able to walk round and inspect the exhibits. Tretyakov noted how he and Eisenstein had 'thought of a performance as a kind of "exhibition of the standard-man, who has to operate under complicated conditions."'[28]

The baby is the symbol of the future, but that future is not spelled out in so many words or theses. The play attempts to open up an important area for questioning instead:

> The play isolates and examines dispassionately the expenditure of sexual energy which has as its aim the birth of a baby. It is not about how to give birth to the biggest baby possible, it is about how to give birth to the healthiest; it is about the direction of Soviet power.[29]

22 *I Want a Baby.* (1) Laskova interrupts Milda's intended seduction of Yakov, at the Berliner Ensemble, June 1989, with Andrea Salter (Milda), Klaus Birkefeld (Yakov) and Dietlind Stahl (Laskova) directed by Günter Schmidt.

23 *I Want a Baby.* (2) Laskova interrupts Milda's intended seduction of Yakov, at the Teatr u Nikitskikh Vorot, Moscow, February 1990, with Vladimir Begma (Yakov), Irina Chernykh (Laskova) and Viktoriya Zaslavskaya (Milda) directed by Robert Leach.

Consequently, *I Want a Baby* was to be a 'discussion-play' which would involve interruption of the action every so often to allow a discussion to take place on the issues and the behaviour of the characters. Whether this idea was originally Meyerhold's or Tretyakov's or someone else's is unclear, but a 'discussion-play' may be seen as the final step in creating that new relationship between the dramatic action and the watching spectator which the revolutionary theatre had sought so desperately. The real and the fictional genuinely would finally coalesce.

The stage setting which Meyerhold commissioned from Lissitsky emphasised this. Constructivist staging had remained something to be looked at from the outside, like a work of art, for all the 'reality' of *The Magnanimous Cuckold*'s 'acting machine' and for all the actuality of the cars, motorbikes, typewriters and field telephones used in *The World Turned Upside Down*. The setting for *I Want a Baby* was to be a sort of 'Milda-machine',[30] a complete environment, using the theatre's galleries and gangways for 'stage' action, seating the audience around the whole interior, and providing spectators with the means to take part in what was happening. Lissitsky 'fused architectural and theatrical elements together to create a new concept of the theatrical stage and the theatrical interior.'[31]

But the design was never realised. The play remained unstaged. Meyerhold accepted it from the author in September 1926, rehearsals began on 16 February the following year, and it was announced for the 1927–1928 season. But Glavrepertkom banned it. Tretyakov rewrote it, changing the setting to a collective farm and excising some of the more distressing material, including the gang rape and the character of the drug-addicted poet. Meyerhold, and Igor Terentiev, who wished to present the play in Leningrad, now re-applied for permission to stage it, and Tretyakov read the revised version to a meeting of Glavrepertkom on 4 December 1928. The members of the committee then gave their reactions, which were almost uniformly unfavourable: Petrov, from the Hammer and Sickle factory, said that it propagandised masturbation, and said it would offend Soviet families who went to the theatre 'for a rest'; Pavel Novitsky, a theatre critic, said it 'vulgarised' its subject; and Abram Gens, representing 'Motherhood and Babyhood', called it 'incorrect: we are not so bad, not such sexual anarchists, as the play makes out'. Valerian Pletnev, still chairman of the fading Proletkult, urged its lack of 'intelligence', and suggested that the public were not yet ready for the play. It was defended by Abram Room, the film director, a former student of Meyerhold, and by Vladimir Blyum, who declared:

> *I Want a Baby* is one of the best Soviet plays . . . Fears connected with this play are analagous to fears of Darwinism. If workers can't

24 El Lissitsky working on the model design for *I Want a Baby*, 1927.

take their families to this play, then their families are philistines. The play is colossally relevant to the present moment.

Before the committee had a chance to come to a conclusion, Meyerhold intervened to suggest that the committee should not consider just the play text, but also the interpretations and intended stagings of the two directors. He also suggested that these should be submitted to a further meeting by each independently. This was agreed, and the committee reconvened on 15 December. The whole affair now acquired an almost surreal quality, as the two directors explained how they would create a 'discussion-play', something which the stalwart Communist bureaucrats utterly failed to grasp. Meyerhold temporised and improvised: 'Of course, you could from time to time send representatives to take part in the discussions. I am completely in agreement with the opinions of Glavrepertkom'. A little later, he suddenly suggested: 'Let Tretyakov come out sometimes from the stalls and say to the actor, "Don't say it like that", and then himself say it or a different line.' Whereupon the aptly-named Raskolnikov, in the chair, added: 'And sometimes, you yourself can come out, Vsevolod Emilievich.' The result of Meyerhold's tactics was that Terentiev, despite Tretyakov's support, was not allowed to proceed, but Meyerhold did receive the committee's permission to stage the play on the lines proposed.[32]

Unfortunately, the crumbling old Zon Theatre could not bear Lissitsky's radical design, so the production was postponed until the time when Meyerhold's new theatre was to be completed. This remained a dream, and *I Want a Baby*, which could have been the highest achievement of the revolutionary theatre, remained similarly insubstantial. Yet the project seemed unique because it was the only one which contained the seeds of the revolutionary theatre's aspirations. The tragedy of an unfulfilled possible masterpiece faced all three artists, Meyerhold, Tretyakov and Lissitsky, as well perhaps as Igor Terentiev, for revolutionary theatre was typically created equally by writer, designer and director – a sort of basic 'comradely collective' in Bogdanov's phrase – and in the projected production of *I Want a Baby*, the democratic collaboration was extended to include the actors and the audience also. The whole experience could therefore have provided an example of Kerzhentsev's sense of community, as it strove to help 'to create an entirely new world from top to bottom'.[33]

The fact that the play was never staged was undoubtedly connected with the struggles ravaging almost every area of Soviet life at that time. NEP was made to give way to the collectivisation and industrialisation of the first Five Year Plan, and the 'Left Opposition', most notably that of Leon Trotsky, was defeated. In 1927 the Agit-Prop Department of the

Central Committee of the Party began its campaign against 'spiritual NEP': among other things, each theatre had to establish an Artistic Soviet now, including trade union and Party representatives, which was to have the power to veto the choice of repertoire and the acceptability of any production before being shown to the public. In January 1928 Stalin declared class war against the kulaks and in March a group of engineers in the Shakhty region of the Donbas were arrested as saboteurs and tried in the very first Show Trial. At the same time a 'cultural class war' was started, typified by Platon Kerzhentsev's speech on 13 November 1928 in Moscow's Red Hall which attacked 'Rightism' in the arts, linking it to the 'Rightist' opponents of the Party line, and specifically singling out for attack Bulgakov's play, *Flight*, then in rehearsal at the Moscow Art Theatre. In January 1929, the rehearsals were discontinued and the production cancelled.

So the struggle for 'the general line', Stalin's policies which never deviated to 'Left' or 'Right', engulfed the theatre. 'Deviation' was anything which did not accord with what came to be called 'Socialist Realism', definitively described by Andrei Zhdanov at the first Congress of Soviet Writers in 1934:

> Truth and historical concreteness of the artistic depiction must be combined with the task of the ideological transformation and education of the working people in the spirit of Socialism. This method of artistic literature and literary criticism is what we call socialist realism . . . [it] presupposes that revolutionary romanticism must enter literary creativity as an integral part, because the whole life of our Party, of our working class and its struggle consists of a combination of the most severe, most sober practical work with supreme heroism and grand prospects.[34]

In other words, the writer's responsibility was to glorify the *status quo*, and certainly not to indulge in that dangerous Marxist practice of critical debate. In theatre, what Tretyakov had called 'reception' theatre was to be preferred to 'action' theatre,[35] the 'spicy stimulants' to 'the operating table'.

In *I Want a Baby*, Saxoulsky's amateur actors play a scene of great emotional intensity and tenderness: a dying father lies in Paris when his Bolshevik son arrives to make his peace with him. 'No Bolshevik's a son of mine,' the old man shouts defiantly. 'There are no commissars in the Polyudov family. In my veins flows the blood of Catherine's court.' The old man dies unreconciled. 'Ideological claptrap,' comments the Factory Club Secretary. Saxoulsky presents the scene again. This time, the dying father lies in Moscow when his White Guard son arrives to make his peace. 'No White Guard's a son of mine,' he declares. 'There are no tsarist cavalry captains in the Polyudov family. In my veins flows the blood of Pugachev's fighters.' The old man dies unreconciled. This time the scene is 'artistically valuable and ideologically consistent', according to the Club Secretary. It is presented with 'truth', 'historical concreteness' and, of course, much 'revolutionary romanticism,' though the character does not say so, and it demonstrates how so-called 'socialist realism' can be adapted to any ruling ideology. Put the two scenes side by side in an elementary montage relationship, and the whole basis of this style of theatre is undermined as a means of social or political expression.

The Soviet Union's descent into barbarism in the 1930s is well documented. 'Trotskyism', that ubiquitous will-o'-the-wisp, was detected in revolutionary theatre as elsewhere, and records were searched. It was discovered that Meyerhold had dedicated his production of Tretyakov's early play, *The World Turned Upside Down*, to Leon Trotsky. Moreover, Trotsky had been to see it, whereas Lenin had refused to attend *Mystery Bouffe* when urged to do so. Trotsky was in fact not a particular supporter of revolutionary theatre: 'When Meyerhold . . . produces on the stage the few semi-rhythmic movements he has taught those actors who are weak in dialogue, and calls this bio-mechanics, the result is – abortive,' he wrote. But he was by no means discouraging to 'Left' art in general, saying, for instance, 'with certainty, that much in Futurism will be useful and will serve to elevate and to revive art.'[36] In September 1923 Mayakovsky had been in touch with him personally about the relationship between politics and art,[37] and the 1924 Blue Blouse sketch, *Herriot and MacDonald*, ends with the boast that though the imperialist powers may have a large navy, the Soviet Union has 'poison gas, aeroplanes and Trotsky'.[38] Trotsky was therefore a kind of icon for the *avant-garde* 'Left' theatre. Meyerhold's own closest connection to the top leadership had been through Olga Davidovna Kameneva, Trotsky's sister and Kamenev's wife, and it is significant that in 1928, once the Trotsky-Kamenev-Zinoviev 'Left Opposition' was disposed of, Stalin told the playwright Bill-Belotserkovsky that Meyerhold was 'not necessary'.[39] On the other hand, Trotsky and his lieutenants were by no means consistent in their attitudes towards revolutionary artists. Lev Sosnovsky, for instance, executed as a 'Trotskyist' in 1937, had accompanied the TEREVSAT troupe round the streets of Moscow on May Day 1920 with much enthusiasm, and had defended RSFSR Theatre No 1 against threats of closure. Yet on his own admission he was no 'admirer of Meyerhold', and he did his best to block the publication of *Mystery Bouffe*. In September 1920, after Mayakovsky had been to Court to force the State Publishing House to pay him royalties owed for the play, and won his case, Sosnovsky wrote an article in *Pravda*, 'Enough of "Mayakovskyism"'.

But truth counted for little in the atmosphere of increasingly feverish cruelty which now overtook Stalin's Soviet Union. As Mayakovsky suggested in his early *Tragedy*, revolutionary 'love' becomes a 'bestial faith' when institutionalised.[40] The *avant garde*'s relationship with Bolshevism was always fraught with tension: to argue for electrification was one thing, to do so by putting an electric wire up the backside of the revered Nikolai Gogol was quite another. On 17 December 1937, Kerzhentsev, by now President of the Committee for Artistic Affairs, published a vitriolic attack on Meyerhold in *Pravda*, under the title 'An Alien Theatre'. The following month the Meyerhold Theatre was liquidated, and in July 1939 the Master was arrested. Significantly, he was accused of being a member of the anti-Soviet Trotskyist opposition, as well as spying for Japan, England, France and Lithuania. His wife, the actress Zinaida Raikh, wrote to Stalin immediately after the arrest, arguing that since theatre people could not understand politics, politicians probably could not understand art. There was a misunderstanding in the arrest of her husband. Soon afterwards, she was brutally murdered in her home. Meanwhile, Meyerhold himself was terribly tortured, then tried and sentenced on 1 February 1940, and shot the following day.[41]

One of the remarks contained in Kerzhentsev's attack on Meyerhold was that 'over several years [he] stubbornly tried to produce the play, *I Want a Baby* by the enemy of the people, Tretyakov, which was a hostile slander on the Soviet family'.[42] Tretyakov had already been arrested in July 1937, and he too had been accused of Trotskyism and spying. The authorities had tortured him to make him name other 'Trotskyist terrorists', but he refused to implicate anyone, and when the opportunity arose, flung himself over the banisters several floors up in Butyrki Prison, Moscow, thus killing himself on the ground below.

The blade of Stalinism was already scything through revolutionary theatre. Mayakovsky had committed suicide in 1930. Olga Kameneva, Trotsky's sister, was 'liquidated'. Eisenstein was effectively silenced through the decade, despite his 1929 film in praise of 'the general line': its rich sensuality was probably not in keeping with Communist prurience. Nikolai Erdman was arrested and exiled, Yuri Olesha was also arrested but spared, and Bulgakov was defamed and virtually silenced, but not arrested. Others dealt with similarly included Afinogenov, Shershenevich, Foregger and Terentiev. Stepanova, Tatlin, Rodchenko and Lissitsky were also reduced to impotence. Proletkult writers Alexei Gastev, Mikhail Gerassimov, Vladimir Kirillov and others were imprisoned, and either executed or died in labour camps. Isaak Babel was arrested and died while imprisoned. Others included Boris Arvatov, *animateur* of the Proletkult in its greatest days, Daniil Kharms, leader of the Left Flank theatre group in Leningrad, and Alexei Gan, once supervisor of Moscow's mass spectacles.

The terrible harvest of Stalinism thus included the revolutionary theatre, which had evolved through extraordinary vicissitudes: artistic, social and political. Because it expressed the energy and the search for renewal of revolution, no later society has been able to recover or redeem it. Its legacy lies partly in those early Soviet films which still have the power to surprise, though film inevitably lacks that vital ingredient of revolutionary theatre, live performance. The Brechtian 'epic' theatre adopted some features of revolutionary theatre, too, though Brecht himself lacked passion, eschewed 'eccentrism' and was never interested in exploring the potential of 'real space'. Other theatres, such as those of Yuri Lyubimov and Augusto Boal, have used some of the features of revolutionary theatre, and wherever this has happened, it has added to the vibrancy of the presentation. From the 1920s to today, various workers' theatres, agit-prop and fringe groups have all developed aspects of revolutionary theatre brilliantly, though they have always been limited, by definition, to 'the fringe'. Revolutionary theatre's heart, by contrast, was located in Meyerhold's major Moscow theatre with its vast number of company members, its central position in the state's theatrical life, and its director's international prestige.

The loss is acute, bewildering. Evgenia Ginzburg wrote in prison at the end of 1937: 'What interesting lives we had led, and how wonderfully everything had begun! What in heaven's name had happened to us all?'[43]

CHRONOLOGY

(*Note*: The following chronology is as accurate as possible, but occasionally discrepancies in historical accounts make for uncertainties or contradictions over specific dates. This is further complicated by the fact that the Russian Empire followed the 'Old Style' calendar and was therefore ten days 'behind' the rest of the world.)

1898

14 October	Moscow Art Theatre opens: A. Tolstoy, *Tsar Fedor Ivanovich*

1899

January	First *World of Art* exhibition

1902

22 November	A. Chekhov, *The Three Sisters*, dir. V. Meyerhold, Company of Russian Dramatic Artists, Kherson

1903

19 December	S. Przybyszewski, *Snow*, dir. V. Meyerhold, Comrades of the New Drama, Kherson

1904

January	Beginning of Russo-Japanese war
1 July	Death of Anton Chekhov
13 December	First appearance of Isadora Duncan in St Petersburg

1905

9 January	'Bloody Sunday' starts year of riots and revolts, compounded by defeat by Japan
5 May	First meeting of Moscow Art Theatre Studio, dir. V. Meyerhold
October	Dress rehearsal of M. Maeterlinck, *The Death of Tintagiles*, dir. V. Meyerhold, attended by K. Stanislavsky. Work at Studio stopped

1906

| 22 November | M. Maeterlinck, *Sister Beatrice*, dir V. Meyerhold, Dramatic Theatre of V. Komissarzhevskaya, St Petersburg |
| 30 December | A. Blok, *The Fairground Booth*, dir. V. Meyerhold, Komissarzhevskaya Theatre, St Petersburg |

1907

| 6 November | F. Sologub, *Death's Victory*, dir. V. Meyerhold, Komissarzhevskaya Theatre, St Petersburg |
| 7 December | Ancient Theatre opens: *The Three Magi*, *The Miracle of Theophilus* |

1908

Theatre: A Book About New Theatre published.

29 February	Bat Theatre opens, dir. N. Baliev
1 September	Meyerhold appointed a director of Imperial theatres
6 December	Strand Theatre (dir. V. Meyerhold) and Distorting Mirror Theatre (dir. Z. Kholmskaya) open

1909

| 8 January | F. Sologub, *Vanka the Butler and the Page Jean*, dir. N. Evreinov, Komissarzhevskaya Theatre, St Petersburg |
| August | Bolshevik training school established in Capri by A. Bogdanov, A. Lunacharsky, M. Gorky and others |

1910

January	*Carnaval*, chor. M. Fokin, des. L. Bakst, Pavlova Hall, St Petersburg
19 April	Calderon, *The Adoration of the Cross*, dir. V. Meyerhold, Tower Theatre
12 October	*Columbine's Scarf*, dir. V. Meyerhold, House of Interludes, St Petersburg
28 October	Death of Lev Tolstoy
9 November	J.-B. Molière, *Don Juan*, dir. V. Meyerhold, des. A. Golovin, Alexandrinsky Theatre
10 December	E. Znosko-Borovsky, *The Transfigured Prince*, dir. V. Meyerhold, House of Interludes, St Petersburg

1911

| February | B. Geyer, *Cinema*, dir. N. Evreinov, Distorting Mirror |
| May | *Tsar Maximilian and his Son*, des. V. Tatlin, Moscow Literary Circle |

13 June	I. Stravinsky, *Petrushka*, chor. M. Fokin, Paris
18 September	B. Geyer, *Aqua Vitae*, dir. N. Evreinov, Distorting Mirror
8 November	V. Soloviev, *Harlequin, the Marriage Broker*, dir. V. Meyerhold, Nobles Assembly Hall, St Petersburg
13 November	B. Geyer, *Memories*, dir. N. Evreinov, Distorting Mirror
18 November	Ancient Theatre second season opens: L.da Vega, *Fuente Ovejuna*, dir. N. Evreinov
12 December	L. Andreev, *The Sabine Women*, dir. N. Evreinov, Distorting Mirror
31 December	Stray Dog cabaret, St Petersburg, opens

1912

20 January	E. Jacques-Dalcroze demonstrates 'Eurhythmics' at Mikhailovsky Theatre, St Petersburg
April	Striking miners shot at Lena goldfield
Summer	N. Evreinov, *The Theatre of the Soul* published
21 October	N. Evreinov, *Back Stage at the Soul*, Distorting Mirror
2 December	N. Evreinov, *The Government Inspector*, Distorting Mirror
December	V. Meyerhold, *On Theatre* published

1913

10 February	Distorting Mirror company perform for the tsar at Tsarskoe Selo
27 July	V. Mayakovsky, *Cinema, Theatre, Futurism*
September	Dr Dapertutto's Studio opens, St Petersburg
2 December	Futurist evening, Luna Park Theatre, St Petersburg: A. Kruchenykh, *Victory Over the Sun*: V. Mayakovsky, *Vladimir Mayakovsky, a Tragedy*, both dir. V. Rappaport

1914

January	First issue of Dr Dapertutto's journal, *The Love of Three Oranges*
January	Marinetti visits Russia
February	Film, *Drama in the Futurist Cabaret*
February	*Pierrot and the Masks*, chor. B. Romanov, Aeroclub, St Petersburg
23 February	M. Kuzmin, *The Venetian Madcaps*, des. S. Sudeikin, house of E. P. and V. V. Nosov, St Petersburg
7 April	A. Blok, *The Fairground Booth* and *The Unknown Woman*, dir. V. Meyerhold, Tenishevsky Hall, St Petersburg

26 April	V. Shershenevich, *A Declaration About Futurist Theatre*
28 June	Assassination of Archduke Ferdinand in Sarajevo
4 August	Beginning of World War I
29 August	Russia defeated at Battle of Tannenberg
16 December	B. Geyer, *What They Say, What They Think*, Distorting Mirror

1915

12 February	'An Evening at the Studio of Dr Dapertutto', Petrograd
3 March	Stray Dog cabaret closed
March	Tramway V, first Futurist exhibition
September	Tsar Nicholas II becomes commander-in-chief
November	N. Evreinov, *Theatre for Oneself*, Pt 1, published
16 November	N. Evreinov, *A Columbine of Today*, Distorting Mirror
December	'0.10', 'the last Futurist exhibition', includes suprematist works by K. Malevich

1916

Spring	Comedians Rest cabaret opens, Petrograd
16 December	I. Zdanevich, *Yanko, King of Albania*, mus. M. Kuzmin, Studio of B. N. Essen, Petrograd
21 December	N. Evreinov, *The Fourth Wall*, Distorting Mirror
30 December	Assassination of Rasputin

1917

6 January	Bi-Ba-Bo cabaret opens, Petrograd
25 January	A. Sukhovo-Kobylin, *Krechinsky's Wedding*, dir. V. Meyerhold, Alexandrinsky Theatre
25 February	M. Lermontov, *Masquerade*, dir. V. Meyerhold, Alexandrinsky Theatre
February	General strike in Russia
8 March	Tsar, overthrown in 'February' revolution, abdicates. Prince Lvov forms new government
23 March	The Burial of the Martyrs celebration day
16 April	V. Lenin arrives in Petrograd
16 June	First Congress of Soviets
July	Comedians Rest cabaret closes
July	A. Kerensky forms new coalition government
7–12 August	Conference to coordinate proletaraian cultural-educational organisations
30 August	A. Sukhovo-Kobylin, *The Case*, dir. V. Meyerhold, Alexandrinsky Theatre
16–19 October	Conference of Proletarian cultural-educational organisations establishes Proletkult

23 October	A. Sukhovo-Kobylin, *The Death of Tarelkin*, dir. V. Meyerhold, Alexandrinsky Theatre
7 November	Bolsheviks under V. Lenin seize power
15 November	O. Wilde, *Salomé*, dir. K. Mardzhanov, Troitsky Theatre, Petrograd
22 November	Sovnarkom puts theatre under control of state
27 November	R. Lothar, *King Harlequin*, dir. A. Tairov, des. B. Ferdinandov, Kamerny Theatre, Moscow
28 November	W. A. Mozart, *Seraglio*, dir. F. Komissarzhevsky, KPSRO Studio Theatre, Moscow
5 December	Russian-German armistice
21 December	C. Debussy, *The Toy Box*, dir. A. Tairov, des. B. Ferdinandov, Kamerny Theatre, Moscow
26 December	G. Hauptmann, *Hannele*, dir. K. Mardzhanov, Troitsky Theatre, Petrograd

1918

January	Constituent Assembly dissolved
January	A. Blok, *The Twelve*, published
29 January	Narkompros Theatre Section (TEO) founded: O. Kameneva chairman, V. Meyerhold deputy
23 February	Foundation of Red Army
23–28 February	Conference of Moscow Proletkult
3 March	Treaty of Brest-Litovsk signed
11 March	Autonomy of state theatres guaranteed by Statute
11 March	Soviet Government transferred to Moscow
15 March	Formation of MONO to oversee educational and artistic functions of theatre in Moscow
18 March	Narkompros transferred to Moscow
12 April	V. Lenin signs decree calling for 'monumental' art
1 May	Streets decorated, May Day demonstrations
1 May	Opening of Proletkult building, Petrograd
1 June	First 'Kino-Eye' newsreels
7 June	H. Ibsen, *Nora (A Doll's House)*, dir. V. Meyerhold, House of Workers, Petrograd
14 June	Mensheviks and others expelled from Soviets
June	TEO opens theatre classes in Petrograd under direction of V. Meyerhold, V. Bebutov and L. Vivien
July	N. Machiavelli, *Mandragora*, dir. N. Foregger, Theatre of Four Masks, Moscow
6 July	Expulsion of S. R.s from Soviets leaves Soviet Union a one-party state
16 July	Execution of Tsar Nicholas II and his family
28 July	All industry nationalised

6 August	Moscow TEO opens
23 August	W. Shakespeare, *Macbeth*, dir. A. Granovsky and B. Romanov, Ciniselli Circus, Moscow
August	V. Meyerhold joins Bolshevik Party
30 August	Attempt to assassinate V. Lenin
31 August	Central Dramatic Studio, Petrograd, dir. V. Shimanovsky, opens
31 August	V. Kirillov, *Dawns of the Future*, dir. A. Mgebrov, Proletkult, Petrograd
7 September	ROSTA established, director P. Kerzhentsev
15 September	TEO transfers to Moscow; Petrograd TEO headed by V. Meyerhold, Northern Oblast by M. Andreeva
15–20 September	Conference of All-Russian Proletkult
10 October	Zamoskvoretsky Theatre opens, G. Hauptmann, *The Beaver Coat*
28 October	First 'wall newspapers' (ROSTA 'satirical windows'), Moscow
7 November	Streets decorated.
7 November	First agit-train inaugurated by V. Lenin
7 November	V. Kamensky, *Stenka Razin*, dir. A. Zonov and V. Sakhnovsky, Vvedensky House, Moscow
7 November	V. Mayakovsky, *Mystery Bouffe*, dir. V. Meyerhold and V. Mayakovsky, des. K. Malevich, Theatre of Music and Drama Conservatory, Petrograd
11 November	World War armistice
7 December	First issue of *Art of the Commune*
29 December	*Pravda* warns against the decadence of Futurism

1919

January	Publication of V. Kerzhentsev, *The Creative Theatre*
January	Workers and peasants Section of TEO established, under V. Tikhonovich
6 February	N. S. Gumilev, *The Tree of Metamorphoses*, dir. K. Tverskoi, des. V. Khodasevich, Theatre Studio, Petrograd
7 February	First TEREVSAT production, Vitebsk
2–6 March	Communist International Congress, Moscow
12 March	*The Red Year*, dir. N. Vinogradov, Red Army Workshop, Petrograd
7 April	Decree mobilising entertainers to visit battle front
1 May	L. da Vega, *Fuente Ovejuna*, dir. K. Mardzhanov, Solovtsov Theatre, Kiev
1 May	*The Third International*, dir. N. Vinogradov, Red Army Workshop, Petrograd

18 May	Special meeting re nationalisation of theatres, TEO
20 May	PUR founded to direct all Soviet agitation and propaganda
May	Meyerhold, with tuberculosis, goes to Yalta; M. Andreeva takes over his post
May	Creation of First Central Theatre Studio of Proletkult, Moscow
6 June	Maly Sovnarkom accepts need to nationalise theatres
2 July	O. Kameneva, 'Why Theatres Must Be Nationalised', *Izvestiya*
12 July	J.-B. Moliere, *The Doctor In Spite of Himself*, Exemplary Theatre, Petrograd
July	TEO theatre classes in Petrograd end
27 July	O. Kameneva resigns from TEO; A. Lunacharsky takes control
1 August	A. Lunacharsky's draft decree on the nationalisation of theatres
21 August	Sovnarkom agrees to amendments to decree on nationalisation of theatres.
26 August	Formation of Tsentroteatr unites TEO and state theatres under Narkompros, effectively nationalises theatres.
1 September	Charges for theatres, circuses, etc. abolished
24 September	L. Tolstoy, *The First Distiller*, dir. Y. Annenkov, Hermitage, Petrograd
4 November	M. Maeterlinck, *Ariana and Blue Beard*, dir. V. Sakhnovsky, Exemplary Theatre, Moscow
7 November	P. Arsky, *For the Red Soviets*, dir. A. Mgebrov, Proletkult, Petrograd
7 November	V. Kamensky, *Stenka Razin*, dir. S. Radlov and B. Romanov, Theatre of Baltic Fleet, Petrograd
25 November	E. Scribe, *Adrienne Lecouvreur*, dir. A. Tairov, des. B. Ferdinandov, Kamerny, Moscow
December	State theatres, including former Imperial theatres, Moscow Art Theatre, etc., become 'Academic' Theatres, independent of TEO.

1920

8 January	*The Corpse's Bride*, dir. S. Radlov, Theatre of Artistic Divertissements, Petrograd
9 January	*Bloody Sunday*, dir. N. Vinogradov, Red Army Workshop, Petrograd
12 February	*The Monkey Who Was an Informer*, dir. S. Radlov, Theatre of Artistic Divertissements, Petrograd

17 February	Theatre of Artistic Divertissements becomes the Theatre of Popular Comedy
19 February	Moscow Soviet closes 'theatres of miniature'
21 February	Reorganisation of Narkompros into five sections; Lunacharsky relinquishes headship of TEO, offers it to M. Andreeva, then to V. Menzhinskaya, who accepts
16 March	*The Sultan and the Devil*, dir. S. Radlov, Popular Comedy, Petrograd
22 March	A. Serafimovich, *Mariana*, dir. V. Smyshlyaev, Second Central Studio, Proletkult, Moscow
22 March	PTO closes Petrograd 'theatres of miniature'
4 April	Declaration of Tonal-Plastic Association
April	TEREVSAT moves to Moscow
27 April	V. Lenin, *Left-Wing Communism, an Infantile Disorder* published
1 May	*The Mystery of Freed Labour*, dir. Y. Annenkov and A. Kugel, Petrograd
14 May	TEREVSAT first performance in Moscow
20 June	*The Blockade of Russia*, dir. S. Radlov, Petrograd
19 July	*In Favour of a World Commune*, dir. K. Mardzhanov, Petrograd
2 August	*International Festival in the Red Countryside*, dir. A. Piotrovsky, Petrograd
13 August	Announcement of the formation of International Proletkult
16 September	V. Menzhinskaya leaves TEO; V. Meyerhold appointed head of TEO
1 October	Tonal-Plastic Department transferred from TEO to Moscow Proletkult
5–12 October	Proletkult National Conference, Moscow
27 October	Meyerhold calls for 'October in the Theatre', *Izvestya*
7 November	Central Arena, Moscow Proletkult, opens
7 November	*The Storming of the Winter Palace*, dir. N. Evreinov, Petrograd
7 November	TEREVSAT triple bill, Nikitsky Theatre, Moscow
7 November	E. Verhaeren, *The Dawns*, dir. V. Meyerhold, RSFSR Theatre No 1, Moscow
November	V. Mayakovsky, *The Championship of the Universal Class Struggle*, Second State Circus, Moscow
10 November	Free Comedy Theatre opens as Petrograd TEREVSAT
14 November	V. Mayakovsky, *And What If . . .?*, and L. Subbotin,

	Skomorokh, dir. A. Zonov and N. Foregger, TEREVSAT Studio, Moscow
16 November	Defeat of Whites at Perekop ends Civil War
29 November	Opening of MastKomDram
1 December	Central Committee of Communist Party denounces Proletkult in *Pravda*
1 December	Former Korsh Theatre votes to become RSFSR Theatre No 3
14 December	V. Meyerhold, 'J'Accuse!': second call for 'October in the Theatre', *The Theatre Herald*
16 December	*Labour*, dir. E. Prosvetov, Ton-Plas Studio, Proletkult, Moscow
31 December	V. Mayakovsky, *Small Play About Priests* and M. Krinitsky, *The New Front*, TEREVSAT, Moscow

1921

30 January	Public meeting: 'Should *Mystery Bouffe* Be Staged?'
20 February	N. Evreinov, *The Main Thing*, dir. N. Petrov, Free Comedy, Petrograd
26 February	M. Kozyrev appointed head of TEO, V. Meyerhold his deputy
9 March	V. Lenin introduces NEP to Tenth Party Conference
10 March	J. London, *The Mexican*, dir. V. Smyshlyaev, des. S. Eisenstein, Second Central Studio, Proletkult, Moscow
14 March	A. Argo, N. Aduyev, D. Gutman, *Bulbus's Journey*, TEREVSAT, Moscow
17 March	Kronstadt mutiny suppressed
17 March	RSFSR Theatres put under control of MONO
21 March	I. Ehrenburg, *The End of the World*, TEREVSAT, Moscow
23 March	V. Kamensky, *Stenka Razin*, dir. K. Mardzhanov, Palace Theatre, Petrograd
28 March	*Theatrical Parodies*, dir. N. Foregger, MastFor, House of the Press, Moscow
5 April	V. Meyerhold, V. Bebutov, K. Derzhavin denounce the growth of bureaucrcacy in the arts
8 April	V. Meyerhold resigns from TEO; V. Tikhonovich becomes deputy head of TEO
April	Lunacharsky invites Evreinov to stage mass spectacle on May Day
1 May	V. Ignatov, *Dawns of the Proletkult*, Central Arena, Proletkult, Moscow
1 May	V. Mayakovsky, *Mystery Bouffe*, dir. V. Meyerhold, MONO Theatre No.1, Moscow

May	Isadora Duncan founds her own school of dance, Moscow
10 June	MONO theatres returned to control of TEO
11 July	PTO announces end of free theatre ticket provision in Petrograd
7 August	Death of Alexander Blok
21 August	*The Theatre Herald* ceases publication
24 August	N. Gumilev shot as counter-revolutionary
6 September	RSFSR Theatre No 1 closed
3 October	Sophocles, *Oedipus the King*, dir. B. Ferdinandov, Experimental-Heroic Theatre, Moscow
11 October	V. Pletnev, *Lena*, dir. V. Ignatov, First Workers Theatre of Proletkult, Moscow
18 October	GVYRM, State Directors' Workshop, dir. V. Meyerhold, opens
November	V. Mayakovsky, *Yesterday's Exploit*, dir. N. Foregger, Ryazin
7 November	*Our Idea of October*, dir. M. Sokolovsky, Petrograd
7 November	S. Minin, *The City Encircled*, dir. D. Gutman, TEREVSAT, Moscow
7 November	I. Duncan dances at the Bolshoi Theatre, Moscow
November	*We Are Collectivists* aligns Proletkult with Left Opposition
22 November	N. Bukharin denounces *We Are Collectivists*
27 November	E. Labiche, *Travels of Perichon*, dir. S. Radlov, Popular Comedy, Petrograd
December	Free Workshop of V. E. Meyerhold founded as 'Laboratory for Actor's Technique'.
5 December	'Dispute on the Eccentric Theatre', Free Comedy, Petrograd
18 December	D. Smolin, *Comrade Khlestakov*, GosTeKomDram, Moscow
31 December	V. Mass, *Kindness to Horses*, dir. N. Foregger, MastFor, House of the Press, Moscow

1922

4 January	MastKomDram closed. Meyerhold Workshop and Nezlobin Theatre amalgamate to form Actors Theatre
January	GVYRM becomes State Theatre Workshop, GVYTM
22 January	*Three Days*, dir. V. Shimanovsky, Central Dramatic Studio, Petrograd
19 February	L. Tolstoy, *The Fruits of Enlightenment*, dir. N. Popov, Actors Theatre, Moscow

February	Theatre of Popular Comedy, Petrograd, disbanded
18 March	*The Paris Commune*, dir. A. Piotrovsky, Petrograd
3 April	J. Stalin appointed General Secretary of Communist Party
20 April	H. Ibsen, *Nora*, dir. V. Meyerhold, Actors Theatre, Moscow
25 April	F. Crommelynck, *The Magnanimous Cuckold*, dir. V. Meyerhold, des. L. Popova, Actors Theatre, Moscow
1 May	*First of May*, dir. V. Shimanovsky, Petrograd
13 May	Crooked Jimmy cabaret opens, Moscow
May	TEREVSAT closes
30 May	B. Arvatov proposes reorganisation of Proletkult's theatre work
1 June	Peretru, Proletkult touring theatre, founded, dir. S. Eisenstein
12 June	V. Meyerhold, 'The Actor of the Future and Biomechanics', lecture, Moscow Conservatoire
26 June	Theatre of Revolution founded, dir. V. Meyerhold
28 June	Death of V. Khlebnikov
9 July	The Factory of the Eccentric Actor (FEKS) opens, Petrograd
July	Actors Theatre and GVYTM dissolved
August	Rezhmas, Proletkult Directors Workshop, founded, dir. S. Eisenstein
17 September	State Institute of Theatrical Art (GITIS) opens, Moscow
25 September	N. Gogol, *Marriage*, dir. G. Kozintsev and L. Trauberg, FEKS, Petrograd
27 September	V. Pletnev, 'On the Ideological Front', *Pravda*
24–25 October	Ya. Yakovlev attacks Proletkult in articles in *Pravda*
26 October	Politburo votes for Proletkult to become self-financing
29 October	M. Martinet, *Night*, dir. A. Velizhev, Theatre of Revolution, Moscow
3 November	E. Toller, *The Machine Wreckers*, dir. P. Repnin, Theatre of Revolution, Moscow
7 November	*Ever-Fresh Flowers*, chor. A. Gorsky, New Theatre, Moscow
24 November	A. Sukhovo-Kobylin, *The Death of Tarelkin*, dir. V. Meyerhold, assisted by S. Eisenstein GITIS, Moscow

1923

22 January	First demonstration evening at Meyerhold Workshop

13 February	*Machine Dances*, chor. N. Foregger, MastFor, Moscow
4 March	S. Tretyakov, *The World Turned Upside Down*, dir. V. Meyerhold, des. L. Popova, TIM, Moscow
9 March	V. Lenin suffers third stroke, loses power of speech
18 March	Second demonstration evening at Meyerhold Workshop
2 April	Meyerhold Jubilee at Bolshoi Theatre; V. Meyerhold created 'People's Artist of U.S.S.R.'
26 April	S. Tretyakov, *A Wise Man,,* dir. S. Eisenstein, First Workers Theatre, Proletkult, Moscow
9 May	V. Khlebnikov, *Zangezi*, dir. & des. V. Tatlin, Museum of Painting, Petrograd
15 May	A. Ostrovsky, *A Profitable Post*, dir. V. Meyerhold, Theatre of Revolution, Moscow
1 June	First performance by Young Ballet, Experimental Theatre, Petrograd, chor. G. Balanchivadze
4 June	*Foreign Trade on the Eiffel Tower*, dir. G. Kozintsev and L. Trauberg, FEKS, Petrograd
14 June	I. Stravinsky, *Les Noces*, chor. B. Nijinskaya, Ballets Russes, Paris
June	S. Eisenstein, 'The Montage of Attractions', *LEF*
6 September	V. Volkenstein, *Spartak*, dir. V. Bebutov, Theatre of Revolution, Moscow
1 October	A. Bogdanov arrested on suspicion of opposition
23 October	Attempted Communist rising in Hamburg, Germany, suppressed
October	Blue Blouse formed by B. Yuzhanin, Moscow
3 November	A. Bogdanov released
7 November	S. Tretyakov, *Are You Listening, Moscow?!*, dir. S. Eisenstein, First Workers Theatre of Proletkult, Moscow
7 November	A. Faiko, *Lake Lyul*, dir. V. Meyerhold, Theatre of Revolution, Moscow
24 December	film, *Fight for the 'Ultimatum' Factory*, dir. D. Bassaglio

1924

1 January	Constitution of U.S.S.R. adopted
19 January	A. Ostrovsky, *The Forest*, dir. V. Meyerhold, TIM, Moscow
21 January	Death of V. Lenin
6 February	V. Kamensky, *Stenka Razin*, dir. V. Bebutov, Theatre of Revolution, Moscow
29 February	S. Tretyakov, *Gas Masks*, dir. S. Eisenstein, First Workers Theatre of Proletkult, Moscow

27 April	film, *The Extraordinary Adventures of Mr West in the Land of the Bolsheviks*, dir. L. Kuleshov
25 May	Death of L. Popova
15 June	*D. E.*, dir. V. Meyerhold, TIM, Petrograd
15 June	*The Crushing Defeat of the Trade Delegation*, GEKTEMAS, Moscow, 5th Congress of Comintern
29 June	S. Tretyakov, *The World Turned Upside Down*, staged as mass spectacle, GEKTEMAS, Moscow
29 June	*Proletarians of All Countries, Unite!*, GEKTEMAS, Moscow
6 July	*The Constitution of U.S.S.R.*, Leningrad Agit-Theatre, Leningrad
20 July	*The July Days, Lenin and the Party*, GEKTEMAS, Moscow
24 October	*John Reed*, dir. I. Terentiev, Red Theatre, Leningrad
25 October	*Harmonious Gymnastics*, chor. L. Alexeeva, Studio of Art of Movement, Moscow
9 November	V. Bill-Belotserkovsky, *Echo*, dir. A. Gripich, Theatre of Revolution, Moscow
9 December	film, *The Adventures of Oktyabrina*, dir. G. Kozintsev and L. Trauberg

1925

30 January	N.Evreinov emigrates
19 February	B. Romashov, *The Meringue Pie*, dir. A. Gripich, Theatre of Revolution, Moscow
3 March	*Joseph the Beautiful*, chor. K. Goleizovsky, Experimental Theatre, Moscow
20 April	N. Erdman, *The Mandate*, dir. V. Meyerhold, GOSTIM, Moscow
28 April	film, *The Strike*, dir. S. Eisenstein
19 November	V. Pletnev, *Over the Precipice*, dir. T. Amtman, Proletkult, Moscow
21 November	A. Gorbenko, *Sashka the Tearaway*, dir. M. Sokolovsky, TRAM, Leningrad
21 December	film, *Battleship Potemkin*, dir. S. Eisenstein

1926

23 January	S. Tretyakov, *Roar, China!*, dir. V. Federov, GOSTIM, Moscow
4 February	A. Afinogenov, *They Came Across*, dir. N. Loiter, Proletkult, Moscow
May	V. Andreev, *Foxtrot*, dir. I. Terentiev, House of the Press, Leningrad

11 June	I. Terentiev, *A Tangled Web*, dir. I. Terentiev, House of the Press, Leningrad
26 September	V. Meyerhold accepts *I Want a Baby* by S. Tretyakov for production
3 December	film, *By the Law*, dir. L. Kuleshov
9 December	N. Gogol, *The Government Inspector*, dir. V. Meyerhold, GOSTIM, Moscow

1927

16 February	First rehearsal for *I Want a Baby* at GOSTIM, Moscow
11 April	N. Gogol, *The Government Inspector*, dir. I. Terentiev, House of the Press, Leningrad
5 October	First performance by Blue Blouse in Germany
7 November	Left Opposition attempts to demonstrate at parades for tenth anniversary of revolution.
14 November	L. Trotsky and members of Left Opposition expelled from Communist Party

1928

26 January	F. Crommelynck, *The Magnanimous Cuckold*, 2nd version, dir. V. Meyerhold, GOSTIM, Moscow
7 March	Arrest of engineers at Shakhty, Donbas, accused of sabotage
12 March	A. Griboyedev, *Woe from Wit*, dir. V. Meyerhold, GOSTIM, Moscow
April	First Five Year Plan inaugurated
18 May	Opening of trial of alleged Shakhty saboteurs
July	Last issue of *The Blue Blouse*
September	V. Mayakovsky and O. Brik withdraw from *LEF*. S. Tretyakov becomes editor of *New LEF*
September	B. Yuzhanin replaced as leader of Blue Blouse
23 October	film, S. Tretytakov, *Eliso*, dir. N. Shengelaya
13 November	P. Kerzhentsev attacks 'rightism' in the arts, Red Hall, Moscow

1929

13 February	V. Mayakovsky, *The Bedbug*, dir. V. Meyerhold, GOSTIM, Moscow
February	L. Trotsky expelled from USSR

1930

16 March	V. Mayakovsky, *The Bathhouse*, dir. V. Meyerhold, GOSTIM, Moscow
14 April	V. Mayakovsky commits suicide
21 April	V. Mayakovsky, *Moscow Is Burning*, dir. S. Radlov, First State Circus, Moscow

NOTES

1 Before the Revolution

1 Lermontov, M., *A Hero of Our Time*, Penguin, 1966, pp.28–29.
2 Kelly, Catriona, Petrushka, *The Russian Carnival Puppet Theatre*, CUP, 1990, p.212.
3 Yershov, P., *Comedy in the Soviet Theatre*, Atlantic Press, 1957, p.9.
4 Kelly, Catriona, op. cit., p.47.
5 Tolstoy, Lev, *The Fruits of Enlightenment*, Eyre Methuen, 1979, p.ix.
6 Gogol, Nikolai, *Dead Souls*, Penguin, 1961, pp.76–77.
7 Benois, Alexandre, *Memoirs*, Columbus, 1988, pp.125–126.
8 See Kleberg, L., '"People's Theatre" and the Revolution', in Nilsson, Nils Ake, *Art, Society, Revolution: Russia 1917–1921*, Almqvist and Wiksell, 1979, p.180.
9 See Valerianov, V. (Pletnev, V.F.), 'K voprosu o proletarskoi kul'tur', *Nasha Zaria*, no.10/11, 1913, pp.35–41.
10 Swallow, Norman, *Eisenstein, a Documentary Portrait*, George Allen and Unwin, 1976, p.24.
11 Benois, Alexandre, op. cit., pp. 129–130.
12 Senelick, Laurence, 'King of the Jesters But Not the King's Jester: the Pre-Revolutionary Durovs', *Theater*, Sept. 1985, p.102.
13 Quoted in Hammarstrom, David Lewis, *Circus Rings Around Russia*, Robert M.MacBride, 1958, p.42.
14 Kamensky, V., quoted in Deák, Frantisek, 'The AgitProp and Circus Plays of Vladimir Mayakovsky', *The Drama Review*, vol.17, no.1, March 1973, p.52.
15 Braun, Edward (ed.), *Meyerhold on Theatre*, Eyre Methuen, 1969, p.56.
16 Ibid., p.60.
17 Voloshin, Maxilian, quoted in Braun, Edward, op. cit., p.60.
18 Eisenstein, Sergei, *Immoral Memories*, Peter Owen, 1985, p.77.
19 Sayler, Oliver M., *The Russian Theatre*, Brentano's, 1922, p. 198.
20 Ibid., p.197.
21 Karsavina, Tamara, *Theatre Street*, Constable, 1950, p.198.
22 Souritz, Elizabeth, *Soviet Choreographers in the 1920s*, Dance Books Ltd, 1990, p.34.
23 See Senelick, Laurence (ed.), *Russian Satiric Comedy*, PAJ Publications, 1983, pp.75–99.
24 Golub, Spencer, *Evreinov: The Theater of Paradox and Transformation*, UMI Research Press, 1984, p.120.
25 Ibid., p.130.

26 See Evreinov, Nikolai, 'Originality at Someone Else's Expense', in Pearson, Tony, 'Meyerhold and Evreinov: "Originals" at Each Other's Expense', *New Theatre Quarterly*, vol.VIII, Nov. 1992, pp.325–329.

27 See Moody, C., 'Nikolai Nikolaevich Evreinov 1879–1953', *Russian Literature Triquarterly*, vol.13, 1976, p.671.

28 Collins, Christopher, *Life as Theatre*, Ardis 1973, p.xiii.

29 Braun, Edward (ed.), op. cit., Eyre Methuen, 1969, p.144.

30 Quoted in Golub, Spencer, op. cit., p.270.

31 Fokin, M., quoted in Rudnitsky, Konstantin, *Meyerhold the Director*, Ardis, 1981, p.147.

32 Eisenstein, Sergei, op. cit., p.77.

33 Fokin, M., quoted in Rudnitsky, Konstantin, op. cit., p.148.

34 See Komisarjevsky, T., *Myself and the Theatre*, Heinemann, 1929, p.98.

35 See Braun, Edward, op. cit., p.131.

36 Lawton, Anna, *Russian Futurism Through its Manifestoes, 1912–1928*, Cornell University Press, 1988, p.10.

37 Matyushin, M., 'Futurism in St Petersburg', *The Drama Review*, vol.15, No.4, p.103.

38 Kruchenykh, A., 'Our Exit', quoted in *The Drama Review*, vol.15, No.4, p.104.

39 This and subsequent quotations from: Kruchenykh, Alexei, *Victory Over the Sun*, translated by Ewa Bartos and Victoria Nes Kirby, in *The Drama Review*, vol.15, No.4, pp.107–124.

40 Matyushin, M., op. cit., p.102.

41 Kruchenykh, A., 'Our Exit', op. cit

42 See Gray, Camilla, *The Russian Experiment in Art, 1863–1922*, Thames and Hudson, 1971.

43 Matyushin, M., op. cit., p.102.

44 Mgebrov, A.A., *Zhizn' v Teatre*, Academie, 1932, pp.276–278.

45 This and subsequent quotations from: Daniels, Guy (ed.), *The Complete Plays of Vladimir Mayakovsky*, Simon and Schuster, 1968, pp. 19–37.

46 Tretyakov, S., 'From Where to Where? (Futurism's Perspectives)', in Lawton, A., op. cit., p.206.

2 Petrograd 1917–1920

1 Bogdanov, A.A., 'The Paths of Proletarian Creation', *Proletarskaya Kultura*, no.15/16, 1920, in Bowlt, John E. (ed.), *Russian Art of the Avant Garde*, Thames and Hudson, 1988, p.179.

2 Bogdanov, A.A., quoted in Sochor, Zenovia A., 'On Intellectuals and the New Class', *The Russian Review*, vol.49, No.3, p.285.

3 See Bentley, Eric (ed.), *The Theory of the Modern Stage*, Penguin, 1968, pp.455–470.

4 For a discussion of this play, see Russell, R. and Barratt, A. (eds), *Russian Theatre in the Age of Modernism*, Macmillan, 1990, pp.155–157.

5 Kerzhentsev, V., *Tvorcheskii Teatr*, GIZ, 1923, ch.5.

6 Quoted in Roberts, Spencer E., *Soviet Historical Drama: Its Role in the Development of a National Mythology*, Martinus Nijhoff, 1965, p.25 See also Bentley, Eric (ed.), op. cit., p.469.

7 Mally, Lynn, *Blueprint for a New Culture: a Social History of the Proletkul't, 1917–1922*, Ph.D.thesis, University of California, 1985, p.247.

8 Rosenberg, William G., *Bolshevik Visions*, Ardis, 1984, pp.64, 65.

9 Ibid., p.432.

10 Ibid., p.432.

11 Quoted in Mally, Lynn, op. cit., p.144.

12 Leyda, Jay, *Kino*, George Allen and Unwin, 1983, p.140.

13 Kleberg, Lars, '"People's Theatre" and the Revolution', in Nilsson, Nils Ake (ed.), *Art, Society, Revolution: Russia 1917–1921*, Almqvist and Wiksell, 1979, p.192.

14 O'Connor, Timothy Edward, *The Politics of Soviet Culture: Anatolii Lunacharskii*, UMI Research Press, 1983, p.11.

15 Lunacharsky, A.V., quoted in Gorchakov, Nikolai A. *The Theater in Soviet Russia*, Columbia University Press, 1957, p.417.

16 Annenkov, Yurii, *Dnevnik moikh Vstrech*, t.2, Inter-Language Literary Association, 1966, pp.45–46.

17 'Rezolyutsiya Pervoi Vserossiiskoi Konferentsii Proletkul'ta po Dokladu V.Kerzhentseva o Proletarskom Teatre', in Yufit, A. Z. (ed.), *Russkii Sovetskii Teatr, 1917–1921: Dokumenty i Materialy*, Iskusstvo, 1968, p.331.

18 Kameneva, O.D., in Yufit, A.Z. (ed.), op. cit., p.56.

19 Fitzpatrick, Sheila, *The Commissariat of Enlightenment*, CUP, 1970, p.18.

20 Benedetti, Jean, *The Moscow Art Theatre Letters*, Methuen, 1991, p.207.

21 See Yufit, A.Z. (ed.), op. cit., pp.380–381.

22 Lenin, V.I., 'Proletarian Culture', *Collected Works*, vol.31, Lawrence and Wishart, 1966, p.317.

23 'Pis'mo Teatral'nogo Komiteta Rossiiskoi Kommunisticheskoi Partii (Bol'shevikov) "O Proletkul'tax"', *Pravda*, 1 Dec 1920, reproduced in Yufit, A.Z. (ed.), op. cit., p.23.

24 See Fevral'skii, A., *Pervaya Sovetskaya p'esa*, Sovetskii Pisatel', 1971.

25 This and subsequent quotations from: Mayakovsky, Vladimir, *Mystery Bouffe*, first variant, 1918, in Mikhailova, A., *Classic Soviet Plays*, Progress, 1979.

26 'Rezolyutsiya Pervoi Vserossiiskoi Konferentsii Proletkul'ta po Dokladu V.Kerzhentseva o Proletarskom Teatrei, Yufit, A.Z.(ed.), op. cit., p.331.

27 'Iz Protokola Zasedanii Osobogo Soveshchaniya po Teatral'nomu Voprosu', in Yufit, A.Z.(ed.), op. cit., p.55.

28 See Gorchakov, Nikolai A., op. cit., p.144.

29 Quoted in Brown, E.J., *Russian Literature Since the Revolution*, Collier, 1963, p.53

30 Quoted in Fevral'skii, A., op. cit., p.73.

31 Jangfeldt, Bengt (ed.), *Vladimir Mayakovsky: Love Is the Heart of Everything*, Polygon, 1986, pp.225–226.

32 Golubentsov, N.A., quoted in Fevral'skii, A., op. cit., p.73.

33 Smirnov-Nesvitskii, Yu.A., *V.V.Mayakovskii i Sovetskii Teatr*, Ministerstvo Kul'tury RSFSR, 1982, p.6.

34 Mayakovsky, V.V., *Teatr i Kino*, vol.1, Iskusstvo, 1954, p.322.

35 See Gerasimov, Y.K., Lotman, L.M., Priima, F.Y., *Istoriya Russkoi Dramaturgii*, Nauka, 1987, p.46.

36 The play is not mentioned in either Segel, Harold D., *Twentieth Century Russian Drama*, Columbia University Press, 1979, or in Russell, Robert, *Russian Drama of the Revolutionary Period*, Macmillan, 1988.

37 Sobolev, Yury, *Teatral'nyi kurer*, 14 Nov 1918, quoted in Rudnitsky, Konstantin, *Russian and Soviet Theatre: Tradition and the Avant-Garde*, Thames and Hudson, 1988, p.43.

38 Bristol, Evelyn, 'Turn of a Century: Modernism, 1895–1925', in Moser, Charles A.(ed.), *The Cambridge History of Russian Literature*, CUP, 1989, p.444.

39 Sobolev, Yury, quoted in Rudnitsky, Konstantin, op. cit., p.43.

40 Wolkonsky, Serge, *My Reminiscences*, Hutchinson, 1925, p.219.

41 Shklovsky, Viktor, quoted in Mally, Lynn, op. cit. p.245.
42 Ransome, Arthur, *Six Weeks in Russia, 1919*, Redwords, 1992, pp.105–106.
43 Carter, Huntly, *The New Theatre and Cinema of Soviet Russia*, Chapman and Dodd, 1924, p.111.
44 Kelly, Catriona, Petrushka, *The Russian Carnival Puppet Theatre*, CUP, 1990, pp.182, 197.
45 See Bablet, Denis (ed.), *Le Théâtre d'Agit-Prop de 1917 à 1932*, t.2 , La Cité-L'Age d'Homme, 1977, pp.65–70.
46 Quoted in Margolin, S., *Pervyi Rabochii Teatr Proletkul'ta*, Teakinopechat', 1930, p.8.
47 Gorchakov, Nikolai A., op. cit., p.120.
48 Carter, Huntly, op. cit., pp.95–96.
49 Quoted in Mally, Lynn, op. cit., p.251.
50 Margolin, S., op. cit., p.25.
51 Sayler, Oliver M., *The Russian Theatre*, Brentano's, 1922, pp.216–217.
52 See Carter, Huntly, op. cit., ch.8.
53 Margolin, S., op. cit., p.12.
54 Quoted in Gorchakov, Nikolai A., op. cit., p.161.
55 O'Connor, Timothy Edward, op. cit., p.11.
56 Yutkevich, Sergei Iosipovich, 'Teenage Artists of the Revolution', in Schnitzer, Luda, Schnitzer, Jean, and Martin, Marcel, *Cinema in Revolution*, Secker and Warburg, 1973, p.15.
57 Ehrenburg, Ilya, *First Years of Revolution*, MacGibbon and Kee, 1962, p.88.
58 Radlov, Sergei, *Stat'i o Teatre, 1918–1922*, Mysl', 1923, pp.41–42.
59 Radlov, S., quoted in Lövgren, Hakon, 'Sergej Radlov's Electric Baton: The "Futurization" of Russian Theater', in Kleberg, Lars, and Nilsson, Nils Ake, *Theater and Literature in Russia 1900–1930*, Almqvist and Wiksell International, Stockholm, 1984, p.111.
60 See Radlov, Sergei, op. cit., passim.
61 Deák, Frantisek, 'Russian Mass Spectacles', *The Drama Review*, vol. 19, No.2, June 1975, p.20.
62 I am indebted to Dr Richard Taylor, of Swansea University, for supplying me with a copy of this film.
63 Zamyatin, Evgeny, 'The Modern Russian Theater', in Proffer, Ellenda and Proffer, Carl R (eds), *The Ardis Anthology of Russian Futurism*, Ardis, 1980, pp.207–208.
64 Carter, Huntly, *The New Spirit in the Russian Theatre 1917–1928*, Brentano's, 1929, p.180.
65 Meierkhol'd, V.E., *Stat'i, pis'ma, rechi, besedi*, vol.2, Iskusstvo, 1968, p.267.
66 Vendrovskaya, L.D., and Fevral'skii, A.V., *Tvorcheskoe Nasledie V.E. Meierkhol'da*, Vserossiiskoe Teatral'noe Obshchestvo, 1978, p.33.
67 Vendrovskaya, L.D., and Fevral'skii, A.V., op. cit., p.34.
68 Il'inskii, Igor, *Sam o sebe*, Iskusstvo, 1984, p.142.
69 *Zhizn' Iskusstya*, 24 September 1919.
70 See p. 32 above.
71 Annenkov, Yurii, 'Merry Sanatorium', *The Drama Review*, vol. 19, no.4, Dec 1975, pp.110, 111.
72 Annenkov, Yurii, quoted in Zolotnitskii, D., *Zori Teatral'nogo Oktyabrya*, Iskusstvo, 1976, p.235.
73 See Gvozdev, A. and Piotrovskii, A., *Petrogradskie Teatry: Prazdnestva v Epokhu Voennogo Kommunizma*, Khudozhestvennaya Literatura, Leningrad, 1933, p.201.
74 Derzhavin, Konstantin, 'Akter i tsirk', *Zhizn' iskusstva*, 30 March 1920.

75 Aleksandrov, A.V. quoted in Gordon, Mel, 'Radlov's Theatre of Popular Comedy', *The Drama Review*, vol. 19, no.4, Dec 1975, p.114.
76 See Gvozdev, A. and Piotrovskii, A., op. cit., p.198.
77 Sylvester, R.D. (ed.), *Unpublished Letters to Nina Berberova*, Berkeley Slavic Specialities, 1979, p.33.
78 Kuznetsov, E., quoted in Zolotnitskii, D., op. cit., p.246.
79 Quoted in Gvozdev, A. and Piotrovskii, A., op. cit., p.196.
80 Yutkevich, Sergei Iosipovich, 'Teenage Artists of the revolution', in Schnitzer, Luda, Schnitzer, Jean, and Martin, Marcel, *Cinema in Revolution*, Secker and Warburg, 1973, p.15.
81 Rudnitsky, Konstantin, *Russian and Soviet Theatre*, Thames and Hudson, 1988, p.59.
82 Radlov, Sergei, 'On the Pure Elements of the Actor's Art', *The Drama Review*, vol. 19, no.4, Dec 1975, pp.117–123. See also, 'Slovesnaya improvizatsiya v teatre', in Radlov, Sergei, *Stat'i o Teatre, 1918–1922*, Mysl', Petrograd, 1923, pp.57–60.
83 Yutkevich, Sergei Iosipovich, op. cit., p.15.

3 Moscow 1920–1921

1 Yufit, A.Z.(ed.), *Russkii Sovetskii Teatr 1917–1921, Dokumenty i Materialy*, Iskusstvo, 1968, p.381.
2 Ibid., p.377.
3 Ibid., p.66.
4 Khudozhestvenno-Prosvetitel'nii Soyuz Rabochikh Organizatsii – Artistic-Educational Union of Workers' Organisations.
5 Il'inskii, Igor, *Sam o Sebe*, Iskusstvo, 1984, pp.177, 178.
6 Ibid., pp.177–178.
7 See Meierkhol'd, V.E., *Stat'i, pis'ma, rechi, besedi*, vol.2, Iskusstvo, Moscow, 1968, pp.10–12.
8 Quoted in Golovashenko, Yu., 'Etapy geroicheskoi temy', *Teatr*, no.2, Feb 1974, p.16.
9 Braun, Edward (ed.), *Meyerhold on Theatre*, Eyre Methuen, 1969, p.170.
10 Yufit, A.Z.(ed.), op. cit., p.139.
11 Ibid., p.381.
12 See 'Theatres of Revolutionary Satire', pp.82–91 below.
13 Lunacharsky, A.V., 'Revolution and Art', in Bowlt, John E.(ed.), *Russian Art of the Avant Garde*, Thames and Hudson, 1988, p.191.
14 See Moses, Montrose J.(ed.), *Representative Continental Dramas, Revolutionary and Transitional*, Little, Brown and Co, 1924, pp.636–665.
15 Il'inskii, Igor, op. cit., p.180.
16 Zagorsky, Mikhail, quoted in Rudnitsky, Konstantin, *Meyerhold the Director*, Ardis, 1981, p.273.
17 See Yufit, A.Z.(ed.), op. cit., p.141.
18 Quoted in Fitzpatrick, Sheila, *The Commissariat of Enlightenment*, CUP, 1970, p.155.
19 See Braun, Edward (ed.), op. cit., p.164.
20 See Meierkhol'd, V.E., op. cit., pp.22, 514–515.
21 Ibid., p.22.
22 Yufit, A.Z.(ed.), op. cit., p.139.
23 Il'inskii, Igor, op. cit., p.178.
24 Golovashenko, Yu., op. cit., p.17.

25 Alpers, Boris, *The Theater of the Social Mask*, Group Theater, 1934, p.143.
26 Lunacharsky, A.V., op. cit., p.192.
27 See Meierkhol'd, V.E., op. cit., pp.24ff.
28 Shtraukh, M., quoted in Mally, Lynn, *Blueprint for a New Culture: a Social History of the Proletkul't, 1917–1922*, Ph.D. thesis, University of California, 1985, p.214.
29 Benedetti, Jean, *Stanislavsky*, Methuen, 1988, p.249.
30 L'vov, Nikolai, 'Trud', *Vestnik Teatr*, No.89–90, 1 May 1921, p.16.
31 See Schnitzer, Luda, Schnitzer, Jean, and Martin, Marcel, *Cinema in Revolution*, Secker and Warburg, 1973, p.17.
32 Carter, Huntly, *The New Spirit in the Russian Theatre 1917–1928*, Brentano's, 1929, p.118.
33 Margolin, S., *Pervyi Rabochii Teatr Proletkul'ta*, Teakinopechat', 1930, p.31.
34 Eisenstein, S., *Film Form*, Harcourt Brace, 1949, pp.7,8.
35 Margolin, S., op. cit., p.31.
36 Eisenstein, Sergei, *Immoral Memories*, Peter Owen, 1985, p.191.
37 Margolin, S., op. cit., pp.30, 31.
38 See Trabskii, A.Ya.(ed.), *Russkii Sovetskii Teatr 1921–1926: Materialy i Dokumenty*, Iskusstvo, 1975, p.270.
39 Ignatov, V.V., *Zori Proletkul'ta*, Teatral'naya Biblioteka Tsentral'nogo Komiteta, Vserossiiskogo Soveta Proletkul'ta, 1921, p.24.
40 See 'An Entirely New World', pp.30–31 above.
41 See Fitzpatrick, Sheila, *The Commissariat of Enlightenment*, CUP, 1970, p.239.
42 Pletnev, V., *Flengo*, Biblioteka Vserossiisk Proletkul'ta, 1922, p.12.
43 Pletnev, V., *Lena*, Repetuar Rabochego Teatra 'Proletkul'ta', 1921.
44 See Margolin, S., op. cit., p.32; and Fitzpatrick, Sheila, op. cit., pp.239–240.
45 Zagorskii, M., 'Protokol Obsuzhdeniya Spektaklya "Lena" v Dome Pechati', in Trabskii, A.Ya.(ed.), op. cit., p.275.
46 Pletnov, V., *Lena*, p.5.
47 O'Connor, Timothy Edward, *The Politics of Soviet Culture: Anatolii Lunacharskii*, UMI Research Press, 1983, p.11.
48 Tikhonovich, V., 'O Proletkul'te. Oshibki molodosti', *Vestnik Iskusstvo*, 1922, No.5, p.4; Pletnev, V., 'Ob Oshibkakh Starosti', *Vestnik Iskusstvo*, 1922, No.6, p.3.
49 Pustynin, M.Ya., 'Vospominaniya', in Yufit, A.Z.(ed.), *Russkii Sovetskii Teatr 1917–1921, Dokumenty i Materialy*, Iskusstvo, Leningrad, 1968, p.185.
50 Chagall, Marc, *My Life*, OUP, 1989, p.162.
51 See Hamon, Christine, 'Le Théâtre de la Satire Revolutionnaire', in Bablet, Denis (ed.), *Le Théâtre d'Agit-Prop de 1917 à 1932*, t. 1, La Cité-L'Age d'Homme, 1977, p.82.
52 See 'Blue Blouses', pp.168–172 below.
53 Mayakovsky, Vladimir, *P'eska pro Popov, koi ne ponimayut, prazdnik chto takoe*, in Mayakovsky, V.V., *Sobranie Sochinenii*, Pravda, 1978, p.244.
54 Mayakovsky, Vladimir, *Kak kto Provodit vremya, Prazdniki Prazdnuya*, in Mayakovsky, V.V., op. cit., p.250.
55 Hamon, Christine, op. cit., p.80.
56 Krinitskii, Mark, *Novyi Front*, Put' Prosveshcheniya, 1923, p.5.
57 See Yufit, A.Z.(ed.), op. cit., p.184.
58 Zolotnitskii, D., *Zori Teatral'nogo Oktyabrya*, Iskusstvo, 1976, p.188.
59 Ibid.
60 Yufit, A.Z.(ed.), op. cit., p.399.
61 Ibid., p.400.

62 Hamon, Christine, op. cit., p.81.

63 Komardenkov, Vasily, 'Vospominaniya', in Yufit, A.Z.(ed.), op. cit., p.188.

64 The film in *The Iron Heel* is not listed in the Filmography in Karaganov, A., *Vsevolod Pudovkin*, Iskusstvo, 1983. It is wrongly credited to Gardin in Leyda, Jay, *Kino*, George Allen and Unwin, 1983, p.426.

65 See 'Stand and Marvel', pp.31–32 above.

66 'Iz Obzora Deyatel'nosti TEO Narkomprosa s Oktyabrya 1920g. po Yanvar' 1921g.', in Yufit, A.Z.(ed.), *Russkii Sovetskii Teatr 1917–1921, Dokumenty i Materialy*, Iskusstvo, Leningrad, 1968, p.70.

67 Zolotnitskii, D., op. cit., p.141.

68 Neverov, Aleksandr, *Grazhdanskaya Voina*, GIZ, 1922.

69 Mass, V. and Subbotin, L., *Prazdnik Mashiny*, in *Derevii Teatr*, Tret'e Izdanie, 1925.

70 Pearson, Anthony G., '"Crooked Jimmy" and "Limping Joe": Russian Theatrical Satire in the 1920s', *Theatre Research International*, vol.4, no.3, p.222.

71 Smirnov-Nesvitsky, Yu.A., *V.V.Mayakovskii i Sovetskii Teatr*, Ministerstvo Kul'tury RSFSR, Leningrad, 1982, p.31.

72 Quoted in Rudnitsky, Konstantin, *Russian and Soviet Theatre: Tradition and the 'Avant Garde'*, Thames and Hudson, 1988, p.49.

73 Ehrenburg, Ilya, *First Years of Revolution*, MacGibbon and Key, 1962, p.89.

74 Quoted in Yufit, A.Z.(ed.), op. cit., p.399.

75 Pearson, Anthony G., op. cit., p.219.

76 This and subsequent quotations from: Mayakovsky, Vladimir, *The Championship of the Universal Class Struggle*, trans. Frantisek Deák, *The Drama Review*, vol.17, no.1, March 1973, pp.55–63.

77 Zolotnitskii, D., op. cit., p.145.

78 This and subsequent quotations from: Daniels, Guy (ed.), *The Complete Plays of Vladimir Mayakovsky*, Simon and Schuster, 1968, pp.45–46.

79 Il'inskii, Igor, op. cit., p.198.

80 Fevral'skii, A., *Vstrechi s Meierkhol'dom*, Iskusstvo, 1967, p.185.

81 Symons, James M., *Meyerhold's Theatre of the Grotesque*, Rivers Press, 1973, p.56.

82 Ralston, W.R.S., *Russian Folk-Tales*, London, 1873, p.59.

83 Golovashenko, Yu, 'Etapy geroicheskoi temy', *Teatr*, no.2, Feb 1974, p.17.

84 Meierkhol'd, *Stat'i, pis'ma, rechi, besedi*, vol.2, Iskusstvo, Moscow, p.26.

85 Cheremin, G.S., *V.V.Mayakovskii v Literaturnoi Kritike 1917–1925*, Nauka, 1985, p.135.

86 Zagorsky, M., 'Kak reagiruet zritel'?', *LEF*, no.2(6), 1924, pp.144,146.

87 Yufit, A.Z.(ed.), op. cit., p.156.

88 Ibid., pp.142, 156.

89 Fülöp-Miller, René, *The Mind and Face of Bolshevism*, G.P.Putnam's Sons, 1927, pp.148–9.

90 See 'October in the Theatre', p68 above.

4 Revolutionary Theatres, 1921–1924

1 Garin, Erast, *S Meierkhol'dom*, Iskusstvo, , 1974, pp.33, 44.

2 See 'An Entirely New World', pp.22–23 above.

3 Garin, Erast, op. cit., p.27.

4 Quoted in Golovashenko, Yu., 'Etapy geroicheskoi temy', *Teatr*, No.2, p.16.

5 Pushkin, Aleksandr, 'On National-Popular Drama and the Play *Martha the*

Seneschal's Wife', translated in Senelick, Laurence, *Russian Dramatic Theory from Pushkin to the Symbolists*, University of Texas Press, 1981, p.10.

6 Translated in Hoover, Marjorie L., *Meyerhold: The Art of Conscious Theater*, University of Massachusetts Press, 1974.

7 See Stanislavsky, Konstantin, *An Actor Prepares*, Geoffrey Bles, 1962, pp.271ff.

8 Diderot, Denis, 'The Paradox of Acting', in Cole, Toby, and Chinoy, Helen Krich, *Actors on Acting*, Crown, 1970, pp.164–165.

9 Meierkhol'd, Vsevolod, 'Printsipy Biomekanika', *Teatral'naya Zhizn'*, Jan 1990.

10 *Stanovlenie Sovetskogo Teatr: Kinovidetel'stva Epokhi*, dir. A.Yu. Tikhomirov, GITIS, 1988.

11 For a full description and discussion of biomechanics, see Leach, Robert, *Vsevolod Meyerhold*, CUP, 1989, pp.46–84.

12 Eisenstein, Sergei, *Immoral Memories*, Peter Owen, 1985, p.79. For a fuller account of *Nora*, see Rudnitsky, Konstantin, *Meyerhold the Director*, Ardis, 1981, pp.288–290.

13 See especially: Law, Alma H., 'Meyerhold's *The Magnanimous Cuckold (1922)*', *The Drama Review*, vol.26, no.1, 1982, pp.60–68; Rudnitsky, Konstantin, op. cit., pp.290–310; Worrall, Nick, 'Meyerhold's Production of *The Magnificent Cuckold*', *The Drama Review*, vol.17, no.1, 1973, pp.14–34.

14 Sarabianov, Dmitri V., and Adaskina, Natalia L., *Popova*, Harry N.Abrams, 1990, p.217.

15 Tretiyakov, S., 'Velikodushnyi Rogonosets', *Zrelishcha*, no.8, 1922, p.12

16 Braun, Edward (ed.), *Meyerhold on Theatre*, Eyre Methuen, 1969, pp.204–205.

17 See Zolotnitskii, D., *Budni i Prazdniki Teatral'nogo Oktyabrya*, Iskusstvo, 1978, p.32.

18 'Frank', 'Otkrytie gitis', *Zrelishcha*, no.5, 1922, p.12.

19 See Rudnitsky, Konstantin, op. cit., p.312.

20 Eisenstein, S., quoted in Yurenev, R., *Sergei Eizenshtein: Zamysly- Fil'my-Metod*, vol.1, Iskusstvo, 1985, p.52.

21 Rudnitsky, Konstantin, op. cit., p.312. See pp.310–313 for a more detailed discussion of this production.

22 Efros, A.M., *Kamerny teatr i ego khudozhniki*, Academia, 1934, p.xxx.

23 Beskin, E., quoted in Rudnitsky, Konstantin, *Russian and Soviet Theatre: Tradition and the Avant Garde*, Thames and Hudson, 1988, p.112.

24 Meierkhol'd, V.E., *Stati, pis'ma, rechi, besedy*, t.2 Iskusstvo, 1968, p.50.

25 Ferdinandov, B., 'Pochemu i ya ushal iz Kamernogo Teatra', unidentified press cutting, TsGALI 2392-1-327-73

26 Markov, Vladimir, *Russian Futurism: a History*, MacGibbon and Kee, 1969, pp.376, 377.

27 Quoted in Lawton, Anna, *Vadim Shershenevich: From Futurism to Imaginism*, Ardis, 1981, p.29.

28 Mass, V., 'Lozhka bez kiselya', *Zrelishcha*, No.11, 1922, p.10.

29 Trabskii, A.Ya. (ed.), *Russkii Sovetskii Teatr, 1921–1926: Materialy i Dokumenty*, Iskusstvo, 1975, p.355.

30 Kuleshov, Lev, *Selected Works*, Raduga, 1987, p.169.

31 Ibid., pp.170–171.

32 Ibid., p.108.

33 Levaco, Ronald (ed.), *Kuleshov on Film*, University of California Press, 1974, pp.163, 164.

34 Kuleshov, Lev, op. cit., pp.220, 221.

35 Shershenevich, Vadim, 'Puti Opytno-Geroicheskogo Teatr', *Teatr i Studiya*, No.1-2, 1922, pp.40ff.

36 See the programme dated 10 November 1924, TsGALI 2392–1–282–4 and 5.
37 Shershenevich, Vadim, op. cit., p.44.
38 Zolotnitskii, D., op. cit., p.34.
39 Shershenevich, Vadim, 'From *Green Street*', in Lawton, Anna (ed.), *Russian Futurism Through Its Manifestoes, 1912–1928*, Cornell University Press, 1988, p.151.
40 Duncan, Isadora, 'The Dance of the Future', in Cohen, Selma Jeanne, *Dance as a Theatre Art*, Dance Books Ltd, 1977, p.125.
41 Quoted in Trabskii, A.Ya.(ed.), op. cit., p.359.
42 Souritz, Elizabeth, *Soviet Choreographers in the 1920s*, Dance Books Ltd, 1990, p.147.
43 Foregger, Nikolai, 'Experiments in the Art of Dance', *The Drama Review*, vol. 19, no.1, 1975, p.77.
44 Foregger, N., 'Charli Chaplin,' *Kino-Fot*, No.3, 1922, pp.2, 3.
45 See Foregger, N., 'Pis'mo Meierkhol'du,' *Ermitazh*, No.8, 1922, p.12.
46 Carter, Huntly, *The New Spirit in the Russian Theatre 1917–1928*, Brentano's, 1929, p.119.
47 *Trud*, 21–8–1921.
48 Foregger, N., 'Iskusstvo Avangarda i Muzykkholl', *Ermitazh*, No.6, 1922, p.6.
49 Publicity handout for MastFor, autumn 1922.
50 The play's title in the original French is *L'Escamoteur*. It was translated into English by Tom Robertson as *Jocrisse the Juggler*. In Russian, the title is something more like, *The Baby Snatcher*.
51 See Carter, Huntly, *The New Theatre and Cinema of Soviet Russia*, Chapman and Dodd, 1924, p.116.
52 See Rudnitsky, Konstantin, *Russian and Soviet Theatre: Tradition and the Avant Garde*, p.98, which quotes *The New York Times*: 'The dancing machine is delighting Moscow.'
53 Fülöp-Miller, René, quoted in Baer, Nancy van Norman (ed.), *Theatre in Revolution*, Thames and Hudson, 1992, p.52.
54 Duncan, Isadora, op. cit., p.127.
55 Foregger, Nikolai, 'Experiments in the Art of Dance', op. cit., p.76.
56 See Goldberg, RoseLee, *Performance*, Thames and Hudson, 1979, p.28.
57 See 'Blue Blouses', pp.168–174 below.
58 Foregger, Nikolai, 'Experiments in the Art of Dance', op. cit., p.77.
59 Trauberg, L., *Izbrannye Proizvedeniya*, vol.1, Iskusstvo, 1988, p.400.
60 Schnitzer, Luda, Schnitzer, Jean and Martin, Marcel, *Cinema in Revolution*, Secker and Warburg, 1973, pp.94–95.
61 Christie, Ian, and Gillet, John, *Futurism/Formalism/FEKS*, BFI, 1987, p.28.
62 Leyda, Jay, *Kino*, George Allen and Unwin, 1983, p.179.
63 See 'Circusisation', pp.50–51 above.
64 L'vov, N., 'Ob Eksentrizme', *Ermitazh*, no.11, 1922, p.6.
65 Kozintsov, Grigorii, et al, 'Eccentrism', *The Drama Review*, vol. 19, no.4, 1975, p.96.
66 Ibid.
67 Quoted in Worrall, Nick, *Nikolai Gogol and Ivan Turgenev*, Macmillan, 1982, p.77.
68 Schnitzer, Luda, Schnitzer, Jean and Marin, Marcel, op. cit., p.100.
69 Kozintsov, Grigorii, et al, 'Eccentrism', *The Drama Review*, op. cit., p.97.
70 Ibid., p.100.
71 Ibid., p.96.
72 Schnitzer, Luda, Schnitzer, Jean and Martin, Marcel, op. cit., p.149.
73 Yeats, W.B., *Collected Poems*, Macmillan, 1956, p.184.

74 Ehrenburg, Ilya, *First Years of Revolution*, MacGibbon and Kee, 1962, p.90.
75 S.T., 'Vsevolod Meierkhol'd', *LEF*, No.2, 1923, p.168.
76 See Meierkhol'd, V.E., *Perepiska*, Iskusstvo, Moscow, 1976, p.218.
77 Trotskii, L., 'P'eca – Vekha', Introduction to Martinet, M., *Noch*', ITG, 1922, pp.3–7.
78 Meierkhol'd, V.E., *Stat'i, pis'ma, rechi, besedi*, t.2, Iskusstvo, 1968, p.51.
79 Also translated as *Earth Rampant, Earth Prancing, The Earth in Turmoil*, etc, the play has never been published, and I am indebted to the playwright's daughter, Tatyana Sergeevna Gomolitskaya-Tretyakova, for my copy. All translations from it are my own. Mme Tretyakova told me that Meyerhold wished to keep the original name, but Tretyakov insisted on his new (almost untranslatable) title: *Zemlya Dybom*.
80 Tret'yakov, S., 'Tekst i rechmontazh', *Zrelishcha*, no.27, 1923.
81 Martinet, Marcel, *Night*, a Drama in Five Acts, translated by Eden and Cedar Paul, C.W.Daniel, 1927. All quotations are from this version.
82 'Polyasnitel'naya zapiska S.M.Tret'yakova "Prinsipy Tekstavoi Obrabotki P'ecy 'Noch' Martine dlya postanovki ee v teatre V.E.Meierkhol'da"', Trabskii, A.Ya.(ed.), op. cit., p.203.
83 Tret'yakov, S., 'Tekst i rechmontazh', op. cit.
84 Nizmanov, P., 'The Soviet Theatre Today', *International Literature*, July 1933, p.140.
85 Schmidt, Paul (ed.), *Meyerhold at Work*, University of Texas Press, 1980, pp.24–25.
86 Il'inskii, I., *Sam o Sebe*, Iskusstvo, 1984, p.182.
87 Lodder, Christina, *Russian Constructivism*, Yale University Press, 1983, p.178.
88 Petronius, 'Zemlya Dybom', *Kommunist*, 27 May 1923.
89 Lesnev, A., 'Zemlya Dybom', *Rabochaya Gazeta*, 8 March 1923.
90 Quoted in Tret'yakov, S., *Slyshish', Moskva?!*, Iskusstvo, 1966, p.192.
91 Federov, V., 'Masterskaya Meierkhol'da', *LEF*, No.2, April–May 1923, p.171.
92 Quoted in Tret'yakov, S., *Slyshish', Moskva?!*, op. cit.,p. 193.
93 See Pike, Chris (ed.), *The Futurists, the Formalists, and the Marxist Critique*, Ink Links, 1979, pp.13–14.
94 Tret'yakov, S., *Slyshish', Moskva?!*, op. cit.,p. 193.
95 Annenkov, Yurii, *Dnevnik moikh Vstrech*, Inter-Language Literary Associates, 1966, p.61.
96 Lunacharsky, A.V., *Sobranie Sochinenii*, vol.1, Khudozhestvennaya Literatura, 1963, p.204.
97 Ibid., p.208.
98 Tait, A.L., *The Literary Works of A.V.Lunacharsky*, unpublished Ph.D. thesis, Cambridge University, 1971, p.303.
99 Blyum, Vladimir, quoted in Rudnitsky, Konstantin, *Meyerhold the Director*, op. cit., p.347.
100 See 'Dawns of The Proletkult', pp.80 above.
101 Also translated as *Even a Wise Man Stumbles, Diary of a Scoundrel, Too Clever By Half*, etc.
102 Shtraukh, M., 'Dva Sergeya Mikhailovicha', in Tret'yakov, Sergei, *Slyshish' Moskva?!*, op. cit., p.182. The script of *A Wise Man* has never been published, and I am indebted to the playwright's daughter, Tatyana Sergeevna Gomolitskaya-Tretyakova, for my copy. All translations from it are my own.
103 Carter, Huntly, *The New Theatre and Cinema of Soviet Russia*, op. cit., p.93.

104 Quoted in Kleberg, Lars, and Lovgren, Haken (eds), *Eisenstein Revisited*, Almqvist and Wiksell, 1987, p.16.
105 Margolin, S., *Pervyi Rabochii Teatr Proletkul'ta*, Teakinopechat', 1930, p.36.
106 Christie, Ian, and Elliott, David (eds), *Eisenstein at Ninety*, Museum of Modern Art, 1988, pp.48–49.
107 Ibid., pp.60–61.
108 Quoted in Aumont, Jacques, *Montage Eisenstein*, Indiana University Press, 1987, p.207.
109 Eizenshtein, S., 'Montazh attraktsionov', *LEF*, no.3, 1923, pp.71–75. Quotations are from the translation in Eisenstein, S.M., *Selected Works*, vol.1, BFI, 1988, pp.33–38.
110 Tret'yakov, S., 'Teatr Attraksionov', *Oktyabr' Mysli*, no.1, 1924, p.54.
111 Schnitzer, Luda, Schnitzer, Jean and Martin, Marcel op. cit., p.170.
112 Rolland, Romain, 'The People's Theatre', in Bentley, Eric (ed.), *The Theory of the Modern Stage*, Penguin, 1968, pp.456, 457.
113 Christie, Ian, and Elliott, David op. cit., p.62.
114 Sadler, Sir M.E., *The Eurhythmics of Jacques-Dalcroze*, Constable and Co, 1920, pp.23, 25.
115 Delsarte, François, *The Art of Oratory*, Edgar S.Werner, 1884, pp.65–6, 84.
116 See Stebbins, Geneviève, *Delsarte System of Expression*, Edgar S.Werner, 1902, pp.91, 94, 193.
117 Bode, Rudolf, *Expression-Gymnastics*, A.S.Barnes and Co., 1931, pp.46–47.
118 Eisenstein, S. and Tretyakov, S., 'Expressive Movement', *Millenium Film Journal*, no.3, 1979, pp.34, 38.
119 Eisenstein, S.M., *Selected Works*, vol.2, BFI, p.231.
120 Garin, Erast, op. cit., p.38.
121 Tret'yakov, Sergei, *Slyshish', Moskva?!*, op. cit., p.10.
122 Eisenstein, S.M., *Selected Works*, vol.1, BFI, op. cit., p.34.
123 Eisenstein, Sergei, *Immoral Memories*, op. cit., p.27. For other examples of attractions in this show, see Leach, Robert, 'Eisenstein's theatre work', in Christie, Ian, and Taylor, Richard (eds), *Eisenstein Re-discovered*, Routledge, 1993, pp.110–125.
124 See *LEF*, no.4, Aug 1924, p.218.
125 Quoted in Christie, Ian, and Elliott, David, op. cit., pp.66, 68.
126 See for instance: Margolin, S., op. cit.; Yurenev, R., op. cit.; Gordon, Mel, 'Eisenstein's Later Work at the Proletkult', *The Drama Review*, vol.22, no.3, p.111.
127 Grimley, Terry, 'Gas Masks', *The Birmingham Post*, 10-8–89.
128 Yurenev, R., op. cit., p.74.
129 Tret'yakov, Sergei, *Slyshish' Moskva?!*, op. cit., p.220.
130 Zavilishin, Evgeny, *Early Soviet Writers*, Frederick Praeger, 1958, p.232.
131 Tret'yakov, Sergei, *Slyshish', Moskva?!*, op. cit., p.36.
132 Ibid., p.225.

5 'What Happened to Us All?'

1 Moldavskii, Dm., *S Mayakovskim v Teatr i Kino*, Vserossiiskoe Teatral'nogo Obshchestvo, 1975, p.75.
2 Khlebnikov, Velimir, *Snake Train*, Ardis, 1976, pp.75, 249.
3 Rudnitsky, Konstantin, *Russian and Soviet Theatre: Tradition and the 'Avant Garde'*, Thames and Hudson, 1988, p.201.
4 Markov, Vladimir, *Russian Futurism: A History*, MacGibbon and Kee, 1969, p.362.

5 Al'perov, D.S., *Sovetskii Tsirk, Sbornik*, quoted in *The Drama Review*, vol.17, no.1, 1973, p.64.

6 Mayakovsky, Vladimir, *Moscow Is Burning*, in *The Drama Review*, vol.17, no.1, 1973, p.76.

7 Ibid., p.82.

8 Report from British Consulate General to the Rt Hon Sir Horace Rumbold, 12–11–29, quoted in Nicholson, Stephen J., *The Portrayal of Communism in Selected Plays Performed in Great Britain, 1917–1945* unpublished Ph.D thesis, University of Leeds, 1990, p.30.

9 Goldfarb, Alvin, '*Roar, China!* in a Nazi Concentration Camp', *Theatre Survey*, 21, Nov 1980, p.185.

10 Meserve, Walter J. and Meserve, Ruth I., 'The Stage History of *Roar, China!*: Documentary Drama as Propaganda', *Theatre Survey*, 21, May 1980, pp.10, 11.

11 See 'The World Turned Upside Down', p.136 above.

12 Nesterov, A., 'God Raboty Klubno-Metodologicheskoi Laboratorii pri Gektemase im Vs. Meierkhol'da', unpublished report, TsGALI, 963–1–1561–5 to 9.

13 See Bablet, Denis (ed.), *Le Théâtre d'Agit-Prop de 1917 à 1932*, t.1, La Cité-L'Age d'Homme, 1977, p.126.

14 'Chto Sinyaya Bluza?', *Sinyaya Bluza*, 1928, pp.9–12.

15 Quoted in Zharov, Mikhail, *Zhizn', Teatr, Kino*, Iskusstvo, 1967, p.153; Moldavskii, Dm., op. cit., p.77 and others.

16 Stourac, Richard, and McCreery, Kathleen, *Theatre as a Weapon*, Routledge and Kegan Paul, 1986, pp.13, 74.

17 *The Christian Science Monitor*, 3–3–28, quoted in Deák, Frantisek, 'Blue Blouse', *The Drama Review*, vol.17, no.1, 1973, p.36.

18 Carter, Huntly, *The New Spirit in the Russian Theatre 1917–1928*, Brentano's, 1929, pp.260–261.

19 Stourac, Richard, and McCreery, Kathleen, op. cit., p.69.

20 Moldavskii, Dm., op. cit., p.80.

21 See, 'The Theatre Epidemic' p.39 above.

22 For a more detailed discussion of TRAM, see Rudnitsky, Konstantin,op. cit., pp.203–205; and Mironova, V., *TRAM*, Iskusstvo, 1977.

23 See Tret'yakov, Sergei, 'Khochu Rebenka', in *Sovremennaya Dramaturgiya*, No.2, 1988, pp.209–237 All quotations from unpublished translation by Stephen Holland.

24 Fevral'skii, A., 'S.M.Tret'yakov v Teatre Meierkhol'da', in Tret'yakov, Sergei, *Slyshish', Moskva?!*, Iskusstvo, 1966, p.198.

25 Ibid., pp.203–204.

26 See Eaton, Katherine Bliss, *The Theater of Meyerhold and Brecht*, Greenwood Press, 1985, p.26.

27 Tret'yakov, quoted in Fevral'skii, A., op. cit., p.198.

28 See Mierau, Fritz, *Zwölf Arten die Welt zu Beschreiben*, Verlag Philipp Reclam jun, 1988, p.103.

29 Tret'yakov, S., quoted in Fevral'skii, A., op. cit., p.198.

30 Mierau, Fritz, op. cit., p.103.

31 Lodder, Christina, 'El Lissitsky's set for Sergei Tretyakov's "I Want a Child", and Constructivist Stage Design', unpublished paper given at conference, 'Tretyakov, Brecht's Teacher', University of Birmingham, January 1989.

32 For the stenographic record by A.Fevral'skii of the debates, see *Sovremennaya Dramaturgiya*, No.2, 1988, pp.238–243. Fedor Raskolnikov had in fact been

married to the charismatic Larissa Reisner, and was an amateur playwright himself, his play *Robespierre* being presented in Moscow in 1934.

33 See 'An Entirely New World', p.24 above.

34 Bowlt, John E. (ed.), *Russian Art of the Avant Garde*, Thames and Hudson, 1988, pp.293–294.

35 See Mierau, Fritz, op. cit., p.102.

36 Trotsky, L. *Literature and Revolution*, Russell and Russell, 1957, pp.135, 160.

37 See Jangfeldt, Bengt (ed.), *Vladimir Mayakovsky: Love Is the Heart of Everything*, Polygon, 1986, pp.133, 246–247.

38 Bablet, Denis (ed.), op. cit., t.2 p.77.

39 Gridina, L., 'Kak Pogibli V.Meierkhol'd i Z.Raikh', *Argumenty i Fakty*, no.29–30, 1992, p.5.

40 See 'The Futrist Theatre', p.20 above.

41 The fullest account of this in English is Braun, Edward, 'Meyerhold: the Final Act', *New Theatre Quarterly*, vol.7, no.31, pp.3–15.

42 Kerzhentsev, P., 'Chuzhoi Teatr', *Pravda*, 17–12–37, quoted in Annenkov, Yurii, *Dnevnik moikh Vstrech*, t.2, Inter-Language Library Associates, 1966, p.94.

43 Ginzburg, Evgenia, *Into the Whirlwind*, Collins Harvill, 1967, p.172.

SELECT BIBLIOGRAPHY

Alpers, Boris, *The Theater of the Social Mask*, Group Theater, New York, 1934.

Amiard-Chevrel, Claudine (ed.), *Du Cirque au Théâtre*, L'Age d'Homme, Lausanne, 1983.

Annenkov, Yurii, *Dnevnik moikh Vstrech*, t.2, Inter-Language Literary Association, New York, 1966.

Arzumanova, N. A., and Kireeva, T. I., *Vstrechi s proshlym*, Sovetskaya Rossiya, Moscow, 1983.

Aumont, Jacques, *Montage Eisenstein*, Indiana University Press, Indianapolis, 1987.

Bablet, Denis (ed.), *Le Théâtre d'Agit-Prop de 1917 à 1932*, La Cité-L'Age d'Homme, Lausanne, 1977.

Baer, Nancy van Norman (ed.), *Theatre in Revolution*, Thames and Hudson, London, 1992.

Bakshy, Alexander, *The Path of the Modern Russian Stage and Other Essays*, Cecil Palmer and Hayward, London, 1916.

Barooshian, Vahan D., *Brik and Mayakovsky*, Mouton, The Hague, 1978.

Benedetti, Jean, *Stanislavsky*, Methuen, London, 1988.

Bowlt, John E. (ed.), *Russian Art of the Avant-Garde*, Thames and Hudson, London, 1988.

Braun, Edward (ed.), *Meyerhold on Theatre*, Eyre Methuen, London, 1969.

Braun, Edward, *The Theatre of Meyerhold*, Eyre Methuen, London, 1979.

Carter, Huntly, *The New Theatre and Cinema of Soviet Russia*, Chapman and Dodd, London, 1924.

Carter, Huntly, *The New Spirit in the Russian Theatre 1917–1928*, Brentano's, New York, 1929.

Cheremin, G.S., *V. V. Mayakovskii v Literaturnoi Kritike 1917–1925*, Nauka, Leningrad, 1985.

Christie, Ian and Elliott, David, *Eisenstein at Ninety*, Museum of Modern Art, Oxford, 1988.

Christie, Ian and Gillet, John, *Futurism/Formalism/FEKS*, BFI, London, 1987.

Christie, Ian and Taylor, Richard (eds), *Eisenstein Rediscovered.*, Routledge, London, 1993.

Collins, Christopher, *Life as Theatre*, Ardis, Ann Arbor, 1973.

Daniels, Guy (ed.), *The Complete Plays of Vladimir Mayakovsky*, Simon and Schuster, New York, 1968.

Dmitriev, Yu., *Tsirk v Rossii*, Iskusstvo Moscow, 1966.

Dmitriev, Yu.A., and Rudnitskii, K., *Istoriya Russkogo Sovetskogo Dramaticheskogo Teatra*, Prosveshchenie, Moscow, 1984.

Eaton, Katherine Bliss, *The Theater of Meyerhold and Brecht*, Greenwood Press, Westport, Connecticut, 1985.

Eder, Boris, *Jungle Acrobats of Russian Circus*, Robert M.MacBride, New York, 1958.

Eisenstein, Sergei, *Immoral Memories*, Peter Owen, London, 1985.

Eisenstein, S. M., *Selected. Works*, BFI, London, 1988, 1990.

Elliott, David, *Mayakovsky: Twenty Years of Work*, Museum of Modern Art, Oxford, 1982.

Ermolaev, Herman, *Soviet Literary Theories, 1917–1934*, University of California Press, Berkeley, 1963.

Evreïnoff, Nicolas, *Theatre in Life*, Harrap, London, 1927.

Fevral'skii, A., *Vstrechi s Meierkhol'dom*, Iskusstvo, Moscow, 1967

Fevral'skii, A., *Pervaya Sovetskaya p'esa – 'Misteria-Buff' V.V.Mayakovskogo*, Sovetskii Pisatel', Moscow, 1971.

Fitzpatrick, Sheila, *The Commissariat of Enlightenment*, CUP, Cambridge, 1970.

Freeman, Joseph, Kunitz, Joshua, and Lodowick, Louis, *Voices of October*, Vanguard, New York, 1930.

Garin, Erast, *S Meierkhol'dom*, Iskusstvo, Moscow, 1974.

Gerasimov, Y.K., Lotman, L.M., Priima, F.Y., *Istoriya Russkoi Dramaturgii*, Nauka, Leningrad, 1987.

Goldberg, RoseLee, *Performance*, Thames and Hudson, London, 1979.

Golub, Spencer, *Evreinov: The Theatre of Paradox and Transformation*, UMI Research Press, Ann Arbor, 1984.

Gorchakov, Nikolai, *The Theater in Soviet Russia*, Columbia University Press, New York, 1957.

Gvozdev, A., and Piotrovskii, A., *Petrogradskie Teatry i Prazdnestva v Epokhu Voennogo Kommunizma*, Khudozhestvennaya Literatura, Leningrad, 1933.

Hammarstrom, David L., *Circus Rings Around Russia*, Robert M.MacBride, New York,1958.

Hatch, John B., *The Formation of Working Class Cultural Institutions during NEP*, University of Pittsburg, Pittsburg, 1990.

Hoover, Marjorie L., *Meyerhold: The Art of Conscious Theater*, University of Massachusetts Press, Amherst, 1974.

Il'inskii, Igor, *Sam o Sebe*, Iskusstvo, Moscow, 1984.

Jangfeldt, Bengt (ed.), *Vladimir Mayakovsky: Love Is the Heart of Everything*, Polygon, Edinburgh, 1986.

Kelly, Catriona, Petrushka, *The Russian Carnival Puppet Theatre*, CUP, Cambridge, 1990.

Kerzhentsev, P., *Tvorcheskiy Teatr*, Gosudarstvennoe Izdatel'stvo, Petrograd, 1920.

Khlebnikov, V., *Snake Train*, Ardis, Ann Arbor, 1976.

Kleberg, Lars, *Theatre as Action*, Macmillan, London, 1993.

Kleberg, Lars, and Lovgren, Haken (eds), *Eisenstein Revisited.*, Almqvist and Wiksell, Stockholm, 1987.

Kleberg, Lars, and Nilsson, Nils A., *Theater and Literature in Russia 1900–1930*, Almqvist and Wiksell, Stockholm, 1984.

Kuleshov, Lev, *Selected Works*, Raduga, Moscow, 1987.

Lawton, Anna, *Vadim Shershenevich: From Futurism to Imaginism*, Ardis, Ann Arbor, 1981.

Lawton, Anna, *Russian Futurism Through its Manifestoes, 1912–1928*, Cornell University Press, Ithaca, 1988.

Leach, Robert, *Vsevolod Meyerhold*, CUP, Cambridge, 1989.

Levaco, Ronald (ed), *Kuleshov on Film*, University of California Press, Berkeley, 1974.

Leyda, Jay, *Kino*, George Allen and Unwin, London, 1983.
Lipkov, A.I., *Problemy Khudozhestvennogo Vozdeistviya: Printsip Attraktsiona*, Nauka, Moscow, 1990.
Lodder, Christina, *Russian Constructivism*, Yale University Press, New Haven, 1983.
Mally, Lynn, *Culture of the Future*, University of California Press, Berkeley, 1990.
Margolin, S., *Pervyi Rabochii Teatr Proletkul'ta*, Teakinopechat', Moscow, 1930.
Markov, Vladimir, *Russian Futurism: a History*, MacGibbon and Kee, London, 1969.
Marshall, Herbert, *Mayakovsky*, Dennis Dobson, London, 1965.
Meierkhol'd, V.E., *Stat'i, pis'ma, rechi, besedi*, tt.1 and 2, Iskusstvo, Moscow, 1968.
Meierkhol'd, V.E., *Perepiska*, Iskusstvo, Moscow, 1976.
Mgebrov, A.A., *Zhizn' v Teatre*, Academie, Moscow-Leningrad, 1932.
Mierau, Fritz, *Zwölf Arten die Welt zu Beschreiben*, Verlag Philipp Reclam jun, Leipzig, 1988.
Mironova, V., *TRAM*, Iskusstvo, Leningrad, 1977.
Moldavskii, Dm., *S Mayakovskim v Teatr i Kino*, Vserossiiskoe Teatral'nogo Obshchestvo, Moscow, 1975.
Nicolas Evreïnoff, 1879–1953, catalogue, Bibliothèque Nationale, Paris, 1981.
Nilsson, Nils A., *Art, Society, Revolution: Russia 1917–1921*, Almqvist and Wiksell, Stockholm, 1979.
O'Connor, Timothy Edward. *The Politics of Soviet Culture: Anatolii Lunacharskii*, UMI Research Press, Ann Arbor, 1983.
Pike, Chris (ed.), *The Futurists, the Formalists and the Marxist Critique*, Ink Links, London, 1979.
Proffer, Carl and Proffer, Ellenda, *The Silver Age of Russian Culture*, Ardis, Ann Arbor, 1975.
Proffer, Ellenda (ed.), *Evreinov, a Pictorial Biography*, Ardis, Ann Arbor, 1981.
Radlov, S., *Desyat' Let v Teatr*, Priboy, Leningrad, 1929.
Radlov, Sergei, *Stat'i o Teatre, 1918–1922*, Mysl', Petrograd, 1923.
Red'ko, A.E., *Teatr i evolyutsia teatral'nyx form*, Izdanie M. i S. Sabashnikovykh, Leningrad, 1926.
Roberts, Spencer E., *Soviet Historical Drama: Its Role in the Development of a National Mythology*, Martinus Nijhoff, The Hague, 1965.
Rosenberg, William G. (ed.), *Bolshevik Visions*, Ardis, Ann Arbor, 1984.
Rostotskii, B.E., *O Rezhissorskom Tvorchestve V.E.Meierkhol'da*, Iskusstvo, Moscow, 1960.
Rudnitsky, Konstantin, *Meyerhold the Director*, Ardis, Ann Arbor, 1981.
Rudnitsky, Konstantin, *Russian and Soviet Theatre: Tradition and the 'Avant Garde'*, Thames and Hudson, London, 1988.
Russell, Robert, *Russian Drama of the Revolutionary Period*, Macmillan, London, 1988.
Russell, Robert, and Barratt, Andrew (eds), *Russian Theatre in the Age of Modernism*, Macmillan, London, 1990.
Sarabianov, Dmitri V., and Adaskina, Natalia L., *Popova*, Harry N.Abrams, New York, 1990.
Sarab'yanov, A.D., *Neizvestnyi Russkii Avangard*, Sovetskii Khudozhnik, Moscow, 1992.
Sayler, Oliver M., *The Russian Theatre*, Brentano's, New York, 1922.
Schmidt, Paul, *Meyerhold at Work*, University of Texas Press, Austin, 1980.
Schnitzer, Luda, Schnitzer, Jean, and Martin, Marcel, *Cinema in Revolution*, Secker and Warburg, London, 1973.

Segel, Harold D., *Twentieth Century Russian Drama*, Columbia University Press, New York, 1979.

Senelick, Laurence (ed.), *Russian Satiric Comedy*, PAJ Publications, New York, 1983.

Seton, Marie, *Sergei Eisenstein*, Dobson, London, 1978.

Sherel', A. A. (ed.), *Meierkhol'dovskii Sbornik*, tt. 1 and 2, Komissiya po Tvorcheskomu Naslediyu V. E. Meierkhol'da, Moscow, 1992.

Shklovskii, Viktor, *Mayakovsky and His Circle*, Pluto, London, 1974.

Souritz, Elizabeth, *Soviet Choreographers in the 1920s*, Dance Books Ltd, London, 1990.

Sternin, G.Yu., *Khudozhestvennaya Zhizn' Rossii 1900–1910kh Godov*, Iskusstvo, Moscow, 1988.

Stourac, Richard, and McCreery, Kathleen, *Theatre As a Weapon*, Routledge and Kegan Paul, London, 1986.

Strong, John W., (ed.), *Essays on Revolutionary Culture and Stalinism*, Slavica, Columbia, 1990.

Swallow, Norman, *Eisenstein, a Documentary Portrait*, George Allen and Unwin, London, 1976.

Symons, James M., *Meyerhold's Theatre of the Grotesque*, Rivers Press, Cambridge, 1973.

Trabskii, A.Ya. (ed.), *Russkii Sovetskii Teatr 1921–1926: Materialy i Dokumenty*, Iskusstvo, Leningrad, 1975.

Trauberg, L., *Izbrannye Proizvedeniya*, vols I and 2 , Iskusstvo, Moscow, 1988.

Trauberg, L., *Svezhest' Bytiya*, Kinotsentr, Moscow, 1988.

Tret'yakov, S., *Slyshish', Moskva?!*, Iskusstvo, Moscow, 1966.

Tret'yakov, Sergei, *Strana-Perekrestok*, Sovetskii Pisatel', Moscow, 1991.

Trotsky, L., *Literature and Revolution*, Russell and Russell, New York, 1957.

Valenti, M.A. (ed.), *Vstrechi s Meierkhol'dom*, Vserossiiskoe Teatral'noe Obshchestvo, Moscow, 1967.

Vendrovskaya, L.D. and Fevral'skii, A.V., *Tvorcheskoe Nasledie V.E.Meierkhol'da*, Vserossiiskoe Teatral'noe Obshchestvo, Moscow, 1978.

Warner, Elizabeth, *The Russian Folk Theatre*, Mouton, The Hague, 1977.

Woroszylski, W., *The Life of Mayakovsky*, Victor Gollancz, London, 1972.

Yershov, P., *Comedy in the Soviet Theater*, Praeger, New York, 1956.

Yufit, A.Z. (ed.), *Russkii Sovetskii Teatr 1917–1921: Dokumenty i Materialy*, Iskusstvo, Leningrad, 1968.

Yufit, A.Z., *Revolutsiya i Teatr*, Iskusstvo, Leningrad, 1977.

Yurenev, R., *Sergei Eizenshtein: Zamysly-Fil'my-Metod*, Iskusstvo, Moscow, 1985.

Yutkevich, Sergei, *Sobranie Sochinenii*, tt.1 and 2, Iskusstvo, Moscow, 1990–1991.

Zguta, Russell, *Russian Minstrels*, Clarendon Press, Oxford, 1978.

Zharov, Mikhail, *Zhizn', Teatr, Kino*, Iskusstvo, Moscow, 1967.

Znosko-Borovskii, E.A., *Russkii Teatr nachala XX veka*, Plamya, Prague, 1925.

Zolotnitskii, D., *Zori Teatral'nogo Oktyabrya*, Iskusstvo, Leningrad, 1976.

Zolotnitskii, D., *Budni i Prazdniki Teatral'nogo Oktyabrya*, Iskusstvo, Leningrad, 1978.

Zolotnitskii, D., *Akademicheskie Teatry na putyakh Oktyabrya*, Iskusstvo, Leningrad, 1982.

INDEX

218